The LEARNING HOUSEHOLD

HOW TO HELP YOUR CHILD GET MORE OUT OF SCHOOL

KEN BAIN
with MARSHA MARSHALL BAIN

THE BELKNAP PRESS OF
HARVARD UNIVERSITY PRESS

Cambridge, Massachusetts
London, England
2025

Copyright © 2025 by the President and Fellows of Harvard College
ALL RIGHTS RESERVED

Printed in the United States of America

First printing

EU GPSR authorized representative:
Logos Europe
9 rue Nicolas Poussin
17000 La Rochelle, France
contact@logoseurope.eu

Cataloging-in-Publication Data available from the Library of Congress

ISBN: 978-0-674-24816-8 (alk. paper)

Education must enable one to sift and weigh evidence, to discern the true from the false, the real from the unreal, and the facts from the fiction.... The function of education, therefore, is to teach one to think intensively and to think critically. But education which stops with efficiency may prove the greatest menace to society. The most dangerous criminal may be the [one] gifted with reason, but with no morals. —MARTIN LUTHER KING JR.

The highest result of education is tolerance. —HELEN KELLER

Let us pick up our books and our pens. They are our most powerful weapons. One child, one teacher, one book, and one pen can change the world.... Education is education. We should learn everything and then choose which path to follow. Education is neither Eastern nor Western, it is human. —MALALA YOUSAFZAI

Contents

	Prelude	1
ONE	Sparking Curiosity	23
TWO	Helping Your Kids Deal with Failure (and Success)	50
THREE	Creating a Home that Supports Learning	86
FOUR	Fostering a Creative Mindset	119
FIVE	Helping Your Kids Learn Deeply	145
SIX	Preparing Your Children for the Slings and Arrows of School	178
SEVEN	Helping Your Kids Get a Higher Education They Can Use	215
	Notes	*245*
	Acknowledgments	*271*
	Index	*273*

THE LEARNING HOUSEHOLD

Prelude

EVERY SUMMER evening around six o'clock, the kids on Roanoke and the surrounding streets played softball at the corner, where the winding avenue crossed the Eleventh Street alley. Giant elms, sycamores, and maples lined the sidewalks leading up to that intersection. Then the skies opened, with no canopy to impede a well-hit, towering fly ball. That's where, after supper, children painted a diamond for their softball games.

The kids created this field of their dreams with no adult supervision. Both boys and girls played—sixteen or so of them, ranging from age six to fourteen. Each night two of the group took their turns as captains and picked their players. Even the youngest were part of the rotation and had the chance to choose their squads.

At first, the kids had umpired their own games, but early on they looked for someone else to make the calls. Someone suggested Mr. Beck, a retired Frisco Railway worker who lived two houses off Roanoke. Seven or eight of the children traipsed over to the former engineer's back door and rang the bell. When the affable but slightly puzzled railman answered, they asked only if he would umpire their game that night. He agreed, and in the evenings to come, the kids came back again and again, and Mr. Beck said yes every time.

Yet the children remained in charge of their own fun. Mr. Beck wasn't their manager or coach. They ran their own game every night, watching out for the rare cars that came rumbling toward them and yelling "hot alley" when they spotted one. The most frequent offender was a college kid named Bob Barker, heading down Roanoke to his mother's house in these days long before he began hosting a famous television game show.

Street ball replaced the graveyard adventures that had played out during earlier summers. A cemetery just across Jefferson Avenue, a block away, had hosted many romps among the tombstones.

At the end of each softball season, the children organized a celebratory picnic across town in Doling Park. They collected money to buy Mr. Beck a shirt or some other present, and some of the older kids took a city bus to Public Square to make the purchase.

One day a player fell backward trying to catch a ball and kissed the curb with his head, and even then the team took control, sweeping around his unconscious body. Mr. Beck wasn't there at the time, so the boys and girls took hold of the kid's four limbs and lifted him, bearing him a block down Roanoke to his home, with his backside occasionally scraping the ground as they went.

Two girls started a newspaper to cover the daily events. It was thanks to one of their fathers that they had access to the technology of the time—a typewriter plus a mimeograph machine and supplies—and he showed them how to use the contraption. But no adults sponsored the enterprise, or even suggested they do it. Nobody's parents edited the paper or told the children what stories to write before they typed them up on the stencil sheets. The journalism project remained in the hands of the kids. They came up with the idea, and they kept going with it because they wanted to do so. They walked around the neighborhood stuffing copies in mailboxes, then joined the evening softball fun.

When children take control of their own play, leaving adults out of the process entirely, they can benefit enormously. The psychologist Peter Gray has studied those dividends. "Play," he argues, "functions as the major means by which children ... develop intrinsic interests and competencies." But the gains don't stop there. When kids meet outdoors and organize games, they also "learn how to make decisions, solve problems, exert self-control, and follow rules." When children engage in free play, they "learn to regulate their emotions," they "make friends and learn to get along with others as equals," and they "experience joy." All this was certainly the case on Roanoke Avenue; in the summertime street games that emerged in Springfield, Missouri, in the 1940s and 1950s, these ingredients boiled to the top of the social soup. And so did the ultimate benefit of that experience. "Through all of these effects," as Gray puts it, "play promotes mental health."[1]

Kids have played freely for centuries, at least whenever they've been allowed to do so. The Roanoke Avenue children departed a little from tradition. Rather than inventing their own games as most earlier generations had done, picking up sticks and stones for some improvised contest, they had borrowed a nineteenth-century adult game with its manufactured balls and bats and embraced it as their own. Yet even with the fastidious Mr. Beck calling balls, strikes, fouls, and close plays on the bases, the Roanoke children called the shots. It was their game and league, and they knew it.

In a book designed to help readers pay more attention to their children's learning, we begin by describing this setting to emphasize how important it is to give young people room to breathe and a sense of autonomy. Maybe you can't recreate the world of the Roanoke games, but you can look for ways to let your children invent. As you settle into a model of helping your kids learn, you can refuse to let it become another example of overwrought and controlling helicopter parenting.

This point is especially important given what has happened in the nearly seventy years since those Roanoke kids played their games. Since the 1950s, as Professor Gray points out, the pattern and nature of children's play has changed dramatically. Kids still play ball in the summer, but they now join adult-supervised leagues, and the adults make the key decisions, not the children.

Please understand that in this Prelude and throughout this book, we are not making a plea to return to some supposedly golden era. Change has produced improvements over the past. We now know more about human learning and motivation, and we can harness recent research to change some of the harmful practices of yore. We have also learned to address some of the social injustices that defined life in those days.

Even in play, change has brought some improvements over the Roanoke Avenue experiences. Today, no one would allow an unconscious child to be hauled awkwardly by his limbs down a city block. (Although that boy emerged largely unscathed and is now coauthoring this book, the bouncing trip home isn't a journey we'd recommend for anyone else.) Many communities have built playgrounds where games can take place more safely, and taken measures to break walls of segregation, although certainly not toppling all of them.

Yet some valuable elements have also been lost in these decades. In the version of play that prevails in the twenty-first century, children aren't always learning to make decisions. They don't as a matter of course gain experience in solving problems, exerting self-control, monitoring their own emotions. They don't necessarily develop the intrinsic motivation of self-driven learners.

Adult managers decide who plays and at what position. Organized sports in school first developed in the nineteenth century, but in the twenty-first, that formalization of play has become all too common in the United States and many other countries. Parents today, especially in wealthier neighborhoods, are the ones who set up the leagues, often buying uniforms, too, and hiring semi-professional umpires and referees. They push from the sidelines. In every Little League matchup or kid's basketball game we've attended over the last half century, through two generations of family members, parents have yelled instructions from the stands and often criticized the kids loudly.

And the result? Gray points out that in the same period that play has changed, so has the mental health of children, with rising rates of "anxiety, depression, feelings of helplessness, and narcissism." He argues that the change in play has contributed to all these psychological problems.

What does this tell us about creating a good learning household—a home where creativity and critical thinking are central to family life? It tells us a lot. It speaks to a fundamental question parents might have as they pick up a book on helping their children get the most out of school: How can you achieve the right balance between helping kids learn and leaving them enough freedom to find their passions on their own? Without guidance, our sons and daughters might miss some of the keys to living a learning life in a learning household. But without freedom, they might not develop the sense of agency that enables them to take control of their own ongoing learning—a theme that runs through this book.

We started with a memory of free play in the mid-twentieth century because it illustrates something powerful about education in general. What does something as seemingly unrelated to school have to do with your children's learning? That question will come up again and again in these pages, even in decisions about when to pick up a crying infant and when to leave it to learn how to self-comfort. And you may be surprised by the answers.

WHAT DOES IT MEAN TO GET MORE OUT OF SCHOOL?

As the two of us, Marsha and Ken, finished doing our exercises, our friends Michael Brown and Charlotte Perks waved from across the gym and asked if we wanted to get some coffee.[2] We had not had a cup in more than twenty years, but we knew the choice of beverage was not the point. The invitation was a way of asking: Do you have time to talk?

We walked to a nearby café with tables spilling outdoors onto the sidewalk. Michael spotted an available one near the curb of this tree-lined street and waved us over. Our New Jersey town spreads gently across a small river valley and up a six-hundred-foot hill. At the top, you can see Manhattan skyscrapers on a clear day. People here pride themselves on how they welcome everyone into their village, and on how much they emphasize education.

Michael, a tall man with Scotch-Irish roots, had graduated from the local community college and then from Rutgers University. Later he got an engineering degree from MIT. His wife Charlotte, a lawyer, grew up in Alabama. Her family had come from Haiti a generation ago. The two had met while she was studying law at Harvard and he was finishing his engineering studies. At home, they had a fifteen-year-old son and a nine-year-old daughter.

For more than three hours, Charlotte and Michael engaged us with observations and questions about their kids and the kind of education they were getting. Would they be ready for life in a challenging world? It was a kind of conversation we'd been party to scores of times, and soon our discussion had branched out into the whole meaning of getting an education.

Early on, Ken asked the couple, "What do you want your kids to learn to *do* in life?" He wasn't referring just to the jobs they might hold but to the thinking and reasoning skills they would cultivate, the emotional and physical abilities they would gain, the values they would cherish, the problem-solving agility and creative skills they would develop, the conversations they could join, and the kind of lives they would be able to live. He was also wondering about the activities they might be able to enjoy. Would Charlotte and Michael's kids have the imagination, grit, skills, curiosity, and knowledge to confront the challenges of a rapidly changing world?

"Of course we want them to flourish economically," Charlotte chimed in, "but will they also learn to see and hear beauty in the world, and to make sometimes tough moral decisions?" As Marsha ordered a bagel and Michael beckoned a refill, Ken took notes.

The two began naming the qualities they hoped to see their children develop and then, laughing at how many began with the letter C, they turned it into a game to make the rest follow suit. In fairly short order they compiled a list of nine goals. They wanted their children to live creative, curious, critically reasoning (constantly questioning), competent (well informed), compassionate (ethical and empathetic), confident, collaborative, contented (happy), and communicative lives, no matter what jobs or careers they might pursue.

"On that last item," Charlotte explained, "it's important that they learn to communicate their thoughts to themselves and others, and understand how valuable that ability can be."

Michael reached over and took Ken's notes, and read them silently as he sipped his coffee. "There are a few more goals that I think are important," he finally offered, "although I can't get them into a word starting with C." We laughed and asked our friend just to say them. "To learn deeply," he replied, "they must come to appreciate how much they don't know. They can't go through life just memorizing 'right answers.' They must learn to question their own ideas constantly, to ask why they believe what they do." After a long pause he added, "I also want our two to be empathetic. To care about other people." Charlotte and Marsha smiled and nodded approval.

"Finally," Michael added, "I've been reading a lot about developing a strong sense of *agency*, which I have come to understand, in part, as taking charge of your own education. You have to know who you are, what you value, and where you want to go." He took a sip of his coffee as Charlotte weighed in. "Agency," she added, "is the opposite of helplessness."

Summing up, Michael laid out his aspirations for his children: "They'll need to be creative, to use the resources around them to overcome problems, and to constantly expand and redefine their goals. They need to motivate themselves and to come back quickly from any failures or defeats."[3]

At that point a light breeze kicked up, and even as we hastened to keep napkins pinned down we were all struck by the pleasant freshness of the air on our faces. Someone joked that the moment felt like a benediction—calling extra attention to the good words just spoken and uplifting our resolve to act on them.

Learning to Live in a Volatile World

Over the last six years, we have talked with several hundred parents struggling with similar questions about their children's schooling and future. Our interviews have included a diverse group. Some parents, for example, had little formal schooling while others seemed to have more degrees than a thermometer. One thing they tended to share was an uneasy appreciation for how volatile the world has become—how uncertain it has turned out to be. One recent interviewee summarized a sentiment that ran through most of these conversations: "I just want my daughter to develop her talents as best she can."

"People must learn to be creative," we heard from more than one parent. "You can't just prepare for a job and expect to live happily ever after."[4] "Your specialty might be obsolete by the time you get out of school," a woman from Tulsa warned. "Besides," added her husband, "life is more than working at a job. We play many characters, from parent to citizen to the person with certain values, and an education must help us fulfill all of those roles."

Children must learn deeply and broadly if they expect to flourish in this new world, reaching a level of achievement and development that very few people mustered in the past. That's challenging, but here's the good news: educators now know how to help more kids meet those high standards. The challenge now lies in unleashing the contributions that parents, teachers, researchers, and children can make by joining in a common conversation.[5] If you are an educator at any level—from early childcare to college or graduate school—and believe this book has little meaning for you, please reconsider.

For parents, our promise is that we're going to help you build what we call a *learning household,* where your kids can find and follow their own passions. In the pages that follow, we will explore this objective thoroughly, providing lots of rich examples and research-based advice at every turn.

As longtime collaborators, the two of us have explored a large and growing body of research and theoretical literature on the nature of learning and how it develops. Over the last century, for example, scientists around the world have probed the human brain and uncovered new insights into how it works. With those discoveries, teachers, parents, and scholars have gained a greatly expanded vision of young people's capacities to learn, grow, and contribute to a better world. We now know enough about brain science to see enormous potential in what kids can learn and do.

Still other important concepts have emerged from practice, from the observations and experimentation of inventive educators and parents. Much of our own previous work has aimed to share the habits of "best teachers" and "best students."[6] Here, we turn our focus to parents, combining past research with our most recent interviews and introducing ideas through compelling stories crafted to inspire and inform.

Redefining the Value of Schooling

In this book, we redefine the purpose of education, shifting the emphasis to the needs and potential of individual students. Our research will help parents think about the big goals of learning, the broader and more important reasons for building capacities to gain knowledge that come to the fore after kids leave the hallowed halls of their alma maters. In other words, this book redefines the value of schooling, recognizing that the objectives of education may be as varied as the students who populate our schools, while also recognizing that the development of some qualities is important to everyone. The notion of helping all individuals realize their full potential might seem old-fashioned, but it deserves a new consideration of what it could mean in the twenty-first century. What role could parents play in helping their children do that?

We will also examine the concept of *deep learning*, an approach that enables students to make connections between disparate ideas. We'll see how it can make a dramatic difference in young people's lives and well-being, laying the foundations for success in whatever career they decide to pursue. More important, deep learning will enrich their lives. When students and parents pay attention to cultivating it, the kids will be happier, will think and act more creatively, and will be better prepared to flourish and assume control over their lives.

Can your child develop such a strong, life-changing learning capacity and still earn high marks in a school that defines the purpose of education more narrowly? That is certainly possible, but is a trickier accomplishment than you might suspect. Indeed, someone choosing the wrong path to academic glory might plant seeds that grow quickly into weeds, crowding out their ability to get much of value out of school, despite what their marks suggest. They may emerge from their schooling not knowing how to learn new things, or without any real drive to do so. We will explore here how an overemphasis on acing tests and making good grades can sour your children on learning and harm them.

Well-educated people know how to question themselves, to ask why they believe what they do, to refine their thinking to meet new challenges. Students who focus only on spouting the answers they need to advance seldom become deep learners. If you go to a bookstore and look for works devoted to helping your kids shine, you'll find many full of keys to passing tough exams and raising grade point averages, but few, if any, designed to help them avoid or uproot those weed patches. This one will do that in spades.

THE CENTRAL POINTS

This book makes three major and interrelated points. First, we now have *solid empirical evidence* about what actually helps kids achieve outstanding academic records, what doesn't much matter, and what downright hurts them. Putting these ideas into practice does not depend on money. Indeed, they are relatively easy to implement, regardless of the size of your bank account. The second major point is that *parents must focus more on fueling children's creative and ethical lives.* While many parents focus on solid academic achievement, and some have discovered good ways to help young people succeed academically, fewer understand how they can foster more creativity and ingenuity in their children. And the third major point is that *kids can learn deeply* and will benefit from doing so.

Central to the second point is the recognition that every child is unique, with life experiences distinct from any other person in history.

That unique mix gives children the opportunity to develop perspectives that no one else will formulate in exactly the same way. It also creates a dynamic of human potential that has huge implications for our understanding of creativity and inventiveness. If each student is unique, then all of us can learn from one another, and from all the important ideas and perspectives that have emerged through human experience.

When children begin to realize that a key element in the creative process is the ability to recognize good ideas when they encounter them and the capacity to integrate those inputs with their own ideas, the world becomes their oyster. With such a perspective, education becomes the means by which learners develop what creativity educator Paul Baker called the "dynamic power" of their minds, and what we will call a creative mindset.[7] It begins by looking inward to understand one's own history and tastes, but ultimately requires looking outward to work with the rich palette of the human genius.

We should add right here that, when we speak of learning to live a creative life, we're not focusing exclusively or even primarily on deepening one's abilities as an artist or involvement in the arts. Creative opportunities and demands pop up in every aspect of life. One can be creative in running a business or holding a job, rearing children, reacting to a crisis, doing research, and myriad other aspects of life.

Our ideas on creativity include what has been called "invention education" by the people at the Lemelson-MIT Program, an organization devoted to providing such preparation to new generations of technology innovators.[8] Invention education focuses on teaching students engineering skills, giving them the opportunity to create and sell new and valuable solutions. Our advice certainly encompasses this approach, but it also includes all kinds of creations in every aspect of human existence—not just products and services to take to market.

Developing a creative mindset requires, in part, acquiring an ability that psychologists Giyoo Hatano and Kayoko Inagaki have labeled *adaptive expertise.*⁹ This is expertise in applying knowledge to novel problems, starting with recognizing where innovation is needed and relishing the opportunity to invent something new. Many students never achieve this. If you believe that your kids are not ready for such ambitious thinking, please reevaluate. Don't sell your children short. At a minimum, try out the ideas in this book to help your kids find their passion and live it.

We will also add that, when you ask parents what they hope their children will get out of school, many will mention the joys of being popular, excelling at athletics or debate, making lifelong friends, or developing good social habits. This book recognizes the value that can come from these achievements, especially if they help kids learn to build good social relationships, which in turn can bolster learning and support lives of creativity.

Deep Learning

Regarding the third major point noted above, that focusing on learning deeply is possible and beneficial for kids, this is a matter on which you cannot retain a neutral stance. Unless you deliberately and actively support deep learning, you (however unintentionally) bar it from your home. We'll explore what this means.

School often presents kids with information they simply need to remember. But how can students make the facts stick? And perhaps more important, how can they learn to use that stored information to think about important questions and solve problems, or see the connection between one item and another?

How can people take something from one corner of their knowledge and see its implications, applications, and possibilities for ideas and projects that seem totally unrelated? When can a child begin to grasp that all knowledge is related and that within that understanding is the key to a creative life? This is called the *far transfer problem* in learning, and we will cut it open and examine its parts so that you'll be able to take it home to your family.

Living Life in a Time of Crisis: the Need for Adaptive Experts

The twenty-first century has already challenged us with new threats and problems, from the pandemic and economic and political turmoil to war, social unrest, and climate change. How will our children learn to live in a world of rapid change and growing dangers?

Some years ago, oil exploded from the ocean floor off the coast of Mexico, sparking a plume of fire and black smoke and leaving a hole. Never had that happened before on such a scale. Since we had no set procedures for addressing that danger, we needed a special kind of expert, an adaptive one who could fashion solutions to a new problem.[10]

Today we have holes in our atmosphere, holes in our social, intellectual, and international structures, holes in our economy and culture. To address a vast array of needs and challenges, we need more than the latest gadgets. How can our kids develop as *adaptive* experts, and not just routine ones who know only standard solutions to old kinds of problems?

We need people who can adjust to evolving conditions and solve new problems for which the answers are not already established. How can we resolve conflicts in values? How can we survive and eventually flourish when fate hasn't allotted our family much of anything? How can kids prepare for a rapidly changing world, for jobs that might not even exist when students go looking for them—indeed, for whole occupations no one has yet imagined? Parents can play a key role in fostering a creative mindset.

In 1929, in an interview in his Berlin apartment, Albert Einstein was asked if he trusted more to his imagination than to his knowledge.

"I am enough of the artist to draw freely upon my imagination," he replied. "Imagination is more important than knowledge. Knowledge is limited. Imagination encircles the world."[11] It was observation about what is important to cultivate in learning that has often been quoted since, and will reverberate through this book.

But must anyone choose between knowledge and imagination? Certainly, Einstein did not consider them to be mutually exclusive, and our belief, too, is that your kids can have it all. We will explore how you can help your children expand and use their own imaginations and creativity as they accumulate vast pools of knowledge.

We live in a world where the facts themselves are changing. Ongoing research in every area often upends what experts once believed. One implication is that your children will constantly need to update their knowledge. They will need to take fresh looks at old problems, and learn new approaches to solving them. How can parents and teachers prepare them for a life of learning?

Whether we drive cabs or lead corporations, mow lawns or manage laboratories, it can feel as if we are only plowing through lives of tedious repetition. Many of us struggle to find meaning and pleasure in life, to make difficult decisions, to laugh and cry, and sometimes to laugh to keep from crying. Our children do the same. How do we prepare them for all the wrinkles of life?

And, yes, how can your children learn *more* deeply and extensively than you have? Good teachers play a key role in this process, but educators and researchers are also beginning to realize the powerful contributions that can and must be made by parents.

My Kids are Different

No two children are alike. All have their own, unique combinations of perspectives, tastes, and habits. Every child is born into a certain place at a particular moment, reared with certain values and religious beliefs (or no religious faith at all) and endowed with an array of ambitions and passions.

Every child has individual quirks and a unique personality and sees the world through a special lens that no one else has. Even a set of twins reared in the same household, who swim together as if their brains are connected, will often surprise everyone with the differences that set them apart.

How can one ideal of a good education meet the needs of everyone? How can it enable all kids to realize their potential, even those who face challenges like dyslexia and attention deficits and other types of neurodivergence? How can it help each child take advantage of their uniqueness? Parents can play a huge role in that process.

Long after grades and school honors have ceased to make any difference, will your children know how to learn and believe they can? Will they appreciate the beauty and wisdom of art and science? Will they remain intrigued by mystery and uncertainty? Can they adapt to changing times, recover quickly from difficult circumstances, become stronger and wiser after defeat or failure? Will they give up and stop trying? Or keep looking for better ways to learn, to work, to play?

How you react to their successes and failures now will heavily influence how they react to life's challenges. Faced with some goal or need, will they give up easily? Will they say, "I'm not a math person and can't do that kind of problem"? Or will they keep pushing forward despite obstacles, simply realizing "I haven't learned that *yet*"?

Can schooling help your kids enjoy life? Think for a moment about a creature that cannot find beauty in the world, who cannot appreciate a good story, a delightful puzzle, a beautiful piece of music, or even a good joke, who cannot grapple with deep moral issues. Human beings have a wonderful capacity to experience the world in ways that other living beings will never know. Yet not everyone achieves the full promise of human life. Shouldn't a good education help them to do so? How can you contribute to that process?

What does research suggest is the best way to motivate students to achieve academic success, no matter how we define that goal? How can we encourage and help our children to take control of their learning and push themselves toward more meaningful goals? Today, a growing body of research is generating new answers to these questions. The simple response is that we all struggle with when and how to get out of the way and allow our kids to fly. But full answers will come in the pages ahead.

Huge social, economic, and political forces shape children's educational opportunities. Anyone who tries to make changes will face major obstacles. Yet our focus will be on what individuals and families can do regardless of the broader system. While this book is not about how to overcome the enormously unequal educational opportunities that exist in the world or the toll that poverty can exact, it does provide resources for all parents, including those whose children face less than ideal learning environments. In short, this book cannot alone erase all of the inequalities that exist, but it can provide valuable ideas that are universally helpful.

Because the development of deep learning and a creative life is a long-term project, we will include material designed to help parents as their kids progress from infancy through college. At the same time, we will emphasize that, while an early start is valuable, parents have not missed the boat if they don't apply this advice the moment a child is born. Those whose children are teenagers or even older can still influence their kids' approaches to school and learning.

As a mother or father, aunt or uncle, close friend, teacher, or neighbor, how do you help children develop beliefs about themselves that will serve them well across their lives? How can you foster good habits and practices, attitudes and concepts, values and goals? Will children believe that their abilities can grow, or instead think their intelligence was determined at birth, and that only geniuses can expand their mental powers? Will they develop a sense of agency that makes them diligent, resilient, and resourceful—or succumb to a sense of hopelessness? Will they be easy targets for anyone trying to fool them?

How can they become people who do not give up easily and who persevere in the face of failure, but who also know when it is time to shift paths and apply what they have learned from their failures to new challenges? To develop self-confidence and a sense of agency they must learn to learn from their own mistakes.

You and your family will benefit most if you build a strong community around the ideas in this book. Bring it to the attention of teachers and neighbors. Organize discussion groups that bring together people to explore new ideas and find points of disagreement and agreement. Your children will benefit if their teachers join the conversation and bring to the table the rich body of literature that stands behind their professional development.

SEVEN KEYS

This book divides its content into seven key realms, each a topic on which we have heard parents wish for more "how to" advice as they try to help their kids unlock more of what a school education should offer. They are as follows:

1. How to spark children's curiosity.[12]
2. How to help kids learn to fail—and succeed.[13]
3. How to make a home that encourages learning.[14]
4. How to prepare children for a world that doesn't exist yet, building their ability to be creative.[15]
5. How to encourage better study and learning habits.[16]

6. How to prepare children for the slings and arrows of life.
7. How to prepare kids to get a higher education that will benefit them.[17]

We are convinced that this set of topics accommodates, if not all, then at least 90 percent of what it takes to bring up children who value learning and will continue to learn. Without doubt, if you influence your children in each of these areas, you will change the way they approach their educations and lives. In the sections of the book that follow, we will explore each of these challenges in depth, offering practical ideas for enabling your kids to get more out of school, no matter what they are studying or what careers they hope to pursue.

INTERLUDE

Within several of these realms of inquiry, we'll devote some discussion—sometimes a few paragraphs, others a few pages—to an important idea that falls outside our main narrative or a point that needs additional emphasis. In these short digressions, which we are labeling *Interludes,* we will address issues that we suspect may be bothering readers, and introduce new ideas that need quick attention. In this first one, we offer a story that may seem like it has nothing to do with your kids and their schooling—but illustrates one of the most important points we make.

Perhaps in all of human history, the person who most spectacularly ignored one of our most valued learning goals was Thomas Midgley. The brash engineer and amateur chemist from Ohio didn't question his assumptions carefully or rethink his conclusions in the way we will encourage you to teach your kids to do. Nor did he seek to anticipate the problems that applying them would create. "Indeed," as writer Steven Johnson put it for a *New York Times Magazine* audience, "there may be no other single person in history who did as much damage to human health and the planet."[18]

Over a roughly ten-year span in the 1920s and 1930s, Midgley churned out two inventions that seemed to offer brilliant solutions to big problems. The first was a new gasoline mix that reduced engine knock. Early car engines would occasionally make a loud rattling or knocking sound, shaking passengers. At the same time, the vehicle would lose power. If you were trying to drive uphill or pass someone on a two-lane highway, that could be catastrophic.

Midgley's solution, which he developed while working for General Motors, was to add a mixture of lead and tetraethyl to the fuel. Introduced in 1923, leaded gasoline made cars run more smoothly. Over the next few years, the number of cars in the United States tripled. But "ethyl," as the company called the new fuel, also released tons of lead into the atmosphere. In high doses, the metal could damage kidneys and cause some people to hallucinate. It could also slow children's cognitive development. Yet Midgley and others never questioned the solution, even though some health experts raised alarms as early as 1928.

In the late 1920s, Midgley and General Motors turned to another problem that cried even louder for a modern solution: how to cool and freeze food. The safety of everything from food to vaccines hung in the balance. An adequate answer required a gas that could be used as a coolant. Before Midgley, the gases used in refrigerators often caused deadly explosions, prompting some states to consider making refrigerators illegal. The dapper and often flamboyant chemist came up with a way to use a poisonous gas that no one else had considered: fluorine.

He combined it with chlorine and carbon, producing a new, nontoxic substance he dubbed freon. The bosses at the world's largest car company, which had bought a small refrigerator business (Frigidaire), decided that Midgley's gas was "altogether without harmful effects on man or animals."

Only later did anyone realize that freon would slowly but surely eat a hole in the ozone layer that protects our planet from the sun's deadly radiation. Without that layer, even a few minutes outdoors could cook your skin in cancerous sores. The decision in the 1970s to ban freon and leaded gasolines came none too soon; the damage to the ozone layer will not repair itself completely until late in the twenty-first century. Meanwhile, lead still poisons people, primarily children, around the world.

Midgley died in 1944 (perhaps from suicide), but his legacy lives on. He and the large corporation for which he worked succumbed to two weaknesses in human thinking. First, Midgley and his colleagues fell victim to old-fashioned greed. They knew about the dangers of lead from the beginning. They even had an alternative to ethyl, but they could not patent and monopolize it the way they could with ethyl. They let their drive for profits dominate their thinking. So they kept churning out ethyl even though they knew about its dangers.

Second, Midgley and his colleagues fell prey to unchallenged assumptions. With freon, engineers didn't have an easy alternative. The problems emerged because they failed to question what they thought they knew.[19]

You will want to help your kids avoid both of these weaknesses.

Recall our friend Michael Brown's addition to the list of desirable qualities, one of the education imperatives he couldn't express in a word beginning with C. "To learn deeply," he said back at that coffee shop, children "must come to appreciate how much they don't know. They can't go through life just memorizing right answers. They must learn to question their own ideas constantly." Perhaps the word "conservative" could serve to remind us that well-educated people should pause and question proposed changes—especially when they involve messing with nature—to reflect on their ethical implications and contemplate alternative perspectives.

How can you help your children develop the mental habits of that kind of conservatism? Emphasize that accumulating money is not the only consideration in making educational and intellectual decisions. Encourage them to seek out new perspectives, to talk with people with whom they disagree—politically, economically, socially, and even religiously. This will help them see that the mark of an educated person is not the memorization of right answers, but a habit of constantly questioning themselves, thinking again, and envisioning problems that might spring from ideas they may hold dear. As psychologist Adam Grant puts it, that means "searching for reasons why we might be wrong—not for reasons why we must be right."[20]

Think of the changes that might follow from artificial intelligence, gene manipulation, nano bots, or other miracle innovations being developed. A kind of conservatism that seldom gets noticed these days might make an enormous difference, if generations of rising scientists and citizens learn to question future technological breakthroughs more thoroughly, wisely, and quickly than Midgley and his colleagues did.

ONE

Sparking Curiosity

IF YOU have spent much time with a child who has just learned to talk and jabbers almost constantly, you know that these young humans can ask lots of questions. Their favorite word seems to be *why*. That is certainly true of the hundreds of children we have encountered, including our own.

We were once driving through Oklahoma with two children who bombarded the adults in the car with everything from "What are those trees called?" to "What makes clouds so puffy?" We thought they had exhausted nearly every topic in sight when they finally turned to each other.

The older of the two looked at his younger sister and asked one of the deepest of all questions: "How do you know for sure that you are *you*? Maybe *I'm* you and you are me and we are both dreaming. How do we know anything for sure?" It was essentially the line of inquiry that obsessed René Descartes and transformed philosophy, but here the question came from the mouth of a five-year-old.[1]

Another time, our niece, at about the same age, took an automobile trip with us from Austin to San Antonio, Texas. In that seventy-eight-mile drive down Interstate 35, the little girl must have asked at least two hundred questions, many of them inspired by the skies above. She didn't know the word *astronomy* until we introduced it in that conversation, but that didn't stop her from asking questions like "Where is the sun at night?" And "where are the stars during the day?" Those are astronomy questions. Her curiosity had obviously been building up for some time, and this long period out on the road seemed the right time to unleash it on someone.

As we motored down the highway, the barrage of questions kept coming. "Why are stars white? Can you ride on a moon beam?" It was as if the ghost of Albert Einstein had drifted up the tailpipe and infiltrated the cabin of the car. But it was not an unusual experience. In one widely cited study, a psychologist recorded young children spending time with their parents and found an average of more than two questions per minute.[2]

If you expect, however, that the conversations you have with the same children a few years later will be equally inquisitive—and perhaps all the more for their additional wanderings through the world, feeding their curiosity—you will likely be disappointed. By the time they are teenagers, you may be worrying that your kids are so disengaged they might only respond to punishments. For some families, the childhood wonder that seems to flow like water starts to dry up and slowly disappear after kids start school.

Children may tell you that they hate going there, or they may simply show no enthusiasm for learning. They may show no interest in reading on their own or visiting the library to find a new book. School becomes a bore. The boundless wonder that filled their minds at an earlier age may be swallowed up as they drag through the day. Oh, they may dutifully finish all (or most) of their assignments, feeling some obligation to keep up their grades, but they may lose their enthusiasm for inquiry, never taking up a learning project just for its own sake.

If you want to help your kids become self-motivated students who get more out of school, you will need to help them revive the wonder that filled their early childhood. To clarify what can be done at home to help rekindle that early experience of awe, or keep it burning, we need to explore some important research on human motivation.

THE SCIENCE OF MOTIVATION

If you have taken your children on many outings or trips, whether to the grocery store or the Grand Canyon, you know that those go best when everyone involved *wants* to be part of the expedition. Proper motivation is a big factor, and that's the topic we take up next.

For years, many people believed that the best way to get someone to do something was to reward them for doing it well and punish them if they didn't. That "carrot and stick" approach guided thinking about learning and schooling. After schools introduced grades in the nineteenth century, they often used them to spark learning. "It will be on the test" became the prod to learn new material. If someone performed poorly on the exam, the failing grade was supposed to turn them around. That approach became deeply embedded in our culture.

Often when the two of us think about these issues, our minds flash to a scene from Ken's family history in the rural American South. On more than one occasion, one of his uncles told the story of how, as a young teacher in an Alabama schoolroom, he had lunged at an inattentive student in the back row, in one seamless motion whipping off his broad belt, pouncing on the troublemaker, and administering multiple lashes. Ken's thoughts of this uncle have ever since featured an image of him flying through the air toward a hapless Appalachian farm boy.

By the mid-twentieth century, the emphasis shifted from the stick to the carrot, favoring rewards over punishments. That change emerged thanks in part to the research of Harvard professor Burrhus Frederic Skinner (better known as B. F. Skinner) and his followers. That hardy crew of social scientists generated a ton of data, some of it from placing rats in mazes and timing their progress under different conditions.

When cheese treats were placed along the best escape path, the rodents would learn more quickly to take that route than they would if they got no rewards. Skinner and his followers surmised that since rats and humans are both mammals, their findings should apply to humans, too. That made sense in a civilization raised on rewards and punishments.

By the time Skinner was nearly ready to retire, however, researchers began to question the line of work he had pioneered. One of those young skeptics was Edward Deci from Clifton Springs, New York, a small town where Victorian houses with gingerbread trim laced the streets. After distinguishing himself as a scholar of motivational psychology, Deci joined the faculty of the University of Rochester in upstate New York and became a prominent challenger of Skinner's claims.

Sure, Deci acknowledged, we can get people to act with promises of rewards and threats of punishment, but what will happen over time to their deep, intrinsic interest in a subject after long exposure to the carrot and stick approach? Will they remain curious and motivated to learn years later? Will their fascination stay the same, decrease, or increase? Is it possible that doling out rewards and punishments actually damages motivation and gradually kills it?

After setting up some elaborate experiments involving people rather than rats, Deci and his graduate student Richard Ryan published a comprehensive explanation of how motivation works.[3] (This will be extremely important to you and your children.) The two psychologists argued, first, that people are born with an intrinsic fascination with the world.

Wait a minute, you might already object: If humans have a natural urge to learn, why do some students get bored with school? The psychologists had an answer drawn from their extensive research. While curiosity is innate, they explained, it can be lost with the wrong experiences.

Deci and Ryan's great contribution was to identify three basic psychological needs that are as important to people's well-being as their physical comfort. The individual who is able to fulfill these needs is as happy as a lark and will seize on new ideas and knowledge-building opportunities like a chicken on a June bug. If these psychological needs go unmet, however, natural curiosity tends to fade.

What Are Those Fundamental Needs?

First, people don't like to feel helpless. They want to believe they can learn to do what life requires of them, and they feel good about doing something well.[4] In part that means that people are not likely to try anything if they don't believe they can succeed at it. But it also means that being successful is its own reward. People feel good when they learn something new and fascinating to them.

Next, they may appreciate wise guidance, but they don't want someone else pulling strings as if they were puppets. They don't like to feel manipulated or have their opinions ignored. As they mature through childhood, they develop an expanding desire to be in control of what they do and what happens to them, a feeling that Deci and Ryan called "autonomy." Any parent who has witnessed the "terrible twos" knows how toddlers exhibit an early version of this strong desire to do things their own way.

Finally, people like to be "part of something larger than themselves." That's why they form families, join clubs, make friends, and engage in activities that give them a sense of belonging and attachment to other people. Because they want to connect socially, they like to help each other, even as they want to set their goals for themselves and control how they get their own projects done, and when, where, and with whom they work on them.

Social science researchers like to come up with big, abstract nouns to express their findings. Deci and Ryan are no different. They summed up their work by naming the needs to develop *competence*, *autonomy*, and *relatedness*. Their research strongly suggests that if life gives us that triple whammy of mental pleasures, our curiosity can run wild; if not, it whimpers, crawls off in a corner somewhere, and maybe dies.[5]

Without the big three of psychological needs, we become sad and even depressed. We lose interest. Curiosity crumbles. And this is why an approach to motivation that relies mainly on rewards and punishments actually backfires. It diminishes long-term motivation by undermining a person's sense of competence, autonomy, and relatedness.

None of this means that parents shouldn't teach children to act according to their values, such as decency, kindness, and compassion. It does mean abandoning some of the traditional ways of instilling those values. For eons, parents have resorted to the quick slap, or more serious physical blows, when kids "act up" or disobey the rules of the family. That certainly went on in Ken's southern Appalachian clan. But we now know that less physical methods work much better—such as a conversation about the proper way to act, or a "time out" to think about why the rules of the family exist or why a child shouldn't slap a sibling or make a mess of their cornflakes.

Most of all, it must be recognized that learning and curiosity don't fall in the same category as childhood misdeeds. You can't build fascination with anything by threatening to sell off a favorite toy, piece by piece, until curiosity improves. Nor can you do it by rewarding obedient shows of interest. Our children are not trained ponies or monkeys, and we wouldn't want them to be. They may become self-motivated, creative, and knowledgeable adults despite our inappropriate care for them. But that hardly counts as evidence that kids should suffer physical or mental coercion to learn something.

Think about the nature of most schooling and you begin to grasp why it sometimes harms that natural drive to learn. Schools do not always give students a sense of control over their own education (and neither do all parents). Even the words we use convey the sense that personal curiosity doesn't count for much of anything. Instructors hand out "assignments" and "requirements" rather than issuing invitations to learn or applauding provocative questions. That's almost universal, even among the best of teachers. Someone else is in charge of the learning.

To maintain order in large and potentially chaotic classrooms, principals and teachers enforce rules and regulations. Promoting free-flowing wonder and an awe for life takes a back seat to managing so many children at a time. Extrinsic rewards and punishments can make kids feel that they have lost control of themselves. They lose interest. Teachers then redouble the rewards and punishments to get them back on track. The cycle continues in an accelerating downward spiral.

None of this means that schools can't have rules, but it does mean that they must help children understand why those rules make sense, and maybe even let the kids draw up some of the rules. As a parent, you can help. Start by changing the words you use. Rather than "homework," refer to "learning opportunities." Ask your kids questions that will entice them. Listen to *their* inquiries.

Some children will come to hate school without losing their curiosity. Kids get bullied, for example, and they don't want to go back. Teachers or other students can intimidate them. Or a child may suffer some embarrassing moment, maybe over something said or a mistake made quite innocently. But some maintain their passion for learning, despite trials and tribulations. The most frequent cause of that hate-school-but-still-love-learning syndrome is respect for another student or a special teacher. Parents often do their parts, as well.

Reviving Interest

What can you as a parent do to revive natural curiosity when it dims? That's extraordinarily important to figure out. To get more out of school, kids need the push of their own intrinsic interests. But parents play a huge role in sparking that drive to learn—or sadly, sometimes, making matters worse.

Our first recommendation is that you avoid focusing on grades. Emphasize instead the joy and fascination of learning new things. Many better schools have completely eliminated grading for the first five or six years. Even if yours has not—*especially* if yours has not—you can be the one your child sees celebrating learning for its own sake.

Ask your kids what fascinates them. Which subjects do they like most? Urge them to find interests and pursue them. Excite their imaginations with questions like "If you had a magic carpet that could fly anywhere, where would you go?" Weave references to math and history into conversations at the dinner table. Show excitement about what they are studying in school. Ask them why they believe what they do: What's the evidence? Yet avoid giving the impression that you are putting them on the witness stand or in any way setting them up for interrogation. Make it a fun experience, a game you play with lots of smiles.

GOING TO SCHOOL

When Ken was just four years old, his mother started teaching him to read and write. She had spent over a decade as an elementary school teacher before he came along. When he was barely five, she arranged for him to spend a day at Phelps Elementary. His biggest challenge on that visit was finding the boy's restroom.

You can imagine what happened once he had spent too much time running up and down the stairs in search of that special and private space. He still remembers the little girl who stopped on the landing where he was huddled against the wall to ask, "Why are you standing in that puddle?" He spent the afternoon trying to cover up his accident.

Springfield, Missouri, didn't have universal kindergarten in those days—only a few programs located in wealthy neighborhoods. That's not where his parents lived, but his mother kept pushing to get him into a program across town, at Rountree School. She finally succeeded. (This may not work for every family from neighborhoods that lack financial resources and political clout).

If your community does not have early education, you can still provide your child with powerful opportunities early in life. Read to them. Show them pictures. Point to things. Teach them everything from language to arithmetic. Arrange for them to play with other children.

But there is considerable evidence that kids who attend preschool, kindergarten, or programs like Head Start go on to do far better later in life than those who don't. So you may also want to work at getting your children into those good opportunities. It may be as important as what high school or college they attend.[6]

What Can Go Wrong?

Unfortunately, Ken's mom's efforts fell victim to that stairwell embarrassment he had suffered a few weeks before at Phelps. He was a nervous wreck as he started school at Rountree, but he tried to hide his fears from his parents. His most vivid memory of that first day of kindergarten was the tissue he had wadded in his hands and dropped crumpled on the floor. We share the image to urge you to be sensitive to the feelings your kid may be hiding.

The happier memory is that all of the embarrassment had melted away by the time Ken entered the first grade a year later. He came to school with enormous excitement and a great sense of adventure. Wow—a globe with all the countries in the world! Microscopes where you could see tiny stuff. Colorful blocks and books with pictures of animals he'd never seen before, not even at the Springfield Zoo. Even the excitement and wonder of learning about new friends tickled his fancy. An interest in learning something new can become contagious. Keep this in mind as a parent and become interested in everything around you.

Both of us remember being intrigued by the equations our teachers wrote out on chalkboards. Our parents had taught us about simple adding and subtracting at home. We now found it fascinating to see people playing with numbers and building new sums. Perhaps in the same way that today's digital games like *Minecraft* draw in young kids, we were intrigued with the possibility of using the building blocks we already knew to create new structures.

Some children learn more quickly and are ready for certain challenges at earlier ages than others, but you can begin to introduce a child to a mathematical process long before kindergarten or first grade. Go slowly at first. Treat processes like adding, subtracting, multiplying, and dividing as a game, and don't worry if a kid doesn't get it initially. Keep coming back to it until it clicks. It's okay if learners make mistakes—how you react to their errors makes the bigger difference in their schooling. Treat wrong answers as chances to learn rather than reasons for impatience or scolding. This is one of the most important points we want to convey, and we will explore it more fully later in this book.

Eventually, we each found out that our teachers would test our knowledge and give us grades in big, red marks. By the third grade, we were sighing over "homework" and "assignments." Even the words hurt. With one notable exception, our teachers told us what to learn and by when we must learn it, rather than offering us opportunities and issuing captivating invitations to build our knowledge. The subtle but relentless message was eventually clear. We were not in charge of what happened. In Deci and Ryan's terms, we could not learn with autonomy.

What the Best Teachers Do and What We Can Learn from Them

The great exception for Ken came in the fourth grade. Ms. McDonald did let her students pursue their own interests. She would introduce a group of topics, each with an intriguing question, and then ask who would like to learn more about them. She encouraged kids to write up the rules of good conduct so that such rules became their own guidelines, not edicts handed down from on high. (Try this at home—you'll be surprised what a big difference such a simple gesture can make.) Her emphasis was on helping children understand what was expected rather than on punishing them for violations.

She might voice displeasure with their actions, but never with any of them as people. She didn't think of them as good children or bad ones. This super teacher never displayed anger. Whether or not you can find a Ms. McDonald at your child's school, you can be one at home. Indeed, more than any teacher's, your own actions and attitudes will shape your children's lives and learning.

Sometimes when she introduced a new question, Ms. McDonald would show a picture or brief filmstrip on the topic at hand (yes, a *filmstrip*—this was the 1950s—so we understand you will opt for new technologies that serve the same purpose). She then asked for anyone interested in learning more to volunteer to do so. Sign-up sheets were posted, and students filled in their names right down to the last lines. Over the course of the year, every child had multiple opportunities to go deeper on practically any topic to be found in a list of fourth-grade learning objectives, and then some. Ken ventured into algebra, for example. It was a subject that usually wasn't taught for another several years, but his parents had served up math problems at many meals already, along with the southern fried chicken, okra, green beans, and lush red tomatoes from the huge garden in the backyard.

You can do something similar with your kids, from their youngest ages. Start a garden for them to tend, even if it is a tiny windowsill box. Take them to a library with instructions to select no more than, say, two books to take home. (It's always better to set a limit than to impose a minimum, for reasons that Deci and Ryan's research and theory help explain.) A family field trip can offer similar opportunities, or the planning of an upcoming vacation, with the children put in charge of researching and selecting some sites to visit. If your finances or work schedule don't allow for a holiday away, a day trip (or, if you live in a city, a bus ride) to something new can serve the same purpose.

So can a sticky situation in a sitcom or movie viewed together. Some films raise terrific philosophical questions, as well as being fun to watch. One that comes to mind is *The Truman Show*.[7] No matter how constrained your travel budget might be, stories can become children's magic carpet, taking them to places far and wide.

Almost any activity that puts kids in position to evaluate or make decisions will work. After all, good decision-making comes from practice and gentle feedback. Children learn from having discussions in stimulating environments about choices and their impacts.

A way to support learning from experience is to encourage reflection on it afterward. We know families who invite their children to be the official reporters for family events, whether they splurge on a trip to Disneyland or pack a picnic to a local landmark. Even tagging along to the grocery store offers reporting potential. The kids keep journals of their adventures, writing up experiences as simple as "what happened at the playground." The parents don't correct or grade these reports, though the accounts may prompt feedback when shared with the rest of the family.

These early reporting efforts might later encourage children to keep journals of their own to take note of things that capture their interest, adding questions these observations spark and speculating about possible answers—perhaps even devising experiments and compiling data. Still later, they might be inspired to dip into the published notebooks of brilliant scientists or writers of the past. There are plenty to be found online with a quick search, from Charles Darwin's pocket diaries to Marie Curie's lab notes and diagrams.[8]

You can introduce road games to engage your children's minds, especially on long drives. One old favorite challenges young kids to point out something along the way that begins with the letter A, then B, and so forth. It doesn't just reinforce the alphabet, it makes them alert to their surroundings, and teaches them that even a boring stretch of road can be turned into fun.

Giving your kids more decision-making power doesn't mean you'll go along with even dangerous ideas, but try to go easy on your vetoes and corrections, especially as they grow older. Don't oppose something simply because it wouldn't interest you, and if you would rather they do something else, explain why. If you think another activity might be better (more interesting, less dangerous, more promising, or whatever), keep smiling as you give your reasons. Make sure your suggestions are grounded in good evidence, not just personal whim. And be open to being swayed by their ideas or finding ways to combine them with yours.

You can set this tone early by making up lists of good children's books and then letting your kids make their own picks. Librarians and teachers can help you compile some great possibilities. The Philosophy Learning and Teaching Organization also maintains a list of recommended children's literature, the value of which will become more apparent once you have read more of this book.[9]

Most importantly, make your kids feel comfortable asking questions. Brighten up when they ask a challenging one and say something like "That's a very good question. Let's see if we can find some good answers." Some children don't ask many questions because they believe that voicing a need for more information will make them look dumb. Sometimes an older child can make a younger child feel that way. Be alert to those possible threats, and help children understand that questions are natural and desirable. As often as possible, respond with an encouraging smile. Build a reputation for liking questions.

Everything Becomes a Learning Opportunity

Think of a day at the beach that begins with the question of how long someone can stay in the open without getting sunburned. How does sunscreen work? How much do we need? You might lead your children on an expedition to find answers before heading outdoors. It's true that the internet is full of worthless content, much of it promoting dubious miracle cures, but it also includes research-based resources, many published by reputable medical schools. Can you prompt your kids to find the good stuff? The trick is often to make your questions seem as natural as heading to a drive-through ice cream stand and asking everyone in the back seat, "What should we order? Has anyone tried the strawberry sandwich? Does that sound good, or what?"

Help your kids understand that humans often do not have easy, definitive answers that people can memorize. Avoid quizzing them with questions that have only one specific answer that they might have committed to memory. Help them realize that some of the most important questions are the toughest to answer. Introduce them to philosophical questions, as we will explore in a later section.

Give kids a sense of control. On that family outing, if you regale them with why the place you are visiting is interesting to you, be sure to engage them, too: "Is there anything I'm leaving out? What questions do you have about San Simeon castle?" Get them to do some reading and report back. Your local historical society or the county government may have a list of historical landmarks that you can explore, perhaps prompting them to investigate who and what has been left out of the official list.

As your children move into high school and college, help them find projects that allow them to contribute to real-world scientific or historical research.[10] Through that process, you can keep chipping away at the notion that everything to be learned is in textbooks and on the internet. "The best way to learn what you enjoy is to get in there and do it," advised more than one person we interviewed. In later pages we'll explore some stimulating examples.

Encourage your children, especially when they get to college, to knock on their teachers' doors and ask them about their research. Urge them to volunteer their assistance on studies in progress, even if no one pays them for doing so or gives them extra credit.

All of these activities become important aspects of sparking kids' curiosity and creating what we call a *learning household*. So can displaying your enthusiasm for learning and encouraging them to follow their curiosity. When children see parents reading or talking about things they've learned, that influences their attitudes toward learning.

Children may express an interest in something that would bore you, but let their fascination draw you in. A single sneer, frown, or blasé look can dampen their ardors forever. Build an environment where enthusiasms are appreciated, and mistakes and failures are never ridiculed.

How you react to a child's first love affair with a turtle found at the edge of a back porch can shape that child's life for years. Your kid should see you responsibly protecting them from danger (turtles can bite and must be handled with care), but not dismissing their emotion and interest. Don't be mistaken: your children can read you like a book, and if your face and rhythm reflect anything less than an awe for life, you will undermine their budding curiosity.

ASK QUESTIONS TO PROMPT INQUISITIVE MINDS

After Isidor Isaac Rabi won the Nobel Prize in physics in 1944, someone supposedly asked him why he became a scientist. "My mother made me a scientist," he answered. "Every other mother in Brooklyn would ask her child after school: 'So? Did you learn anything today?' But not my mother. She always asked, 'Izzy, did you ask a good question today?' That difference—asking good questions—made me become a scientist!"[11]

To teach your kids to raise good questions, ask them some. Make them open-ended inquiries that invite lots of speculation and explanation, rather than simple yes-or-no answers. You can ask them about matters that scientists and scholars have already explored but that are still mysteries to them. Ask for their opinions. Then inquire about the evidence that led to their conclusions.

"Why are there so many different kinds of animals and plants in the world?" you might ask casually in the backyard or on a stroll through a park. "Why does it get cold in the winter and warm in the summer?" Ask questions about values, too, or how to change things for the better. An ambiguous question like "How could we get more love into politics?" or "Why do history lessons seem to lack compassion?" might get an older student thinking creatively.

You need to listen to their questions—and answers. Find out what topics intrigue your kids. Do they like talking about sports or the arts? Or both? About religion or values? About friends or enemies? All of the above and more? The answer may depend on how old they are. Go with the flow before injecting your own preferences. Slowly expand their horizons with questions from philosophy and science. Or wait for one of them to pose those big questions themselves.

Fifty years ago, when Ken first began teaching, he used a process to spark inquiry that he borrowed from some other source, now long forgotten. Recently we found the techniques in the work of the Right Question Institute, an organization that tries to get teachers (and parents) to "make just one change," as Dan Rothstein and Luz Santana put it in a fine little book they published in 2011.[12]

In the 1990s we used the process in workshops we organized for faculty members at Vanderbilt and Northwestern. When we picked up *Make Just One Change,* there it was, all neatly laid out, pretty much the way we remembered it, but with all the brilliant insights, perspectives, and language that Rothstein and Santana had employed to breathe new life into it. It was like finding a beloved dog scratching at your back door after many months on the lam.

After someone from our local library dropped the book off at our house, we found it in a rumpled brown sack on a front porch chair. Like kids at their own birthday party, we eagerly tore back the paper wrapping and began to read.

At its heart, the process begins with something interesting, anything that might provoke questions. It could be a rock or a feather, a sculpture, a swath of colorful cloth, a facsimile of some historical document, a smell or poem, a cacophony of sounds followed by the most melodious of music. Almost anything. It could be a magical trick that seems to defy the rules of nature. It could be a statistic that shocks you: "In 1970 a hundred thousand people were in jail in the United States. Today, there are over three million. What happened?" The people from the Right Question Institute called this object of interest the "Question Focus."[13]

Next, the process invites brainstorming about some possible questions they might ask. By the rules of brainstorming, you simply spit out whatever comes to mind. No one can ask for further elaboration or object to a suggestion. If you think it, say it, and someone writes it down, but you keep going, churning out possible questions with no judgments attached. As your children grow older, the topics might change, but the process is the same for a six-year-old as it is for anyone older.

Finally, everyone participating examines the list. Divide the examples into open-ended and closed-ended questions, into those that can be settled with an observation, and those that require an abstract concept. Do the questions involve assumptions that haven't been resolved yet (sometimes called double questions)? Do any involve value judgments or expressions of preference, as in the question, "Which is a better drawing?"

Which question do you want to ask first, second, and third? Do you want to review any questions now that you have the whole list, or perhaps combine some? Can you rephrase any questions to make them clearer, or to get at something that otherwise isn't being said?

Rothstein and Santana called these last steps *metacognition*, which is a fancy way of referring to thinking about one's own thinking. It's when your kids examine and label their thoughts and make judgments about them. Sometimes we call that *critical thinking*, but the labels don't matter. It is something you will want to help your kids learn to do. Over the years, we've employed this approach repeatedly.

More to Learn from Going to School

In Ms. McDonald's class, the sign-up sheets usually filled rapidly. The teacher divided kids into groups of five or six. The room brimmed with excitement. It was like a great museum with work stations and exhibits in every direction. At any given time, a couple of small groups might be working together in one section of the room or another.

You can imagine setting up something similar in your own home, places where your kids can explore different areas of itnerest. We know one family that placed a small workbench in one corner of their living room, where their six-year-old could make his own toys, sawing and hammering to his heart's content. In other homes, we found tables with microscopes and telescopes by the windowsills. If you have such instruments in your home, show your own enthusiasm for them, but let your kids show you how they work, creating a family culture of exploration and adventure. If they fiddle with something the wrong way and damage it, don't rage at the carelessness—calmly help them learn from the experience. Next time, try to point out what is fragile and vulnerable before they begin.

For that matter, gadgets aren't even necessary to create this magic. You can summon it with riddles and questions. Get a good book of brain teasers and bring it out from time to time. Make sure you treat it like a game and not a test of your kids' intelligence. And keep the problems age-appropriate or just slightly more advanced. Pages to come will offer some important insights on making questioning adventures with your children run more smoothly.

One of our favorite puzzles is this one from computer science: Let's say you need to send a highly secret message to someone. You put it in a box locked up with a padlock so that no one can access it. You drop the box in the mail. When it gets to its destination, the recipient will need the key to open it. But if you send both lock and key through the same mail system, couldn't both be intercepted and stolen? How do you get the key to your friend by more secure means?

Give that puzzle to your children and invite them to speculate about how they would solve the problem. Do it all with a sense of delight and play, with no sense that a wrong answer will earn a parental "gotcha." What are some alternative first steps? Where would the step you're considering lead you next? Treat the whole experience as an adventure of fun, not a measure of intelligence. Keep smiling and laughing. Then hand over your book of puzzles or riddles and challenge them to find one that will stump you.

Do you want to know the answer to the secret message puzzle? Here it is, but don't tell your kids (unless they beg for it). Send the message in a locked box, but keep the key. When it arrives at your friend's house, have them put their own lock on the box and send it back to you, while keeping their key. When you get it back, take your original lock off the box and send it back to the friend. They can then use their key to remove the single lock, open the lid, and read the message. It has been locked throughout its travels with one or two locks. If you want to make this especially memorable, have your kids actually send such a secure message in a box back and forth to a friend. You can also mention to them that the same principle is used to send encrypted messages over the internet.

Here's another puzzle. Imagine you have eight balls, and all are of equal size, but one ball is slightly heavier than the other seven. How can you use a balance scale to find the odd ball, and do so in only two weighings?

If you put half of the balls on one side of the scale and the remaining four on the other, you can easily find which group of four is lighter. But how do you find the heavier ball once you know what group it's in? Assume the difference in weight is so slight that you can't feel it with your hands.[14]

Intrigued? The answer requires imagination. Here it is. Again, don't give away the solution until your children beg for the answer. If possible, get a balance scale and let them watch and even participate as you show them the solution.

Put three of the eight balls on one side of the balance scale and three others on the other side. If the six balls balance evenly (three on one side and three on the other), you know that the odd ball isn't among the six you have arbitrarily chosen. So you take all those balls off of the scale and put the remaining two balls on opposite sides of the scales from each other. Now you know which one of those two is heavier in only two weighings.

If, however, an imbalance results when you put three balls on one side of the scale and three on the other, you proceed differently. You now know that the heavier ball is in the heavier group of three. For the second weighing, you set aside the lighter group and then choose any two balls from the heavier group to weigh against each other. If one side of the scale dips, you have identified the weightier ball. And if they weigh the same, it is equally clear that the ball you didn't select for this second weighing is the heavier one.

These puzzles require some imaginative thinking. Have fun, and go look for other good examples. Yet math and science are not the only way to encourage learning outside of the classroom. You can bring history, philosophy, great literature, politics, sociology, the arts, and a variety of disciplines and topics into your discussion as well. Ask your local librarian and teachers for examples. The *New York Times* has a weekly Sunday game that challenges players to put seven events in chronological order. Try working on it with your children.

When David Grant was president of the Geraldine R. Dodge Foundation in New Jersey, he established a poetry festival in the state, but he also took his love of verse home with him. He and his wife, Nancy, had their own poetry festival at family dinnertime every day. They asked their two sons to each bring a poem to the table, read it, and then offer thoughts on it.

We know families who begin every meal with a good math problem or poem, or both, adjusting the level to fit background and age. In an ideal setting, everyone joins in the process, with older children forming teams with their younger siblings to struggle with or guide them, asking good questions rather than providing all the answers.

As you solve these puzzles or read those poems, take note of any biases you harbor that could ruin the fun and cheat some of your children. Make sure you react to all of your kids with the same level of inviting smiles, subtle glances, and body language. We all have preconceived notions about others that can cloud the atmosphere we are trying to create. Do you expect the same from all your children, or do you perhaps make assumptions based on gender, anticipating that the boys will sail through some types of questions and the girls will ace others?

Stop and think about all that could go wrong, even in what some would regard as a stimulating environment. Weigh the special burdens (and benefits) that each of your children carries, their unique backgrounds, the subtle factors that change their lives. In a later section, we will explore how you can mine their differences. Then, even further down the road, we will explore the worst slings and arrows that can stop students in their tracks.

For now, realize that even siblings can have dramatically different experiences. One size does not fit all. Birth order matters, and so does gender. A family event like the death of a relative can affect one child differently than another. Consider how dramatically life and learning have changed for boys and girls over just the last hundred years. In our youth, boys and men had a distinct advantage and were far more likely to go to college and graduate school, and to study law, engineering, and medicine. Few women received PhDs. All that has changed dramatically, although some people think and act like it hasn't.

Women are now more likely to go to college. The gender balance in the total population is roughly equal, but as of 2024 women make up nearly sixty percent of higher education students and are far more likely to graduate.[15] During the Covid-19 pandemic, more men dropped out of college than women.[16]

Is that because women do better in school, or is it because men can get better paying jobs without advanced degrees and are more seduced by money? The answers to these questions don't matter for the larger points we're making. It's difficult to provide equal educational opportunities for all children in a family, and you should always be aware of the challenges that each child faces. We'll help you do that in a later section.

What Happens If Your Kids Don't Volunteer?

One day, Ms. McDonald announced that we were beginning a unit on "outer space." She came to class with the same level of excitement she did for other topics. Yet not as many people signed up to participate in the unit. Ken was one who didn't.

For reasons he still doesn't understand, outer space was just spooky to the nine-year-old Ken. Ms. McDonald took the news in stride as if he'd said he didn't want mayonnaise on his hot dog. No signs of approval or disapproval. But other kids did sign up and formed study groups. In the days to come, the outer space volunteers met to pursue their interest in the vast universe while the rest of the kids stuck to their usual fare.

One day, as Ken skittered around the room, looking at this and that, he brushed by the planets-and-stars people gathered in a circle in the middle of the room. He must have paused for a second or two, because Ms. McDonald looked up and asked if he would like to join the space travelers.

No fanfare. Just a quiet invitation, a second chance to take up something he had rejected earlier. When he paused even longer, the nonjudgmental teacher got up and brought a chair for him to use. In no time at all, he was part of the group. But no one said, "You should have signed up earlier. Now you are terribly behind everyone else."

In the days to come, other holdouts joined the fun, and by early the next week everyone in the class had joined in. And soon enough, their discussion of planets, moons, stars, and comets branched into interests in rocketry and the laws of Newtonian physics.

Built into each lesson was an opportunity to speculate. Our guess is that the kids most eager for that opportunity were the ones whose parents had introduced that imaginative aspect of learning at the breakfast, lunch, and dinner table. You can do the same for your children.

Challenge them on one occasion to find the square roots of various numbers, and on another day, to comment on some political event, or the causes of a war or economic crisis. Create a positive and supportive home environment that helps your children sustain their natural curiosity.

INTERLUDE

When you ask parents of young children to name the most important reason for going to school, many will say it is to learn to read. Reading "influences every aspect of your life," said one Michigan mother.[17] But here's the "dirty little secret" that many teachers and parents don't know or won't admit. Hundreds of schools (and some parents) use a method of teaching reading that will most likely produce poor readers.

Cognitive research has debunked this approach and the theories that stand behind it. Yet scores of school districts refuse to abandon it or discard the textbooks and other materials that support this disproven technique. As education reporter Emily Hanford put it, "Elementary schools across the country are teaching children to be poor readers."[18]

The results have been disastrous. In 2022, two-thirds of fourth graders in the United States did not meet minimum standards in reading ability.[19] This problem is woven into the very fabric of our educational system. Years ago, administrators and their advisors made decisions that are still haunting us.

Publishers didn't have much research on what worked best, so they just made guesses, selling stuff that was popular. And they made tons of money as school districts, as early as the 1960s, spent millions of dollars buying those materials. Today it costs millions more to revise and replace them, so some sellers still push the old, discredited approaches.

Too many teacher-preparation programs still instruct future educators in the unsupported way to teach reading. So do many school districts with their on-the-job training. Today, schools would need to spend lots of money they don't have, and overworked instructors would require hours of study to retool themselves with research-based approaches to reading. Only wealthy parents and districts can afford the expense.

Outmoded Approaches, Better Alternatives, and What to Do

The old approach that cognitive scientists have repeatedly debunked goes by various names. One that has had great influence is the "whole word" method. It assumes that if you read to kids, they will naturally and easily learn to read. They won't. Reading isn't a natural process for *Homo sapiens*. Our species has been around for over two hundred thousand years (and earlier forms of humans first walked the earth six million years ago), but the first written language didn't appear until about five thousand years ago. Our brains were pretty well formed by that point, and they weren't designed for easy reading.

In the last hundred years, scientists have developed a systematic and evidence-based method for reading instruction that is called *phonics*. Children who learn with a pure phonics approach are better readers and spellers. To make the transition to the better way easier, some people have tried to mix the two methods together. The result is a toxic combination. It's like stirring your orange juice into your brilliantly brewed morning coffee.

To understand what we mean, consider listening to Emily Hanford's podcast, *Sold a Story*, which explains the background of the whole-word approach, how it became ubiquitous, and why it is wrong.[20] Her criticisms of the whole-word approach focus on only one part of the reading process. She assumes students have already heard the words they are learning to read and understand their meanings from hearing them. Reading in that situation means turning printed text into sounds that a child already knows. But what if your kid has never heard a word and must acquire some new vocabulary? Phonics won't always help them much with that second part of learning to read.

How do you help your kids add new words to their vocabularies? We asked Hanford about this. She suggested that once students learn to use the phonics approach, and can read the words they already know, they can go on to learn the meaning of new words by looking up their definitions. Your children may find the flashcard app Word of the Day useful.[21] She also advised that parents should teach phonics at home. In interviews with parents, we've heard hundreds of them echo the same advice.

A Young Kid's Discovery

Almost twenty years ago, when our grandson was two years old, he watched his mom use her computer, surfing the internet. One day when she was out of the room, he tried doing it and stumbled onto a site called starfall.com. Maybe his mom had left the site up so that he would come across it. As he clicked various icons on the screen, he discovered games and songs. In the days to come, he returned to the site frequently.

Those activities were part of an ingenious phonics course that taught him to read. By the time he was three, his preschool teacher asked him to read to some kids in school while she tutored a few others. The site he discovered is still free and accessible through the Starfall Learn to Read app.[22] You can use it to help your kids learn to read. Some kids will learn faster than others. That doesn't really matter.

One Little Girl's Challenges in Reading

Carol Greider had an even bigger reading challenge that not even phonics or vocabulary study could solve easily. She had dyslexia; the part of her brain that looks at letters on a page and turns them into sounds and meanings didn't work well. This didn't mean she had low intelligence or had bad eyesight, as some people once believed. It meant that for her, the process of reading was extremely slow and tedious. (For that matter, reading isn't a natural process for any of our brains.) In Carol's case, it also meant she was put into remedial classes in grade school.

"It was quite embarrassing," she told us, "to have someone come into your classroom in the second and third grade and take you out to go to remedial classes." That experience made a lasting impression on her. "I thought I was not as smart as everyone else. So I was determined that I would just work harder." Others might have given up. Her parents set good examples, making reading an important part of their regular routines.

Greider worked hard enough to get into college and enrolled in the College of Creative Studies at the University of California, Santa Barbara. Her advisor urged her to find a job working in someone's research lab. "I could not learn by just reading about research," she explained. "I had to get in and do it."

That experience changed her life. She continued doing medical research throughout her undergraduate years, her graduate school, and later, her career. In 2009, this woman who was embarrassed in the second grade—and still is dyslexic—was honored with the Nobel Prize in Physiology or Medicine.

Your child, too, even if he or she initially struggles with reading, can learn to think deeply and go on to enjoy an immensely rewarding life.

TWO

Helping Your Kids Deal with Failure (and Success)

SOME YEARS AGO, the Andrew W. Mellon Teaching and Learning Institute at Bryn Mawr College in Pennsylvania appointed Ken their first visiting fellow. On seven different occasions over the course of that fellowship, we drove to their historic and bucolic campus outside Philadelphia to conduct seminars for faculty.

On the first occasion that we met with anyone there, an English professor announced, "I don't like your new book." Taken aback by that blunt statement, we asked why, thinking this would at least be a good opening to a hardy discussion. "It uses the word *failure* too many times," she announced. "I don't use that nasty word in my classes. I emphasize success. My students don't fail. I teach them to have confidence and succeed."

Her desire to be positive is understandable. Yet when we think about that brief encounter, we remember a past conversation with Nobel laureate Dudley Herschbach, who stressed that you can't learn without failure. In the realm of science, he noted, you have an idea about how nature works. You test your notion with an experiment. When it fails, you devise a new and better hypothesis, and you keep doing that until you develop a deeper insight. "Nature doesn't change," Herschbach said, and it "waits patiently for you while you screw up." When scientists do finally arrive at an accurate understanding, he added, "It's not because we are particularly smart but because we are stubborn."[1]

Before this section of the book is over, you will understand why parents should heed Herschbach's wise observation and help their kids develop that healthy kind of stubbornness that has done so much to fuel human progress. May your children embrace their mistakes and learn from them.

GROWTH MINDSET

Let's imagine for a moment that, among the people who study human learning, someone has discovered a new way for kids to bounce back from defeat stronger than ever. Suppose that this approach is so effective that it doesn't require expensive new technology. Students can develop new abilities within themselves. They can conquer new areas of study with powerful success, reaching levels of personal achievement that no one would think possible. Over the last fifty years, social psychologists have in fact made such a discovery. It's called a *growth mindset* approach, and it fosters the idea that intelligence can grow. So why don't we use it?

Actually, we do—at least some of us. Educators in hundreds of schools around the world employ this important breakthrough with impressive results. While most of the work behind it consists of rigorous research on human learning, it has also been developed as families have stumbled upon its precepts themselves or had them passed down from earlier generations. And together, the researchers, educators, and families keep discovering even better ways to make it work.

The growth mindset approach does, however, have at least two major weaknesses. While millions of Americans know a little about it, far fewer comprehend it deeply. The importance of having a growth mindset has become a hot topic in parent groups and school discussions—even in corporate board meetings, employee training sessions, and dozens of other forums. Yet that has not led to widespread understanding. Nor has it kept some people from mangling some of the key ideas at the heart of this approach.

In the business world, the fundamental notion here is often expressed as a simple aphorism: "You can always do better." It's easy to imagine that laconic expression appearing on the cups and caps and other swag handed out at employee gatherings or on the kind of strategically placed motivational poster that sometimes pops up on the wall of a workplace. Yet no such tidy distillation can do justice to the rich set of ideas that make up this approach.

Some of its critics say the growth mindset approach amounts to little more than an admonition to work harder. If it is within the power of every individual to make an essential change, then doesn't this imply that any students who fail (and their parents) can only blame themselves for not applying enough energy to the task? Effort becomes king, argue these naysayers, and that can be harmful to kids. But we will help you understand how misguided that objection is.

Meanwhile, a richer and more nuanced version of this crusade has blossomed thanks to some well-designed and well-funded experiments—real-world projects implementing the best current thinking about fostering growth mindsets, and devised to measure outcomes. While such carefully managed applications of the social science behind this movement have produced some impressive results, one additional challenge remains.

The programs are difficult to ramp up for everyone. Because good learning environments are so complex, they work better in some cases than they do in others. Furthermore, while this approach can make schools better, it can't address all problems. That's where you and your family can play a big role. This book can help you understand this important innovation and learn to introduce it to your kids, potentially transforming their lives.

You can also introduce it to friends and neighbors in a way that will benefit your kids. If millions of moms, dads, aunts, and uncles do that, we can collectively change the way people in our culture talk and think about schooling, and thereby improve the learning environment for nearly everyone. That's especially true if this approach is linked to other major ideas discussed in this book.

A word of caution before we continue. This approach seems to work best among younger children, and it has had some significant triumphs even among teenagers. It is not, however, a miracle cure. As with any human endeavor, a variety of social forces can make it less effective in some communities than in others.

For example, it seems to work better in places where nearly everybody buys into it—teachers, other students, and parents. As we will keep emphasizing, it is important to build a wide community of friends and neighbors who discuss this work and understand both its weaknesses and strengths, and all of the major social forces that can undermine it. Community-building around shared commitments to young people's success can also allow us to address the social and psychological concerns that many parents mentioned to us, from bullying to the threat of deadly violence on campus.

What Are these Ideas and Where Did They Originate?

We previously described the research behind fixed versus growth mindsets in a 2021 book, *Super Courses,* but it's worth revisiting its origins here.[2] We could start the story at various points, but let's begin with events soon after World War II. According to a widely repeated account, Albert Bandura, a young psychologist from Stanford University, encountered a group of people at a carnival having their first experience of handling snakes. After watching them for a while, he noticed something important about their efforts.

After the trainers showed them how to pick up a reptile by the back of its neck, the volunteers first tried the hold on toy snakes and most passed this test with flying colors. When the same people switched to live varmints, however, they failed. They clearly lacked the confidence that they could do it right, despite having just demonstrated mastery of the technique.

Bandura concluded that to become a good snake handler, you need to know the correct procedure—but you also need to *believe* you can implement it successfully. Otherwise, you will not try hard enough to succeed. It was like Peter Pan, who needed a sprinkling of pixie dust to be able to fly (by analogy, mastery of technique) but also needed faith in his ability, for "the moment you doubt whether you can fly, you cease for ever to be able to do it."[3] The Stanford professor suspected that his simple observation was a broader formula for success in life. Some people believe, he reasoned, that with the correct effort they can overcome, or at least manage, the challenges of life, while others surrender to expectations of defeat and failure.

Psychologists like Bandura earn their livings stating such succinct observations and then setting up experiments to see if they apply broadly and reliably to human behavior. If a theory checks out and the researcher then gives the newly proved phenomenon a fresh name (creating the impression of an insight that no one has ever had before), that social scientist has the makings of a career as a research psychologist.

Bandura coined the term *perceived self-efficacy* to describe the quality that the star snake handlers possessed.[4] The Stanford professor further argued that good problem-solvers generally have this quality. They know the right techniques, and they believe they can use them successfully. They focus boldly on the problem to be cracked, while others hold themselves back with reservations about what they can't do and concerns about how tough it will be to find an answer. People who lack perceived self-efficacy often give up too soon. But whose who have plenty of it keep trying, too stubbornly confident to admit failure.

Why do some people have large doses of this stubbornness—this perceived self-efficacy—and others don't? Fast-forward a few decades. In the same postwar era that Bandura was watching snake handlers, a future Stanford psychologist was growing up in New York City. This little girl did well in school and then enrolled as an undergraduate at Barnard College on the Upper West Side of Manhattan.

After Barnard, young Carol Dweck went on to Yale University to work on a doctorate in social psychology. By the time she finished her graduate degree at the Ivy League school, still in her mid-twenties, she had become fascinated with the problem that would consume her professional attention for the rest of her career. In many ways, her work took up where Bandura's left off.

Why, she wondered, do some people fall apart when they fail at something? What makes them conclude that they lack the mental tools to succeed? Meanwhile, others bounce right back from a setback, even exploiting that experience to adjust their thinking and soar to new heights the next time around. How are some people able to use even embarrassing mistakes to come back with roaring triumphs, while others can't bring themselves even to mention their smallest missteps?

A traditional answer chalked it up to well-studied mental capacities. Some kids had the intelligence and ability, the determination and talent, and yes, the self-efficacy and grit to power through any failure while others didn't have "what it takes." Dweck suspected that such an easy answer didn't explain much and set out to find a better way to think about the problem. After more research and thought, she and her colleagues decided that the predicament stemmed from how people imagine intelligence works.

Some kids (and often their parents) think that mental abilities, such as remembering, understanding, problem solving, raising important questions, doing math, and so forth can't change much after birth. "You're either born with the mental wiring to do calculus and higher mathematics, or you're not," one parent told us. "You can't change your basic IQ and you can't change your brain." To these people, intelligence is frozen, a product of birth, an inherent advantage or disadvantage. You may have more marbles or fewer than the average, but either way, that's what you have to work with for the rest of your life. According to this view, a few special children are gifted and talented, but most are not. And therefore, if you fail at some cognitively challenging effort, it must mean you weren't so smart after all. We're going to insist that this is not the case.

Before we explain why, however, we want you to focus on another key point. It's not difficult to see that children who do not believe they have the potential to excel at school often do not invest the effort that could prove them wrong. But this is not just a story about kids who lack self-confidence. Children who consider themselves really smart can also believe that one's cognitive capacities are fixed and that people can't do anything to alter that. These kids will often protect their images as advantaged members of the population by declining to take on challenges so difficult that they could expose a lack of competency. They will perform tasks they know will shore up their reputations as talented students, but not attempt more.

The problem is not that they are lazy or uninterested in learning more. It's how they think intelligence works. When they fail at something big—which almost everyone does at some time or another—they come away not only discouraged on that front but less eager to try other new things. As their intellectual playground shrinks, they may arrive at the extreme form of self-doubting timidity called a sense of helplessness. A once-capable student can melt into a pool of anxiety, even while projecting a sense of self-assuredness. It is hardly the state of mind in which to get the most out of school.

Dweck wasn't saying that learners need to give themselves more credit for their intelligence or motivate themselves, perhaps surrounded by upbeat slogans on posters and mugs, to try harder. She was arguing that all of us need to revise our fundamental understanding of how our talents and capabilities develop through experience. That sounds hard, and Dweck understood that difficulty in a way that many others never do. To benefit from her research, we need to appreciate this vital point.

People's basic beliefs about how the world works—including how intelligence is gained—are rarely called to the forefront of their thinking and subjected to deliberate consideration. Yet those beliefs are always operating in the background, shaping interpretations and decisions. As Dweck noted, such convictions are implicit—seldom directly stated but strongly implied by actions. If, in your own household, you want to establish prevailing beliefs that will help your child get more out of school, you must start by confronting any deep-rooted notions you may have about an individual's being inherently smart or dumb, and wash those from your mind.

Again, this may require a little of Peter Pan's boldness. You have to believe that you have it in you to do something you have not attempted before. And, yes, we're talking about having confidence and a healthy dose of perceived self-efficacy.

Dweck had some ideas about what caused such misconceptions and how one could change them. She would soon supercharge Bandura's theory into what she termed the "new psychology of success."[5]

Proof of the Pudding

In one of her early experiments at the University of Illinois, Dweck and a graduate student, Carol Diener, placed ten-year-olds into two categories.[6] In one-on-one interviews they had invited the kids to talk about various disappointments they had suffered in school, whether scoring low on a test or getting a bad grade on an assignment—and asked them why they felt they had failed.

Some of the children were identified as "helpless" because they tended to attribute their failures to uncontrollable factors such as inherent cognitive deficits. "I have a bad memory," one might say, or "I'm not a writing person," or "I'm no math whiz." Later, Dweck would identify attributions like these as evidence of a "fixed view." In these kids' minds, whether they succeeded was largely out of their hands, the product of endowments that could not be altered.

Other children, meanwhile, described their disappointments as times when they had mistakenly failed to prepare enough or to use the right technique. For these kids, the problem wasn't that their brains weren't equal to the task. They had just not figured it out yet, or tried hard enough to succeed. These children were pegged as "mastery oriented," given their evident faith that, by setting their minds to an intellectually challenging task, they could learn how to succeed at it. By extension, these kids thought they could improve other things about themselves, including their intelligence.

Having identified the ones who believed that intelligence was fixed, and the ones who believed otherwise—those with what Dweck would later call a growth mindset—the researchers then gave the children a series of puzzles to solve. The first eight of these brainteasers were challenging, but all the kids eventually solved them. It didn't matter if a kid had a fixed or growth mindset. Everyone seemed to be having fun, talking about how much they enjoyed the challenges and sometimes asking for more. Everyone used good strategies to find their solutions—something Dweck and Diener could gauge because they asked their subjects to talk aloud as they struggled with the challenges.

With so much excitement and interest in the room, the psychologists pulled out four more puzzles and let the kids have at them. But these new ones were designed so that no one in the room could solve them. The researchers were deliberately setting the kids up to fail to see what would happen. For the fixed-mindset kids, the ones who believed that whatever intelligence they had been endowed with by birth couldn't be altered, everything changed. It was as if someone had plunged those children in some kind of I-am-a-bad-student cold bath.

These children soured quickly on the activity of working through problems, voicing pessimism about their abilities to solve them. Some said the exercises weren't fun anymore. Others tried to divert attention away from their failed attempts by, for example, blurting out comments that had nothing to do with the problems, such as mentioning what they would be doing in the days to come. Were these the same children who shone on the first set of problems, and asked for more? They sure were, but they couldn't stand to fail. Dweck ascribed the changed behavior to their fixed view of intelligence.

What about the group who believed that intelligence expands with experience and that failures serve up valuable lessons along the way? They kept trying, changing their methods for solving the problems. They didn't mind making mistakes. In fact, the flubs made it more fun. They enjoyed the challenge of a hard problem and said so. Rather than retreating with a sense of humiliation, they were more likely to seem energized by a puzzle and to appreciate the ways it turned out to be informative.

As part of the experiment, the researchers asked the children why the last four puzzles were proving to be so tough. The kids in the helpless category typically made comments about their own limitations. None of the kids that Dieter and Dweck had identified as "mastery-oriented"—the ones who assumed that brains could improve—offered that kind of explanation.

Abilities Deteriorate

Perhaps most disturbing, the skills of kids who believed they could not change their intelligence deteriorated when they took on exercises they could not crack immediately. Again, all of the children failed to solve the tougher puzzles, but because the kids talked aloud as they worked on them, the researchers knew what kinds of strategies they used.

Growth-mindset children continued to try out approaches, some of which might have worked if they'd had more time. Not so for their classmates in the other group. As those in the helpless group struggled to solve the problems and experienced failure, their abilities actually deteriorated. More than half of them resorted at some point to problem-solving approaches typical of five-year-olds. Meanwhile, the kids who did not assume they were hindered by factors out of their control continued to use more sophisticated approaches.

You will probably not be surprised to learn that the students who believed they were just not smart enough to succeed lost interest in the exercises, while those with faith in their ability to improve their abilities stuck with them and continued having fun.

What Does This Mean?

It began to occur to Dweck and her colleagues that if they could change the way a student understood intelligence, they could improve that kid's abilities and performance in school. Even more important, they could endow those students' lives with greater creativity, critical thinking, compassion, and competence. Having a growth mindset was the key to success. To understand how to bring that shift about, however, the psychologists wanted first to know why so many kids were in the fixed-mindset camp. Where had they picked up their ideas about how intelligence works? Did these impressions just form spontaneously in the mind of some kids and not others? Were they innate or a result of conditioning? Likewise, how had children in the growth-mindset group acquired their beliefs? To answer these questions, let's start with a story from the early twentieth century.

THE BIRTH OF IQ TESTS

In 1903 Alfred Binet was already an accomplished psychologist working at France's leading university when the Ministry of Education in Paris contacted him. They asked the forty-seven-year-old professor to help identify very young kids who might later have trouble in school. The ministry wanted to provide early intervention so that these children wouldn't struggle in the classroom later on. This sounds like a close cousin of a growth mindset.

Educators around the world were already debating whether nature (what you had when you were born) or nurture (what kind of help you got in life) determined who would be star pupils. Binet was more on the nurture side of the debate, but what he did helped win millions of converts to the opposite position.

The test he and a colleague devised to help the ministry would become widely accepted as a way to measure an individual's brainpower relative to the average of their age cohort. Soon enough, another interested party—Lewis Madison Terman, a psychology professor at the newly minted Stanford University in California—had the idea to translate the results into an "intelligence quotient," which was calculated by dividing one's "mental age" by one's chronological age and then multiplying that fraction by 100. After "IQ" scores had been assigned to over a million members of the US military during the First World War, the idea that intelligence levels could be expressed as simple numbers became ingrained, and in time, an IQ culture and industry grew up around it. People increasingly talked and acted as if a test taken on a given day captured how superior or inferior a thinker you were—and would be for the rest of your life.

It was all done as if examiners were assessing people's heights or weighing sacks of potatoes. Just as a pediatrician might say by how much a six-year-old was tall for her age, an IQ test administrator could declare by how much the child was smart for her age—as if the two qualities were equally measurable and meaningful.

To Terman, a great believer in eugenics, the best way to achieve human progress was to produce more smart humans through well-informed breeding. If especially gifted people could be identified, they could be encouraged to marry each other and have lots of children. Others should see their mating prospects reduced. Build a better society with superior human beings. Higher IQ scores came through your genes, Terman and his disciples proclaimed, not from anything schools or parents might do.

Until the Nazis used such notions to justify the Holocaust in the 1940s, millions of people believed in eugenics. Its ultimate decline in the latter half of the twentieth century came, however, not simply because of its association with Hitler but because of what it did to many children with seemingly high promise of success. More on that a little later.

Even after schools stopped using Binet's test or the Stanford one, the idea of a fixed IQ became deeply ingrained in our culture. Children heard the discussions, and by the age of five or six, some kids began to wonder whether they were smart or dumb. By the early twenty-first century, it was not unusual for six-year-olds to come home from school and announce, "I guess I'm smart," or "I guess I'm dumb." We've spoken to hundreds of parents from various cultures whose children have made similar announcements.

When Ken was a child growing up in Springfield, Missouri, he and his sisters listened each week to the *Quiz Kids* radio program, which was broadcast from Chicago. The popular show featured five high-IQ children who would dazzle audiences with their supposedly superior brains and seemingly endless knowledge. They could spell words Ken had never heard before and rattle off details about historical events and scientific work that seemed magical. Without explicitly saying so, the program preached the questionable gospel of gifted kids versus less gifted ones. It helped popularize the idea that some kids have the marbles, but most don't.

It's not just eugenics and IQ culture that have cultivated fixed mindsets. Parents and other significant adults in a child's life can prop up that frozen view of intelligence without ever intending to do so. Researchers have shown that the poison of fixed mindsets can creep into a family because we want to bolster a kid's self-confidence.

The Costs of Too Much Praise (or the Wrong Kind)

Think for a moment about two different ways you can compliment your kids. In the first, you can heap praise on them for something they did. "You really worked hard on that science project." That's called "task praise." In the second, you could talk about some quality they supposedly have. "You're really good at math and science." That's called "person praise." You can also offer negative comments or suggestions in both of these scenarios. ("Let me show you a better way to learn science" versus "you're just not good at science.")

It's easy to recognize that the second way of offering criticism can discourage your children. You should avoid person praise. When adults praise children for a quality like intelligence ("you are really smart"), that sounds to many kids like something that's fixed for life. You either are smart or you aren't. They will then try to do things that will prove that they have this quality called intelligence and avoid acts that might suggest otherwise. Later, if they face challenges or fail at something, there's a good chance they will conclude they don't have the smarts to get it right after all. They may also decide that they will not even try certain things because they might fail, and that would make them look dumb. Some kids won't ask questions because that suggests they don't already know the answer, and that makes people look less intelligent.

A growing body of research has demonstrated that person praise encourages kids to develop a fixed view of intelligence rather than a growth mindset. Rather than praising your kid's intelligence, you should say, "You must have worked very hard on that paper," or "You used good strategies to solve those problems," or "Let's remember what those tactics are so you can use them again." With that kind of feedback, most kids usually focus on how they must act. Outcomes will depend on what children do, not on something they are and can't change. Effort and the right strategies matter.

If you don't think this small shift in language from person to task praise can make a huge difference in the way your children handle failure—and success—then consider the research. In one study, researchers exposed some children to short periods of person praise ("you are smart") and other children to task praise ("that's good effort"). They then put both groups in a situation where they would fail. Children who got the thirty minutes of praise for their intelligence often began saying, "I can't do this. I'm just not smart enough." The kids who were praised for their efforts were more likely to stick with the task, even with repeated failure. They might say, "This is tough," and "I've got to find a way to solve this problem," but they wouldn't stop working and sour on the whole experience.[7]

When adults encounter kids who don't think much of themselves, they are likely to pour on the praise, and the kind they choose is the type that does the most harm. "But you are really smart," will flow like a fountain from the concerned adult.

It's tempting to say, "I wouldn't do that now that I've read this book," but research suggests it is as easy to do as slurping down a cold drink on a hot summer day. When we were writing this book and showed parents this section on person versus task praise, many of them said something like, "That's fine if kids have self-confidence, but if they don't, you've got to build that up first."

Yet the wrong kind of attempt to "build up self-confidence first" invites a vicious cycle that ultimately backfires. Parents pour on the person praise, causing their kids to develop a stronger fixed mindset, which makes it hard to accept failure. Kids don't try challenging work. They don't learn as much. They fall behind other children, which provokes even lower self-esteem. All of that leads parents to lather up the person praise. It's no longer just "you're smart," but now it becomes "you're just brilliant," and the cycle begins anew.

Yet is that always true? How do kids hear and understand, "You did a good job"? For younger children, no problem. Task praise makes them feel proud and believe that they can get better with plenty of the right attempts. But watch out once they hit middle and high school—and puberty.

In the elementary grades, teachers often emphasize personal growth, not how you rank against other people. Words that tell you what a good job you did sound reassuring in a kid's personal journey to grow and learn. No mixed message. But by the time young people hit puberty at around eleven, schools are changing too, especially in the United States and Western Europe.

Good old Central High begins to rank kids, or puts them in special classes that say either they are extra smart (gifted and talented or college track) or not quite up to snuff. In this "performance-oriented" world, scores on tests become more valued than the individual growth of any kid. Children might also notice that those who are judged to be a little behind the pack get the task praise because no one really expects them to meet the highest standards. It can take on a whole new meaning for some people in this environment.

If kids hear it for themselves in high school, they may think it's because teachers don't have anything positive to say about the work they are doing. In a culture that is trying to pick winners and losers, "you did a good job," becomes a sorry consolation prize. As psychologists Jamie Amemiya and Ming-Te Wang from the University of Pittsburgh argue, "Effort praise [for some kids] unintentionally communicates to adolescents negative messages about abilities and consequently reduces their motivation to learn and overcome failure."[8]

So what do you do? In general, we would be reluctant to feed them a steady diet of person praise, but you may need to see what works best for your child. Be careful, however, and think about your kid's reactions thoroughly. Children with low self-esteem will need the right feedback (task praise) far longer than other kids before they will begin to acquire a growth mindset. For many of them, any use of person praise will set them back, whether it comes from parents or other adults. You need patience and perseverance, but you also need help from every member of your community.

Does that mean you should give everyone you know a copy of this book for their birthday and circle this section with a big red marker? Maybe. It does mean that you should establish a habit of finding solutions and ways for children to improve rather than just finding faults. Show your kids how they can improve their work or study habits, but do so without being critical. If you do not feel comfortable giving your kids good feedback on their math or writing, look for free tutoring opportunities in your community. Talk to friends and neighbors about where you can get help. Teach your kids to seek assistance without hesitation or shame by doing so yourself.

What to Do?

It seems increasingly clear that one size does not fit all. You may need to change your feedback to adjust for age and the kind of learning environments your children face in school, the level of confidence they have in themselves, and maybe their birth order in the family. Is there an old reliable that you can use when you are not sure what to do?

Claude Steele, a psychologist at Stanford University, and his colleagues may have found such an escape hatch from this conundrum. Back in the 1990s, the Stanford folks set up an experiment that can inform how you help your children. Any response needs to reassure kids that adults think they have potential, that they can grow into excellent performers. Steele, Geoffrey Cohen, and Lee Ross invited some college students to submit essays for possible inclusion in a special journal of undergraduate writing.[9] Then they tried three forms of feedback to see which one would prompt the most students to take the comments home, make changes, and return with revised essays.

With the first of three comparable groups, the researchers used the "sandwich method." Here are some good things about your work; here are some weaknesses; and here are some more positive items. Sounds almost as delicious as barbecued salmon on rye. With a second group, they employed a "cut to the chase" method. Here's everything wrong with your work. Now go fix it. Both approaches worked fairly well. Still, some students did not use the suggestions they received.

In the final group, however, nearly all of the students took the feedback to heart, made sometimes extensive changes, and resubmitted their work to Steele and his colleagues. What did the psychologists do that could become a model for how you help your kids? In essence, they said, we have some high standards for this work, but we think you can meet and even surpass them. To do so, however, you will need to make some changes. Here are some key places in your writing where you need to revise your work.

That method clearly said, we have faith in your ability to improve your work if you learn and apply the right approaches. "It won't be easy, but the right kind of diligent work can help you improve." When you give students good suggestions on how to fix all the problems, they can respond with improvements. As Steele put it, "The combination of high standards and assurance was like water on parched land."[10] The approach encouraged everyone, especially those who had traditionally not done well.

Notice something important here that some researchers and journalists have failed to recognize. This whole approach depends on convincing kids that no one is going to judge them on the basis of some unfair stereotype. Trust becomes extremely important to curing this problem. Children must believe that adults will not be prejudiced, either for or against them. When psychologists have been unable to replicate these results, trust is the key ingredient that's often missing—in some cases because researchers didn't think the method would work and that attitude came shining through to the research subjects. It was like making a cherry pie and forgetting the cherries.[11]

Praising children presents special challenges for parents. When you say to your kids that a class or assignment has high expectations, but those can be met with the proper effort, they may not believe you, because after all you are their parent. You may need to add something like, "it's your choice, but you will succeed only if you try and use good methods."

Parents will enjoy more success if they have worked hard to build that sense of trust and have helped their kids understand how brains work (topics later sections of this book will explore). If you have tried to be honest and optimistic with your children but also kind and sensitive to their feelings, you have increased your chances of success. That can be hard to do if parents believe old prejudices like "intelligence is fixed for life, and you can't change it." It is essential that your family culture cultivates a growth mindset.

Build a community that includes your children and other kids in their classes. Invite their friends to your house to study and read, creating social occasions out of such gatherings. Begin that process early in their lives. Talk to your friends about these ideas and issues. Most important, keep pushing the message that basic abilities can grow but only if you use the right techniques and work on deep understanding. Furthermore, do so with lessons about how brains grow.

As we go forward, we will show you how your kids can learn deeply. In the meantime, please consider a powerful approach to these issues that could transform your family.

VIEWS OF FAILURE VERSUS IDEAS ABOUT INTELLIGENCE

In 2016, a graduate student at Stanford did some pioneering research that could enable you to transform your family. Kyla Haimovitz began to consider whether we've been barking up the wrong tree when it comes to understanding children's attitudes toward learning. What if something besides misguided beliefs about how intelligence works was the real culprit?

After all, in most families, kids don't know whether their parents have a growth or fixed view of intelligence. It's not exactly something that comes up frequently around the breakfast table. Parents can believe that smarts can grow like an Iowa cornstalk bathing in a warm spring shower, or that IQs remain frozen no matter what the weather outside. Yet those notions seldom become clear to their children.

Indeed, because fixed mindsets are implicit ideas, lying in the back of our minds, rather than explicit ones, many parents never think aloud about what they believe on the matter. Rarely do kids hear their parents say, "I think you were born dumb and you will stay that way until the day you die," or something in the other direction. Let's hope they don't.

Does that mean parents should discuss the possibility of improving intelligence directly, offering evidence that intelligence can grow, and showing kids how it does so? Sure, we'd agree with that. We're going to show you how you can communicate your belief in growth mindsets to your children. First, however, you have to consider the possibility that something else you are saying to your kids may be undermining your message that brains can change. Every time you push growth mindsets, another conversation might be saying to your children, forget it. No way that can happen.

What is this other conversation? Kyla Haimovitz and Carol Dweck argue that it is how we express our attitudes toward failure.[12] Remember the teacher from Bryn Mawr we mentioned above? She had a failure-is-bad mindset, and so do many parents—even when they believe intelligence can change. They easily convey those notions to their children. How so?

Imagine your kid comes home with a D in math. How do you react? Do you take the advice of some people and threaten your child with punishment if he or she doesn't improve their grades? Or do you think, "maybe my child is just not that good at math," and then console them with words like "not everyone can excel in every subject. You're really good at making friends," or something similar.

Do you say to yourself, "I hope their grade on other tests will make up for this one," or "let's wait and see what other kids did on the exam"? Do you pity your child's "lack of ability" and begin to act a "little nervous . . . because [you] know how hard it can be"?[13]

The threat of punishment runs the risk of harming intrinsic interest by using an extrinsic motivator (the punishment), but all the other approaches have their own downsides. They say to your children that "performance" on an exam is more important than long-term deep learning and understanding, and that a bad performance indicates they don't have what it takes. It's the same as saying, "intelligence can't be changed and you, my dear, don't have much of it."

Think about how different you will sound to your kids if you respond to their failures with more positive behavior that says to them "mistakes are wonderful opportunities to learn." Rather than reacting to their low grades with shame and pity, or horror, you can respond in ways that whisper reassurance: *Experiencing failure facilitates learning and growth.* When a psychologist asks your kid what they think about those times when they didn't do so well in school, they will reflect on it as part of the learning process, appreciating on some level that "experiencing failure enhances my performance and productivity *if I try to learn from it.*" It's like having a miniature Nobel laureate perched on their shoulders urging them to change up their approach and keep at it. Comments like "you can't learn unless you make mistakes" are reminders that intelligence is constantly evolving and whatever brainpower you wind up with was not predestined from the start.

In some households, the behavior of the adults sends a strong signal that, when something goes wrong, some culprit must be called to account. Much energy goes into identifying who's at fault, who's to blame.

Kids may hear an argument erupt between their parents that culminates in, say, their father telling their mother, "this is all your fault." The first order of business is not to find a way out of a predicament but to mete out the punishment for it, starting with identifying who's the bad person. That pin-the-tail-on-the-guilty-party becomes especially harmful when the squabble is over a child's performance in school. Likewise, when children fail, parents may tell them, "You've got to own your mistakes." That sounds like a reasonable demand for accountability, but it shouldn't be the first and most frequent response to a mistake. Instead, the strongest emphasis should be on finding solutions.

Another Kind of Reaction

When Marton came home with the grades from his first term in middle school, the D he had earned in math was a shocker. He had always been good with numbers and seemed to enjoy wrangling with difficult problems. The boy was often like the kids we described earlier, who reacted to tricky puzzles with responses like "I was *hoping* this was going to be fun!"

When Moday, his mother, saw the report, she had several options for how to react. She could have thrown what Ken's southern cousins liked to call "a hissy fit with a crocheted tail," screaming at her son and maybe even throwing a few objects at the walls. She could have turned stony on him, and calmly announced the loathsome punishment he would suffer until he brought his grades up: "That train set in the basement you like so much is going to be taken apart piece by piece until your grades improve." Or she might have shamed him by wailing in her slight Texas accent, "Don't ever embarrass me again with a grade like this." There are scores of ways to convey that a failure is intolerable or disgraceful, and with that message drive a child toward a fixed mindset. Thank goodness she chose none of them.

Instead, Moday calmly asked Marton what they could learn from this experience. "This will be a terrific chance to learn something valuable," she smiled at her son. "The important thing we need to do is try to understand the concepts behind the problems you got wrong."

As they continued to talk, she asked what kinds of problems Marton was doing in his math class. "Oh, you know," he explained, "adding and subtracting, multiplying and dividing."

It suddenly hit her. He hadn't been overtaxed by a challenging teacher. He'd been doing arithmetic since at least the first grade. He was bored with a class that was too easy and reteaching him material he had already learned. (This may not always be the cause of a poor performance, but keep our larger point in mind. How you react to failure can shape the influence it will have.)

Moday didn't say anything about boredom to Marton, but she concluded their discussion with the promise that they would use this occasion to learn. "Your deep learning and advancement in math, a subject you have always loved, is more important than the report card. But let's get some input from your teacher. I'm sure he'll have some good ideas." That afternoon, she made an appointment with Mr. Dunne.

When she met with the teacher a few days later, he confirmed that the class was doing problems in basic arithmetic. "What about algebra?" she asked with a smile.

"We don't offer algebra at Crockett Middle School," he explained. "The students aren't capable of that." It appears that Mr. Dunne, and perhaps the school administrators, had a fixed mindset. Worse than that, it was attached to another form of bias. When Moday reacted with some surprise, aware that algebra was offered at the town's other middle school, he elaborated: "That's true, but Jefferson has a different population than we do. We have many students who are . . ." He stopped himself mid-sentence, but finally finished, "who come from ethnic groups that are just not that good at math."

When Mary Murphy and Elizabeth Canning from the Department of Psychological and Brain Sciences at Indiana University analyzed the grades of some fifteen thousand students who had taken science courses, they found that in classes led by teachers who thought intellectual capabilities were in-born, the racial achievement gap was on average twice as large as in classes taught by teachers endorsing "the idea that ability is malleable and can be developed through persistence, good strategies, and quality mentoring." One implication is that any educators who remain captive to the "fixed mindset culture of genius" so prevalent in science education—the idea that "some students have strong, innate intellectual abilities, while others do not"—actually harm their students with their prejudices and conceptions of how intelligence works.[14]

As for Moday, encountering such an attitude in her own son's school, the enterprising mother paused for a minute, thinking calmly about how she should respond. She could feel her heart beating more rapidly, but she focused on staying positive—on treating a low grade as a step toward learning rather than an occasion for blame. She wanted Mr. Dunne to know that her concern was with deep learning rather than performance in the grade book.

"I want to propose something unusual," she finally managed to say. "Give Marton the algebra textbook that they use at Jefferson and let him sit in the back of the room and study that more challenging subject on his own. We'll get a tutor for him if necessary. At the end of this term, give him the same final they use at Jefferson, and his grade this year in math will come from how he does on the test." After considerable hemming and hawing, Mr. Dunne accepted.

Over the next few days, Moday also learned of other kids who were not thriving in their math class at Crockett Middle School. They hadn't all brought home disappointing grades for the first term, but they all shared a preference to tackle algebra rather than wait for another year. Other parents went to school administrators and asked that their kids be offered the same path Marton was taking.

Soon, more than half the class was studying algebra, each student doing so on an individual basis. Parents pooled money to hire several tutors, while making sure that no family had to chip in more than it could afford. The kids began making social events out of studying algebra, holding several picnics attended by nearly everyone, forming small groups who could gather at someone's house to work together, and getting on the telephone nearly every night to confer with friends about problems that were stumping them.[15]

This experiment occurred more than forty years ago, but if it took place today such a program might incorporate online resources, including games. An early one of these that impressed us was launched in 2011 by Jean-Baptiste Huynh and his colleagues. To help children develop an understanding of the concepts of algebra, they created an online adventure about a shy dragon who doesn't like to be with other objects. The goal is to isolate the dragon, using algebra's method of isolating an unknown in an equation.[16]

At the end of the Crockett Middle School year, the children who took Marton's path were tested with the same final exam in algebra used across town at Jefferson, and none scored lower than 85 percent. All went on to study more advanced math. Marton remained fascinated by the subject and, after college and graduate school, made his career in a math-intensive field.

This story is based on real people and events, with only names and a few incidental details changed to protect people's privacy and to help us make the key points clearer. The tale shows the power of a community of parents and their children acting together. Was this sit-in-the-back-of-the-room approach the best way to learn algebra? Probably not, but it was an available option, and in some ways did more to make students appreciate that how deeply you learn a subject is more important than the grades you are given in it. Gaining that perspective was a big step in their schooling and it's a perspective you can help your kids achieve in various ways.

At the very least, Moday and Marton's experience should illustrate why the most productive response to a student's failure is to engage them in thinking creatively about solutions rather than assigning blame for what went wrong. The story should emphasize the importance of growth mindsets, not only among students but among their teachers and parents. We hope it also helps you see how too much focus on test scores and course grades can undermine the deep learning of a subject—and reinforce fixed mindsets, with even more lasting damage.

How you react to your children's triumphs and missteps can shape their conceptions of intelligence, which in turn will influence how they deal with success and failure and what they get out of school, no matter what they study. If your kids believe they can become more intelligent, they will learn more and become highly productive people.

But must you wait until they fail at something before providing any assistance? Isn't there some way to teach them that intelligence can grow and begin chipping away at the concept of frozen mental abilities before that happens? Educators have been struggling with these questions for several decades, trying one way and then another to shift minds toward believing that all learners have the ability to get "smarter." Unfortunately, these efforts have not yielded instructions that can be followed in paint-by-numbers fashion. They have, however, left us with important insights into how some children have come to realize that their intelligence can grow. We'll still need to react well to their failures, but the lessons we are about to explore will advance the cause.

As mentioned earlier, some researchers created a bit of controversy when the results of their mindset studies proved hard to replicate. Consider the wise questions that Carol Dweck, working with David Yeager, raised about that mini-tempest: "Why should the idea that students can develop their abilities be controversial? And why should it be controversial that believing this can inspire students, in supportive contexts, to learn more? In fact, don't all children deserve to be in schools where people believe in and are dedicated to the growth of their intellectual abilities?" But none of this is easy. "The challenge of creating these supportive contexts for all learners will be great," Yeager and Dweck concluded, "and we hope mindset research will play a meaningful role in their creation."[17]

LEARNING LEARNING

What does it mean to take the journey we call learning? To help your kids shake loose of the tyranny of fixed mindsets, you must answer that question. To understand it better, let's go back to the beginning of the process. How does learning start? If you think about that, you can grasp something important about your children that will enable you to help them flourish as learners in school and elsewhere.

No matter the age of your kids, they all had some common experiences when they were born. We need to understand their experiences if we want to help them from this point on, no matter how old they are now. Some people reading this book will have children who are already teenagers or older. Some will have newborns or toddlers. That doesn't matter. All humans have some common experiences in the beginning of their lives.

While some learning takes place in the womb, let's start with that magic day you will go on to celebrate annually: your birth date. What was happening to you as you lay in a crib moments after that big event? What happened to your child on their own birth date? A thunderstorm of light, sound, touch, tastes, and smells bombarded their senses. That was their only contact with the outside world.

Before that day, each kid had a cluster of many billions of brain cells housed in a little skull. But with the sensory input flooding through their ears, nose, eyes, tongue, and skin, they got information about their surroundings. Some people are born without sound or sight, but the same ideas apply. Sensory stimuli begin and sustain education.

What did your children do with all of that input? They tried to make sense of it. But how did they do that? They made sense of the environment by doing something that human brains can do quite well. They noticed patterns and built mental models, or paradigms, about how the world works: *I cry, I get fed. I cry, I get my diaper changed.*

They didn't have those words yet, just the perceptions and feelings, and the models they built were simple. But over time they began to construct more complex ones and to combine them into more intricate and extensive sets of ideas. Eventually, they started associating sounds they heard with the models they constructed, and they had the beginnings of spoken language.

Most important, they began to use the mental models they fashioned to understand subsequent sensory input. They had a model of something we call a chair. When they went someplace new and saw one of those objects, they understood what it was because they already had a model of it in their minds.

Why Dogs Are Dogs

Junhui was born in rural China, and for the first eighteen months of his life he heard only the words of Mandarin. He learned to call that big, hairy, friendly kind of creature that sometimes licked his face or stole his food a *gou,* but when he came to the United States at the age of eighteen months, the word changed. That lively beast became a *dog.* Junhui adjusted easily and began learning a second language even before he had mastered the first.

Just like you and your children, he also continued to build a rich collection of mental models and to use those frameworks to understand new sensory input. Whether he used the word *gou* or *dog,* he could transfer his understanding of this four-legged creature from one example to another. Even when he saw a collie that had been injured and lost a leg, he still understood that this was the same kind of creature as the boxer he met in his new home in Washington, DC.

That ability to transfer mental models and even to adjust them slightly is one of the more remarkable skills human brains master without formal instruction. You can go to a completely unfamiliar country and still understand a new sensory input in terms of an already existing model. You can walk into a place where you have never been and understand that you are in a *room* and that is a *chair* and there is a *table,* no matter what sounds are used to refer to them.

An electromagnetic field we call light tickles the retina of our eyes and we have a sensation we call seeing. We understand what we see in terms of our previously constructed mental models, not just in terms of the light that floods our nervous system. Something similar happens with sounds, touch, and other sensations. They are the pathways for all learning, the way the world communicates with us.

That's a beautiful system that serves us well, but it does have one tiny problem that you must understand if you hope to help your kids get more out of school. Here's the catch: since we are building our mental models out of patterns we experience, it is possible to form them from a few early examples that are actually not typical of the whole. It would be like watching some bush-league baseball players sweeping the New York Yankees during spring training and then proceeding to place bets on the conviction that this minor team from Hoboken was better than the Bronx Bombers.

To make matters worse, this is a problem that can grow into a monster. Once we form our models, we tend to fall in love with them and don't want to let them go. It's just too easy to go with the old familiar way of thinking. As such, our way of forming paradigms, wonderful as it may be, is the source of all false stereotypes, the origin of every nasty prejudice.

We All Live in Our Own World

Consider for a moment the plight of a fictional character named Truman Burbank. Jim Carrey played this young adventurer in a movie we've already recommended, *The Truman Show*. It's a comic film with a storyline that illustrates something quite important and complex.

In it, Truman Burbank has lived his entire life as the central character of a highly popular reality television program. But he doesn't realize it. Because he has been in this show since birth, he does not understand that all of the people around him are actors playing roles. He is the only one who doesn't know that his village is a giant television studio with hidden cameras that follow his every move and broadcast his life to a worldwide audience eagerly tuning in to his round-the-clock reality show.

In an important sense, we are all prisoners of our own studio settings. Our brains have constructed mental models, sometimes quite elaborate ones, and we use those models to look at the world and understand how it works. Part of the goal of deep learning is to question our existing paradigms and perhaps to construct new ones, or at least to realize that alternatives are possible. It's an idea we will explore later in this book.

How Does This Relate to Intelligence and Growth Mindsets and Your Kids?

Let's illustrate how such mental models work with the ones we have formed about the way intelligence functions. For various reasons—some of which we have already discussed—millions of children have built in their minds the idea that intelligence is something that can't change or grow. In their thinking some human brains are "smart," and others are "mediocre" or downright "dumb" and can't change their basic ability level. They then use that notion to tell themselves why they and other people do well or poorly with certain subjects in school.

For the most part, they develop that mental model because so many forces have taught it to them. Once humans form such conceptions, they stick in their minds like glue. The mental models are convenient answers to life's experiences. They become deeply embedded in our minds, so firmly fixed that we don't even need to think about them.

Do we ever change those frameworks after we form them? Yes, but that's quite an operation. To do so we must experience what some learning theorists call a model failure. That is, we need to go to a place and get in a situation where our model does not work. And we have to care that it fails.

We must expect a certain result, and not get it. In other words, we must encounter ideas and information that are inconsistent with our mental models. If we deeply care that our paradigm does not explain something, we might begin to grapple with it, to change it, to twist it one way and then another to try to make it fit. In the process, we might build a completely new paradigm.

Some scientists began to question the prevailing theory that brains and intelligence can't change when they considered infants. Newborns can't read or write, speak or understand any language. Yet we don't consider them dumb. We assume they will change as they grow older. Yet if their abilities can grow, why can't older children or adults continue to improve over time?

That was not the only evidence that brains could change and "get smarter." A few people began to consider evidence that accumulated in, of all places, zoos. When lions, tigers, monkeys, and other big mammals died, some of their doctors sliced up their brains, studied those slices, and found something quite astounding.

If those animals had spent most of their lives alone in isolated cages with no toys to entertain or intrigue them or other creatures to challenge them, their brains looked very different from those of other zoo animals. The isolated animals had fewer connections between their brain cells. It was those connections that allowed them to think, to learn how toys worked, to deal with other animals who tried to take their goodies. To make those connections sprout and grow, the animals needed to problem-solve.

As psychologist Lisa Blackwell noted, "the adult animals who were exercising their brains by playing with toys and each other were also smarter ... better at solving problems and learning new things."[18] The old mental model that brains and intelligence couldn't grow didn't explain these new findings.

But the clincher came when a group of researchers studied the brains of people who could not juggle.[19] The researchers began by scanning the brains of all study participants. They then taught half of the participants how to perform the trick. After months of practice, they brought everyone back to the lab and scanned their brains again. The brains of those who had still not learned the circus maneuver (because no one had taught it to them or they hadn't practiced it) looked the same.

But what about those who had been taught how to juggle, went home and practiced, and could now perform the old trick like a vaudeville comic? Just as you might expect, the brains of people in that group had changed considerably. The parts that controlled motor and visual skills, enabling them to keep three balls rotating in space, had grown. You could actually "see" how their brains had changed as they learned something new. If intelligence was an indication of how well your brain functioned, the standard mental model that said IQs couldn't change now required an alteration of its own.

But do you think that every psychologist and neurologist in the world suddenly declared, "by golly, I was wrong—intelligence can actually grow if you get the right kind of help and then practice what someone has taught you"? You tell us. If you came into this chapter believing in fixed mindsets, did the last few paragraphs change your mind? (We can hear a few books slamming shut out of frustration and unwillingness to alter a deeply seated mental model constructed long ago.)

Some years back, Ken shared these studies with a physician who ran a major state university. That school leader simply pronounced, "I don't believe those studies." But he was wrong and just couldn't let go of an old mental model. On other occasions, we sensed that some people just didn't think about the implications of what they heard or read.

After some occasion later arose when it would be logical to think and act like brains can change and diligence can grow, the old mental models still triumphed. To these people, kids are either smart or dumb and will remain that way until the curtain closes. They are either highly diligent and full of grit, or they are not. They are either gifted and talented, or not.

Can Your Kids Change Their Mental Models about Intelligence?

So how can you help your kids change their mental models if they now fall on the frozen side? If your children are not part of the small segment of humans who have severe limitations on their cognitive functioning and development, you can help them improve their intelligence. Put them in a situation where their existing model does not work and they care that it doesn't. We can take clues from some programs that have successfully done just that.

Over the last twenty years, a number of efforts have managed to move people from a fixed to a growth concept of intelligence and in the process improve their learning performance and their abilities to triumph over failure. You can begin to utilize those experiments by building what we call a learning household. We've seen this kind of family practice and arrangement in scores of homes. We've already begun that conversation in earlier pages. As we take it forward in pages to come, we will provide you with more in-depth examples of how that kind of home works.

INTERLUDE

We know what some readers are thinking: "Can't students get ahead just with better study habits and good learning techniques?" That's what many books on doing well in school preach ad nauseam.

Certainly some approaches to studying and learning work better than others. We will explore and share the latest research later this book. Yet considerable work has found that even the best of good study habits alone will not turn the trick.

Nearly forty years ago, Susan Bobbitt Nolan found that adults could teach students the best ways to do homework until the cows came home, but the kids wouldn't use those highly recommended techniques consistently if they had the wrong priorities in school.[20] If they primarily wanted to get the highest grades (basically, to beat everyone else in an academic competition), then any class time devoted to how to learn had little influence on what they did. Only those who valued learning for "its own sake" went on to employ those good approaches when studying.

Growth Mindsets Make a Difference

In 2007, researchers put some seventh-grade kids through eight solid weeks of training in best study skills.[21] This group was not distracted with any teaching about growth mindsets or deep intentions. With a second group, however, the researchers mixed it up. As well as being instructed in better ways to read, understand, and solve problems, they also encountered the research on growth mindsets. Which kids did better?

When students enter big transition years like the seventh grade without a strong growth mindset, their learning and grades start tumbling. That is what happened in the 2007 experiment. Both groups suffered lower grades initially, as kids of that age often do in what's called the "seventh-grade slump." But once some of them began learning that their brains could grow smarter, those students began to improve. By the end of the year, they had recouped their losses and then some. The kids who heard only about better ways to study continued to spiral downward. Time and again, gaining awareness of how your brain can grow, and is growing, does more good than spending hours looking only at favored study techniques.

Please don't get us wrong. Researchers have discovered some powerful ways to study and learn that easily outrank the traditional methods that many books still peddle. We'll help you with those in our later discussion of how to help kids learn deeply. Yet if we didn't spend time on the great influence that growth mindsets can have and how to ignite them, even the best study techniques would leave your kids underprepared for school. They need a solid foundation of both deep intentions and the understanding that their intelligence can grow. Only then are they likely to apply the best approaches to studying.

THREE

Creating a Home that Supports Learning

SOME FAMILIES create dynamic environments where children's educations flourish. Some have built learning households around religious texts that everyone reads and discusses together. Others have crafted them around sports enthusiasms. Still others have done so with the study of nature or history or the human brain. You can create yours around learning anything from politics to poetry—whatever captivates your children's attention. Anyone can build that kind of setting. We will help you do so.

You may need more than one focus to serve the interests of multiple children, creating an open environment where they stimulate each other. You may find that your children's favorite subjects change as they grow older, acquire new friends, and have different experiences. Welcome that eclectic mix and evolution. Constantly help your kids see the intersections of their dominant interests and other matters. They might not take a shine to everything you introduce, but keep trying, floating new topics, and making connections to what you know is already on their minds.

Families who fashion their homes into learning households weave the process into every aspect of their lives. Parents model learning for their kids by reading, studying, practicing, taking on new projects (perhaps to learn a new language), talking openly about goals they have and any difficulties they are figuring out how to overcome. Parents set good examples by diving into topics of particular interest and discussing important ideas. A climate of inquiry runs through every day.

Yes, these parents also help their kids with fundamental skills, reading to them frequently and giving them math problems and writing opportunities. But they do so especially thoughtfully, informed by research in areas from phonics to growth mindsets.[1] When they lack a strong background in some area, they use the opportunity of their children's education to brush up. "When I was your age, I didn't learn much about how the human brain works, so it's great to learn about it now together," they might say. "I'm amazed by this new book—look at these fantastic pictures." Become the enthusiastic learner you want your kids to be.

Perhaps most important, parents recognize when their children harbor potential passions, and they let those interests bloom, even when they might not fit some preconceived notion of what is necessary to a good education. Introduce everything with a question and an opportunity rather than a requirement.

Consider beginning a breakfast or dinner discussion this way: "I was reading today that a lot of people make the mistake of thinking they are just naturally smart or not so smart. But actually, their ability to learn new stuff can change quite a bit over time and they can do things to increase it. How do you kids think someone could do that?" At first you may get a lot of silly responses, or simply, "I dunno."

Be patient. Smile. Pass along a short, kid-friendly article on the topic and urge them to check it out because you'd like their thoughts.[2] We've done this with children as young as five (basically, any kids that had learned to read). On the subject of growth mindsets in particular, Ken recently pulled out an old article that a student had first read in the first grade and put it in front of the same kid as a high school senior. The young man did not remember reading it when he was much younger, yet its message that brains can grow (probably a message he continued to hear across the years) had clearly made it through. Its influence on his thinking showed up in the unmistakable growth mindset he brought to many subjects and activities.

You can stir up a powerful conversation about what an article means. What's the evidence it offers to support its claim? Ask for thoughts about it: "Do you accept the contention? Why or why not?" Help your student see the strength of the argument. Return to the topic from time to time to reconsider whether that argument still holds.

Doing the Same with Phonics

This engaging approach, using casual conversation to pique a learner's interest in a subject, doesn't only apply to the realms of big ideas and world affairs. It can work just as well at the level of skills building. Take the mastery of phonics—normally a matter of rote exercises, but potentially more interesting to a kid. Do they read often and well? Ask them. Do they spell well? Do you?

We know some parents who like to begin with a confession: "You know, I need to get better at spelling." Or "It would be nice if whenever I came across a new word while I'm reading I could figure out how to pronounce it. I wouldn't have to ask someone else how to say it." The follow-up is an invitation: "I guess I better learn about phonics. Want to do that with me?"[3]

PASSION-BASED LEARNING AND THE HOUSEHOLD THAT SUPPORTS IT

A few years ago, a radio show host invited Ken to be a guest on his morning program. As the conversation turned to the keys to deep learning, Ken began to make the case for encouraging students to follow their passions and delve into subjects they want to understand better. But the interviewer was not willing to concede that students must be motivated to learn, and that motivation largely springs from positive attitudes and feelings toward the material to be mastered. His focus was on whether students were graduating with the skills that would make them employable, whether they had to be force-fed that instruction or not.

The objection he raised was one we've heard often—in his case, summoning up thefanciful subject of "underwater basket weaving." It might have its passionate adherents, but no school should indulge that preference because no one could make a living from such a skill. "You can't just let students follow their own passions—they have to learn practical stuff. We have to require them to take essential courses whether they like them or not."

What this interviewer did not grasp is that a person who has developed into an avid, capable learner will be highly successful at whatever work and study they later go on to do. When they encounter something new that their job or school requires of them, they will know how to find joy in the challenge and tap into their passion for what they are trying to achieve because they have had experience with those sensations. And how did they gain that experience? By going all-in on some realm of learning they loved exploring in the past. Passion breeds passion. People learn to become passionate by becoming passionate. By the same token, if someone has never experienced the satisfaction of making progress in an area of deep, intrinsic interest, or going at a problem with real fervor and commitment, they don't know to seek it out.

We know a young man named Nate who, in grade school, fell in love with the saxophone. He discovered free lessons on YouTube and practiced what they had to teach. Before long, he was filling his home with the sounds of Charlie Parker, and winning first chair in his school band. No one told him he had to play the sax. He took it up as a passion.

In those same years, he became serious about drawing and learned to wield a pencil like a magic wand, sketching faces and people in intricate scenes—again learning from resources he found on the internet. Later, when Nate moved on to other interests, these early passions served him well. He had tasted the fruits of his fascinations and learned to savor the joys of his own diligence. In high school, he immersed himself in many endeavors and subjects, from history and creative writing to statistics and basketball.

Parents, more than educators, have the freedom to let those feelings well up within their children. Listen to your kids. Watch their eyes and actions, their faces and shoulders. Ask them questions about what they like. Accept whatever they say about their interests. Remember, you aren't following a curriculum. Families don't have curricula.

You can let your kids pursue interests that enthrall them, however fleetingly, and test the waters with activities they might later decide aren't for them. Give them a chance to flex their passions. Go with the flow. You can also support them in growing the set of interests that endure. When they display a deep interest in something, you can help them see connections to dozens of other matters.

Every time your kids follow their own interests and become more knowledgeable and capable in a realm they care about, they will deepen their appreciation of how it feels to be exhilarated about learning. They will grow their ability to generate that zeal for themselves, even in the face of learning challenges that may not at first hold much appeal.

Stories about Finding Passion

Imagine a four-hour, voluntary, Saturday morning class that students never miss—indeed, that they attend with joy and enthusiasm. Imagine also that the kids who take this course have struggled in school and had no interest in learning until they got to this program. Think you can learn a thing or two from that example? We suspect you can.

Steve Rees, a former architect and amateur race car driver, co-founded that Saturday class with Linda Buchner. He had gone to lunch one day at De La Salle Education Center, and by the time he left the building, without much planning, he found himself volunteering to teach a class on creativity and entrepreneurship. Most of the kids attending this charter high school on the south side of Kansas City were there because they had run afoul of the public schools for poor behavior or academic failure, but the inventive architect and his colleague thought they had an idea that could change hundreds of students' lives. The remarkable educational experience they went on to fashion also offers powerful lessons you can use with your children.

Rees had little experience with teaching or exposure to education research, but he had arrived at some important insights about how to help others learn. For the most part, these were drawn from his own life and commitment to fostering a creative mindset (an idea explored in pages to come). When we asked him to describe his childhood, we heard about elements that other highly inventive people have mentioned in recounting theirs. His parents encouraged the kind of play that involved making stuff, even setting up their garage as a "kind of laboratory" where he and his friends could tinker and build, test and imagine.[4] The kids went there for the fun of learning and growing their abilities, not because any grade depended on it. Their projects were exciting and intriguing. The chance to create was its own motivation and reward. The satisfaction of making something they were proud of drove the young Steve and his friends.

It was in 2008 that Rees offered his first course at De La Salle, to an ethnically diverse class made up of young men and women in equal numbers. He called it MindDrive. By that point retired from his architectural firm, he could play with the moment. At first, the students in the class learned to build small stuff. Mostly they constructed models of objects around them—gluing toothpicks or welding pieces of metal to make little buildings and bridges. Yet from almost the first day they clamored to build their own full-size car.

Why was this their passion? Maybe because automobiles were such a central part of the world around them, and all of modern industrial culture. Or maybe because these students were acutely aware of being at the bottom rung of society's economic ladder and lacking the means to purchase any fine example of that symbol of success and power. Maybe it was just because they had found out Rees was an amateur race car driver and knew other such drivers, including actor Paul Newman.

The important thing is that, for whatever reason, it was their passion—and Rees and his colleague Linda Buchner were smart enough to seize the moment, even though it meant shifting the course in a new direction. As we shall see, that pivot paid off in many ways, as a very energized group of students not only produced a car they were proud of, but one that would not pollute the environment they lived in. And on top of that, their enthusiasm for solving the challenges of this one passion project carried them into new areas of learning they had never known about or expected to find interesting.

We need to pause here and underscore how impressive a move this was by Rees and Buchner. You might already, at this point in the book, see it as only logical. You might consider it obvious that students are most likely to take a deep approach to their learning when they are trying to answer questions or solve problems that they regard as important, intriguing, beautiful, and perhaps fun. If so, we need to remind you of the unfortunate reality: that's not the way schooling usually works.

Most of the time, teachers are in charge of posing all the questions the kids are expected to answer. They make assignments and outline the requirements to fulfill them. That practice creates a gap between what happens in school and the conditions needed to foster deep learning.

To be sure, a strong case can be made that teachers and parents should control most of the questions that kids pursue in school—after all, wise adults can imagine inquiries that will never occur to young people. But denying students a role in framing the questions still creates a gap. How that gap is filled makes a huge difference in the whole business of education, and in how you help your kids get more out of school.

So, again, what did Steve Rees and Linda Buchner do that was so special? When the architect-turned-teacher and his colleague were presented with a precious opportunity, they jumped on it. Their students were expressing a passion, and Rees recognized that it would take them further and faster on their learning journey than his originally planned approach could. He and Buchner quickly made the students' goal the backbone of a revised syllabus, and recast their own roles as providing timely, expert support to the students' project—while also looking for those moments when a particular step could serve as a point of departure to provide instruction in one of the broader concepts the course was intended to teach.

Maybe it was the race car driver in him, the well-honed instincts to decide when to zig right or zag left, zoom ahead, or stay back in the pack. However they develop it, creative people like Rees seem to gain the ability to see possibilities that others miss. He and Buchner grasped that they must build on the bedrock of their students' passion and find ways to help their charges expand their interests to broader foundations. That's one of the key notions of this entire book. If you want to help your kids get more out of school, you should meet them where they are, and be prepared to help them grow into something new.

Students started with cars but the MindDrive program helped them understand that to pursue that quest they must also understand science, math, engineering, communications, environmental studies, problem solving, history, and more. The kids traipsed happily down these new paths because they came to them on their way to a deep passion. They found new loves that would never have emerged without their original interest in cars.

The whole journey fostered a deep and wide curiosity and improved academic performance across a range of disciplines and courses. It was an entirely voluntary program that took place outside of class but spread its influence across its participants' entire school experience.

Perhaps most of all, the students learned to succeed at something and experienced the joy of having done so. They could now go into new areas of learning, knowing what success felt like and that such moments were possible. You can help your kids do the same.

Rees procured an old wreck of an Indy car and challenged the kids to turn the broken-down vehicle into a high-mileage electric automobile. They learned about environmental issues in the process and learned how to communicate the story of their project more broadly.

From the beginning, Rees and Buchner made a point of shining a spotlight on the MindDrive program, posting photos of all the students in the hallway outside the classroom to instill a sense of pride and ownership of this special enterprise. As they worked with administrators to set a broad vision for MindDrive and raise awareness of the course, they developed a companion communications program that sang a rich chorus of achievement.

"Our mission," they wrote on their website, is "to inspire students to learn through mentoring and project-based learning, to expand their vision of the future, and for them to be a positive influence on the community."

That theme resonated through the field trips they began to take. When Rees challenged the students to devise a rechargeable electric car that could be driven all the way from San Diego, California, to Jacksonville, Florida, the students weren't satisfied with a theoretical achievement. They wanted to drive from coast to coast to see if their vehicle really could make it. The old Indy car was the perfect starting point. It was already lightweight, and the students could make it lighter.

As the young people began their drive across the country, stopping occasionally to recharge their battery, they arranged in advance to make presentations to local schools, clubs, an occasional university, and other groups. The kids expanded their ability to communicate, to speak publicly, and to tell their story. Later they drove from Kansas City, Missouri, to Washington, DC, gaining the opportunity to interact with government on the highest level and adding politics to the list of disciplines they studied.

In the stories we tell throughout this book about creativity and passion, be prepared to notice some common elements with this one. Creative people learn to examine themselves and how they work. As Paul Baker, a renowned teacher of creativity, put it in one of his classes, "Get used to the pattern by which things come up in your mind and your imagination. Find out when and at what times of the day you work best and what motivates you."[5]

In building your learning household, help your kids find out what's inside them. Help them discard the parts that are old and stale, and enhance and use the elements that are unique, beautiful, and useful. Get them involved in running the household—helping with cooking, shopping for food, cleaning, preparing meals, dusting, mowing, tending gardens, and planting flowers.

What tickles their fancy? Encourage them to spend time reflecting on what motivates them, to talk with themselves and other people, to visualize themselves working. Help them figure out what conditions they need to do creative work. Do they work best when they're in certain moods? Do certain attitudes help get their ideas churning? How about physical activity? Make a ritual out of writing about creative work and thoughts. Urge and equip them to keep a journal on their creative thoughts and lives.

The Boy Who Became Passionate about a Conversation with Nature

Imagine a young kid growing up in the 1930s in what is now Silicon Valley. In his boyhood, before Hewlett-Packard, much less Apple and other high-tech companies, started up their businesses there, Dudley Herschbach remembered the walks he took all alone with his own thoughts.[6] He recalled the birds and pools of water, and how nature swirled around him.

Or imagine Marsha's childhood in a small town in north Texas, with warm afternoons devoted to fishing for crawdad in the long ditch running alongside the road near her house. It was an era of good stories and time to daydream—and it didn't require a semi-rural environment. Similar elements shaped the worlds of children living in urban Brooklyn and other densely populated communities. Perhaps more important, it isn't an era that has to be over. You can recreate it, and we urge you to do so. You can get your children outdoors with no tightly scheduled agenda, rambling through a cityscape or along a creek bed, discovering intriguing bits of nature and human influence on that environment.

Play the story game with your kids. Start telling a tale. After getting the ball rolling for forty-five seconds or so, point at one of your kids and ask them to keep it going, adding their own characters, plot twists, or details. Let them take the story in any direction they want. Then it's their turn, after a minute or so, to point at someone else, who continues the narrative until they pass it along to a next contributor. If you're stuck for ideas, you can use the introduction of a familiar story to launch the game. Once we started with *Charlotte's Web* and another time with *Of Mice and Men,* taking care to choose a work appropriate to the age of our children or grandkids but still using the same basic technique.

What does this tell us about creating a good learning household? A lot, but before we go there, let's add one more ingredient to this mix. Something else has changed, and we must understand those changes to build a successful home where learning flourishes.

Too Perfect

We might not be able to rebuild the world of rural California that lit up Dudley Herschbach, or recreate mid-century Missouri, where kids organized their own play on Roanoke Avenue and explored the caves at Doling Park. But we can recapture some of the key elements that fostered deep learning without much anxiety and worry.

If you build a learning household to help your kids make higher grades, and that goal is apparent from what you say and emphasize, your assistance can drive your kids toward perfectionism. That's not good. If you become involved only right before a big exam or as they prepare for a major assignment, you are shouting, "I care only about your grade." That's not good either. Instead, make learning more casual, woven into the fabric of life. Play games that give them a chance to learn to reason and draw conclusions (like *Clue*).

Chess can help kids improve their memory, problem solving, and planning skills and habits. Experienced players learn to put themselves in someone else's shoes, to anticipate the moves their opponents might make. Some research has found that kids who play chess will learn to recognize and remember visual patterns more easily than nonplayers. They can become deeply involved in concentrating on the moment and the work they are doing. Chess players often excel at inventing alternative approaches to problems. Oh, and here's a benefit that your children may realize years after you teach them chess. Some research finds that chess players are less likely to suffer from dementia as they age. In the meantime, chess players learn to pay attention and are less likely to experience attention deficit disorders.

Some kids think that all knowledge comes from books and the internet. We'll help you broaden and change your children's perspectives. You can begin to engage them in original research. Once they become creators of knowledge, and not just consumers, their world will change. Their ability to understand complex ideas will blossom, improving their performance in school. We'll help you begin that process.

We know what some readers are thinking. "My kids can't do original research when they are young." But we'll show you how they can and why that is so important. Maybe some skeptics will object, "they have to learn the basics first." We'll help you understand how mixing original research into their learning at an early age can help them conquer fundamental skills that schools often emphasize.

Provide them with the help they need but leave them to their own devices as much as possible. Let them play outdoors with other kids and invent their own games. If your kids are still young, you can take them on their first walks along a creek bed or through a park. You can enchant them with your own stories and adventures, but let them find their own fascinations.

Make it all casual, and as they grow older, let them take time to daydream. Share your own fantasies but never intrude on theirs unless they invite you. Play the submarine parent instead of the helicopter type who monitors their every move. You can raise your telescope from time to time to quietly check on their safety, but don't hover over them constantly.

And here's the great irony: if you want to help your kids get more out of school, make the learning household about learning that has no direct connection to school. Make it about awe with life, about inventing stuff, about their passion.

Get Your Kids Involved in Building Stuff

You can build a workshop home the way Jeffrey Hawkins's parents did. When the guy who invented the first successful handheld digital assistant (the Palm Pilot) was growing up on the north shore of Long Island, his entire family invented stuff. Tinkering in the garage with his father and two brothers helped him discover the joy of learning and experimenting.[7] It might help your kids too.

Other children might learn in the kitchen or on the outdoor grill, helping their parents to fix a meal, or bake a cake. These kids (and maybe their older siblings) are invited into that enchanted place where pies and cakes, and even the morning coffee, emerge like some mysterious concoctions. Importantly, their parents let them help with breakfast rather than requiring them to do so. Or maybe their first taste of adventure is making a floral arrangement that decorates the table. Either way, they learn how to calculate, to plan and take responsibility. Perhaps the most powerful ingredient is the passion that burns in the mind but can go out without enough space and oxygen.

All will go better if you let them take responsibility for their own lives and all the little acts that help people and families live together. Do your kids set their own alarm clocks every night? Do they choose which clothes they will wear to school? Every night do they pull together all the materials they will need at school the next day, and perhaps put them in a particular place or in a satchel or backpack?

Every act they do that allows them to plan their lives helps them to learn to be mindful, to plan and execute, to make decisions. Avoid the temptation to mock their choices, or to step in at the last minute and say something like, "I think this shirt (or skirt) might work better with your outfit." (Hopefully, they won't run into their version of Mr. Ford, the fashion tyrant vice principal who objected to calypso pants—at the height of the Harry Belafonte craze—and sent the eleventh-grade Ken home to change.)

If your kids are, say, in middle school or later before you begin trying some of these suggestions, expect some trouble at first. Ten years of living without responsibilities and chores may be hard to change, but be patient and persistent. Help them have fun and feel good about their new roles.

Human beings must eat to survive but if they never contribute to the preparation of food and drinks, they miss important chances to make decisions and to develop a sense of responsibility toward themselves and others in their community. You can find ways for them to contribute to the preparation of food that are appropriate to their age.

Even when they are still young they can help cut up vegetables, stir ingredients, put out dishes and gather them up, and help wash them when the eating is done. Let them make mistakes, but mind how you respond when they spill everything on the floor. Remember, how you react to their blunders will influence how they understand the workings of intelligence. Avoid driving them toward fixed mindsets. Remember also to avoid putting them in harm's way. When one of Ken's sisters was three, his mother handed her the bag of picked-over chicken wings that had been the stuff of a tasty meal and told her she could help by putting this in the trash. On her way out the door, she remembered how delicious the meat was and gave in to temptation. One of the bones stuck in her young throat and nearly choked her before the family knew what was happening.

Creating a learning family doesn't mean banishing all televisions, computers, and smartphones, but it does involve changing how you use them and what you watch. As James M. Lang argues in his brilliant book on distractions, the solution isn't to crack down on uses of digital devices but to create better alternatives, offering enough engagement, or sheer hustle and bustle, to hold a young person's attention.[8] If kids' brains are mesmerized by playing mindless games and scrolling through endless social media feeds, make them a better offer.

Get your kids to design a family policy on screentime that they think is fair and best for everyone's well-being. (It may be as tough on parents' television watching and emailing as it is on kids' online gaming and meme sharing.) But mainly focus on diverting their reach for distracting electronics with opportunities for play or work in real life that is absorbing and offers gratifying rewards.

When they are watching or playing a game on a screen, don't hesitate to ask for their take on what's happening in it, or why they think this game is so popular. Or, if a drama is on television, what issues does it raise? What conflicts in values does it invoke? A crazy game show can provoke questions about why they have broad appeal. Even a sports event offers chances to learn. When your kids offer some opinion, respond with a robust, "Could be. How can we decide?"

"How do you suppose these players get ready to play this game? What kind of exercises do they do? What parts of their brains are involved in catching that ball, running, jumping? Let's do some research on how they do it. Does throwing a ball at a hundred miles per hour do harm to your body? Or make you stronger? How can athletes protect themselves?" How can you find reliable answers? How can you weigh the quality of the material you find on the internet?

Even a birthday party is full of stimulating possibilities. In an earlier book we told stories of parents using these milestone events to bring some exciting learning adventures to the table. One couple hired a "traveling reptile company," whose expert animal handler helped any guest who was willing touch and interact with a range of snakes, lizards, and turtles. Another year, they put together a "science is magic" show that amazed the young partygoers with chemistry-based stunts and other mysteries of the natural world.[9] Turning a family celebration into a learning environment isn't hard to do—you must only be determined to do it, and to let your imagination run wild.

Almost any occasion offers those learning moments. A scuffed knee can call for research on the best treatment and a discussion of germs and infections. "When I was a kid, they always said to put mercurochrome or alcohol on a cut, but now doctors say not to do that. Maybe after we wash this with soap and water instead, we can find out why."

That kind of comment can help a kid appreciate that learning is a constant process, and reinforce the importance of keeping an open mind. It can also open up a further line of inquiry—in this case, perhaps, leading to germ theory. "We know we're cleaning this up because we don't want it to get infected from germs—but we can't even see those, so how do we know they are there? Physicians haven't always known about germs. I wonder who first began to explore their existence and how they could cause illness?" You might use the tragic story of President James Garfield, who survived an assassination attempt in 1881 only to die of a bacterial infection, possibly introduced by his surgeons in their attempts to extract the bullet. Candice Millard's *Destiny of the Republic* offers a gripping account.[10] It's a book you may want to read together if your kids are old enough (and after that scuffed knee is fully healed). They will be glued to the story from the opening pages. Let them do part of the reading aloud.

The Girl Who Became Passionate about Flowers and Beauty

A few years ago, we got to know Trinity Marshall, a young woman who grew up and still lives in the sprawling Dallas metroplex. If you come from outside the Lone Star State, you might think of Texas as all small towns and cattle ranches—an impression that flows from popular movies and Texas lore—but the real Dallas, where Trinity lives, has little of the rural flavor of those venerable images.

It is a land crisscrossed with concrete overpasses and massive buildings, home to large corporations, shopping malls, and more than four million people. What was once open farmland now sprouts row upon row of housing projects, with their tight suburban lawns and winding streets staking out the property lines. In this territory, west of the tree lines that mark the prairies, wood is more expensive than bricks.

Color often comes in subtle brown, yellow, tan, and other earthen hues, with only rare pops of rose, lilac, and the purples of vibrant iris beds. Only for a few weeks in the spring is one treated to the occasional field of brilliant bluebonnets carpeting the terrain. The land lies mostly flat, but with ripples and rolls here and there like a well-exercised forearm. On the edges of civilization, where the crawling spread of house contractors has not yet reached, nature dresses up in these famous Texas wildflowers for a short time in April.

Along the edges of highways and up embankments that road construction crews have fashioned to accommodate the high-speed thoroughfares, blankets of ocean blue drape the Texas landscape. Sometimes on an already hot north Texas spring day, you can see those bright carpets for miles, a product of a vigorous highway planting program and alkaline and moderately fertile soil. But by summer, all this azure terrain has burned brown and will stay that way until the seasons roll back around.

In the local high school culture, the boys play football and the girls try out for the drill team. But when Trinity rose to her senior year, something happened that kept her from taking her place on the marching brigade. She signed up for a floral design class instead. It would turn out to be a life-altering move, introducing her to what would become her passion. "That is what really got me into the field. It was part of the Future Farmers of America program," she told us. Part of the FFA's approach to agricultural education is to stage competitions where kids can show off the fruits of their learning. Sure enough, Trinity's teacher soon invited her to join the floral design team.

In some households a choice like the one Trinity made that semester might spark dismay if not derision: "What, you're taking flower arranging now? I suppose next you'll sign up for basket weaving. Why don't you study something that will lead to a well-paying job? You'd be much better off with an accounting or coding class." Trinity's parents didn't object—while they didn't imagine that spending time with flowers would put her on her career path, they gave her a free hand to pick the subjects she wanted. "They *did* pressure me on grades," Trinity told us—but that almost cost her dearly, as we will see.

Trinity fell in love with the beauty of flowers and the creative artistry of filling a vase or anything else with them. "It was the first time I was really motivated and interested in learning about something." Before long, she was eagerly devouring all the information she could about plants and their flowers, curious to understand more about all the thriving, if sedentary, organisms that sprang from the ground. "All of a sudden, I found myself carrying around note cards about different plants," she said. "I was really motivated about that stuff and learning deeply." When she considered colleges, she picked Tarleton State University, just east of Dallas, because it had an outstanding agricultural program.

In that advanced educational offering, Trinity's learning became more conceptual as she focused on the science of botany. One interest led her to a fascination with something else and a newfound pleasure of exploring broadly. "You learn about the biology of plants," she proclaimed proudly. She majored in agriculture with a minor in horticulture, developing a deep understanding of important natural principles. She could not succeed by just memorizing answers. "In growing things, it is not going to be exact," she observed. "Not every situation is going to be the same." She was confronted with unstructured (or ill-structured) problems and had to learn to think and reason. "I learned a lot about maintaining plant life from seeds to leaf growing."

Her associations began to grow. In high school she had hated the study of many of the standard, college-prep subjects. But her passion for flowers and their arrangement drew her to explore those disciplines as they related to plants and the discoveries and industries that grew up around them. Math, science, and art history now had relevance, and almost anything even remotely related to flowers could spark her curiosity.

Her grades zoomed with that new emphasis and enthusiasm: "After I was in FFA, I focused more on my interests and not grades. My scores went up." Her fascination even changed how she acted in class and later studied. "While a lecture was going on, I took notes on my laptop. Then, when studying outside of class, I would write down additional notes that helped me understand even more." It was a form of retrieval practice linked to deep learning—a topic we will return to later in this book.

Still, one cloud hovered over her education. Her family emphasized high grades rather than learning and creative growth. "The relationship with my parents was like a business transaction," Trinity recalls. "If I didn't meet their standards, I would be punished. I would constantly get into hot water."

In college, she joined a sorority and that group had the same focus. "There were grade requirements. So for the first two years I had this leaning over me." Trinity had to make a decision. "At the end of that time, I realized I didn't function well or enjoy that. So I ended up leaving the sorority. The last two years my grades got better. Then, for the first time, I made the Dean's List. I had been too worried about the outcomes, so I did better after I got out of the sorority and the pressures of grades."

It is a pattern we have seen over the years and by now know to expect: an emphasis on grades often lowers them, while a focus on deep understanding and passion-based education can cause both learning and marks to improve. Trinity says it best: "My parents were very strict and controlling, especially about grades. And the pressure of that caused me to do worse." In college, the same kind of pressure attached to sorority membership undermined her motivation to study again. Once she changed her situation to remove that pressure, she was able to rediscover the satisfaction of gaining knowledge she really cared about.

She went on to take challenging courses, from ranching to farming. "Those classes made me think about how agriculture affects everybody every day. I learned everything about the agricultural world." Her original passion seeded new thoughts and interests that flowered, morphed into something new, and continued to change. In her senior year, she had an opportunity to do an internship. "I taught the horticulture lab, helping people to learn floral design who had never studied the matter before." By the time we talked to her, Trinity could sum up the journey she took from a class that sounded fun to thriving as a professional florist: "As I learned more, my interests grew. I decided this is what I wanted as my career."

THINKING GALORE

We've saved the best for last. Some of the problems and questions your children will face in life defy easy answers. In another book, Ken tells the story of a young kid who asked the deepest of questions. "Where do we go when we die?" he inquired. When he saw that Ken hesitated, he tapped the screen of the adult's laptop computer and urged, "Google it."[11]

But we know life isn't that simple. Our existence is full of ill-structured problems, or, as we sometimes call them, "fuzzy" areas. What do we mean when we say something is morally wrong? Do we know anything for sure? What is beauty? What is our purpose in life? Do we have the power to make choices between good and evil, or does some higher power—whether God or nature or luck—predetermine the decisions we will make in life?

People often regard such "philosophical" questions as being beyond the reach of children. Yet, over the past half-century, scholars have collected a growing body of evidence that young children actually crave such levels of inquiry. When we listen to their talk with each other, we can sense that appetite, and almost see the enthusiasm bubbling to the surface.

Indeed, we have considerable reason to believe that the reason many children lose their curiosity when they go to school is because those places don't focus on or even put up with such fuzzy questions. They fill the day instead with information that can be expressed and memorized as fact.

Kids love to ask questions, but they also want to grapple with some of the biggest and most difficult matters that *Homo sapiens* encounter. We want to have a purpose for our lives, to decide what's morally right and wrong, to find beauty in the world, and to find good reasons for our choices. That too often begins to decline when children go to school. But with some ingenuity, you can begin to rebuild some vital practices for your children that will transform their lives.

Before you throw this book against the nearest wall for offering such imprecise guidance, please consider the story of Matt Lipman.[12] He was teaching at Columbia University in New York City in the 1960s when he noticed again and again that many of his students could not think adequately. They couldn't take a body of material and draw rational conclusions from it. They couldn't defend their decisions. They committed logical errors, both formal and informal.

Oh, they could memorize like crazy, but they couldn't think rationally and consistently, like good scientists or historians. They were too credulous, even when someone Lipman immediately recognized as a charlatan was trying to propagate some outlandish social or political hoax. Lipman wasn't trying to control what these young adults thought, but he did care deeply about *how* they thought, and how they arrived at their own conclusions. He cared that they displayed so little ability to analyze (take ideas apart) and to synthesize (put concepts together). The young people at Columbia were supposed to be the elite students in American society, ready to enter the ranks of the nation's future leaders, but in their logic courses he saw them commit fallacy after fallacy.

As he looked at their weaknesses and how they could be addressed, it struck him that any education system that expected colleges to teach young people how to think well was waiting until too late. What if that process could begin in the first grade? What if teachers began helping young children learn how to think philosophically, to live reflective lives, even when they were in kindergarten and the early grades? (Don't worry, we'll explore what this could mean in a moment.)

Some of his colleagues thought he was crazy. No doubt they envisioned the typical college philosophy course of the day and said there was no way little kids would sit through boring lectures and take notes while some philosophy teacher stood at the front of the room and droned on about *post hoc ergo propter hoc*.

Lipman agreed and responded that teachers would need to change the way they taught. You don't learn how to ride a bicycle by listening to lectures. You learn by—get this—*riding a bicycle*. Falling down, getting up, and trying it again. Maybe you first use a balance bike, dangling your feet down on either side and coasting until you get the hang of staying upright, but you learn by putting your muscles into action and getting feedback through your whole body. You don't start by reading books or hearing lectures on, say, how the body balances itself and which parts of your torso engage in that activity.

Children learn to think philosophically, Lipman realized, by doing philosophy. But few of his colleagues at Columbia University wanted to join him in creating a philosophy for children program (P4C, as he called it). So he left the hallowed halls of the prestigious Ivy League school, where future presidents and CEOs, composers and filmmakers, Nobel laureates and Pulitzer Prize winners roamed the floors.

He went across the Hudson River to New Jersey and joined the faculty of Montclair State. There, he and new colleague Ann Margaret Sharp launched one of the most significant movements in philosophical education since the days when Plato created the first academy outside Athens, nearly 2,500 years ago. Their P4C (later revised to Philosophy *with and for* Children, or Pw4C) program has since spread around the world, across Europe and Africa, South America and Asia, demonstrating repeatedly, among rich kids and poor ones and within all sorts of cultures, that children take to philosophy like ducks to water. It helps pick up their zeal for learning, and learning deeply, not just memorizing isolated facts as if they were preparing for a quiz or trivia contest, but understanding deep concepts and learning to think critically.

Joining the Fun

As it turned out, kids love to tackle fuzzy problems and when schools don't give them a chance to do so, they get bored with the old "memorize this" game. If you want to pump up their zeal for learning, get them involved in a Pw4C program. We'll show you how to do that. You can even do it at home.

We're going to show you some major examples of this approach—including one in a kindergarten in a working-class neighborhood in Greece, and another in one of the best universities in the world. We're also going to share some rich online resources, where some organizations have created materials specifically for parents and grandparents who want to bring the advantages of philosophy to their kids, even the young sprouts.

While the techniques that Lipman, Sharp, and others have fashioned have spread to hundreds of schools worldwide, this movement is still in its infancy and you also can join the ranks of its pioneers, receiving salutes from your kids, grandkids, great grandchildren, and more in generations to come. We're not making this up or exaggerating. Don't believe us? Stay tuned.

To launch this approach, Lipman had to find a way to tune in to kids' philosophical questions and to migrate them to the center of every child's education. How would he do this? He saw his path as going through the arts, and more specifically through enticing literature written specifically for kids. The only problem was that there were few good examples of such literature in the early 1970s. He would need to write some.

Lipman would help craft a new type of children's book. He published his first in the 1970s. Soon, other writers began penning good examples. And some people noticed that such literature already existed—from *Charlotte's Web* to *Alice in Wonderland*. Today, scores of richly philosophical children's books are available.

In this account, we've emphasized philosophy for young children, primarily because that will be new and unusual for many parents. But what if your kids are older, in middle school, or beyond? You can still introduce them to philosophical thinking, to the practice of struggling with fuzzy questions in civil and measured conversations. Your teenagers will take to the quest just like the younger kids. A little later, we'll look at a college version of this approach, too. You'll use different material to spark the discussion for teenagers, and the philosophical questions can change, but the rewards can be just as substantial. Kids of all ages learn to think carefully, to exchange ideas in a civil manner, to respect each other, to listen carefully, and to test their thoughts in an open forum.

What is Philosophical Thinking and Why Should Your Kids Do It?

Let's look at what philosophical thinking means and what value it has in the twenty-first century. Philosophy is the oldest discipline in all of human learning, older than biology, history, computer science, or any kind of science for that matter. Too many parents ignore its value because they can't see how there is any money to be made in practicing it: "What are you going to do, son? Open up a philosophy shop down on the public square or in the shopping mall?"

Yet if you survey CEOs of large corporations and ask them what qualities they value most in new employees, especially in those they hire into leadership tracks, they will mention abilities most naturally learned in philosophy classes, like critical thinking, wisdom, common sense, and the capacity to collaborate with others.

But don't computer science majors make the most money? They may get the highest starting salaries, but if you look at earners over ten years, philosophy and history majors come out on top. (We'll come back to this salary race later, although we'll also argue that other considerations should come into play.)

But what is philosophy? The simplest definition is that it is the study of common, ordinary ideas and making sense of them by taking them apart and looking at them in new ways. It looks at abstract ideas that we often fail to define, making the familiar strange, and the strange familiar. What does it mean to have a friend, for example? Or to love someone, know something, think well, reason, find beauty in the world, or act ethically? How should loyalty or friendship, or beauty or truth, be defined? What counts as good evidence that one should or shouldn't do something? What's the right thing to do?

These are matters that students can't just look up and then memorize. They require deep thoughts and a willingness to struggle with them. Is lying ever a good thing? What if it saves someone's life? If you steal money, but then use it to find a cure for cancer, does that justify the theft? If children struggle with such matters, they can develop strong moral fiber. As they do, they can grow more comfortable with uncertainty and begin to realize that when life presents its hardest dilemmas, the answers won't come from a search engine or AI tool. A person needs to learn to grapple with them. This requires gathering evidence carefully and honestly, asking tough questions, always trying to find out why you shouldn't believe some popular notion, and always probing for the problems in accepting any line of thought. You can't just barge ahead like Thomas Midgley without questioning your convictions.

Such a sophisticated approach to knowledge isn't going to emerge immediately from a "philosophy for children" program. But it will blossom eventually. In the meantime, as hundreds of programs have demonstrated, kids can readily learn to listen to each other, to think carefully before they speak, and to disagree respectfully. We live in a world of bitter political, social, cultural, and religious conflicts that threaten to tear our planet apart. The Lipman approach to children's philosophy has helped kids become better thinkers and listeners, and to calm the wars of ideas and ideals.

What do these questions have to do with restoring curiosity or getting the most out of school? Experience has shown that kids from all sorts of backgrounds love tackling these fuzzy matters. As they do, they learn to think critically, to reason carefully. And because they love it, they become more curious.

Let's take just the simple question of what it means to disagree or agree. Are all agreements and disputes of the same type? Are disputes about the concrete facts the same as fights over attitudes? If John says that Thomas Jefferson was born in Virginia and Sally claims he was born in Maryland, is that the same kind of disagreement as when John reports that the third president was a good man and leader because he gave us the Declaration of Independence and the idea that everybody has basic rights, while Jill declares him a bad man because he kept people in slavery? How should we resolve disagreement about the facts? By appealing to the evidence. But should we resolve disputes in attitudes? Lipman and Sharp (and other philosophers) found that, if you introduce such conflicts through intriguing stories, you can spark a great deal of curiosity and help kids learn how to disagree and sometimes resolve their differences.

It's All Greek to Me

In Patras, Greece, the third-largest city in that ancient Hellenic country, researchers and educators started a "Philosophy with and for Children" pilot program more than a decade ago.[13] The large metropolitan area lies at the foot of Mount Panachaiko, overlooking the Gulf of Patras, a branch of the Ionian Sea—an area of spectacular beauty. It was one of the first such programs in that country. That alone made it significant, given that its location only about a hundred miles west of Athens was where western philosophy first emerged in the minds of Socrates, Plato, and Aristotle.

It was also significant because it was one of the first anywhere that brought philosophy to four-, five-, and six-year-old children. Yes, kindergarten kids. The teachers read carefully selected stories about friendship and diversity to the children, then engaged them in philosophical discussions.[14]

Rather than calling on kids to report what happened in the story (as teachers often do just to make sure students have been paying attention), they raised philosophical questions. If a story raised themes of friendship, they asked the children to reflect on, for example, how they chose their own friends: "What makes a good friend? Should one be similar to us in order to call him/her a friend? In what aspects do we expect our friends to be similar to us? Have you ever felt that other children don't want to play with you? What did you do to make them change their mind?"[15]

They got the kids to talk to each other in pairs, in small groups, and in whole class discussions. Yet they also made sure they gave everyone a chance to think carefully before they talked, often asking them to gather their thoughts before turning to their neighbors. (This is sometimes called "think / pair / share.")

Before beginning any discussions, the teachers helped the kids draw up guidelines for their behavior during the conversations. Check out the rules drawn up by the first group of children:

> Do not make fun of other children.
> Listen closely to other children.
> Do not harm other children.
> Raise hands when someone wants to talk (so one person is to talk at a time).
> Be polite and use the words "thank you," "please," and "sorry."
> Respect other children's opinions and not say they are correct or incorrect.
> Do not interrupt other children when they speak.
> Do not misbehave.
> Do not lie.[16]

Pretty good, right? Maybe governments should have similar guidelines drawn up by children.

Because the kids hadn't learned to read and write yet, they drew pictures to represent some of the rules and the routine became to hang up those rule-drawings as a signal that a philosophy session was about to start. The children took to the exercise like they might seize on ice cream cones. They thought carefully and logically, using words like *because, why, in order to, namely,* and *since.*

The people running the program set up comparison sessions across town where privileged kids just listened to stories and then had a discussion of what the characters in them did. No philosophical questions. Just the rehearsal of "facts" from the stories. No rules drawn up by the kids.

Those classes did not display the same level of critical thinking. And the same is true around the world: a conventional rehash of what happened in a story just doesn't provoke the same excitement and interest. Neither does pounding "the facts" of any subject into students' heads. We're telling you, children love to do philosophy. It lights their fuse, sparking their natural curiosity about everything back to life.

In too many school experiences, the emphasis isn't on asking questions. It's just on memorizing answers. Oh, and if you are worried about students "getting the facts," the more engaged ones do that, too. What's not to love?

Bringing It Home

You can find plenty of resources online if you implement such a program at home. Philosophy Learning and Teaching Organization (PLATO), for instance, offers buckets of materials for little kids, middle schoolers, high schoolers, and even college kids.[17] You can keep these efforts within your family, but you might also think about forming a larger "community of inquiry" that invites other families to join in discussion and solution sharing.

But no matter what you do to bring philosophy to your children, let the kids have their own dialogues with each other. If you have just one child, and can't invite in some of your neighbors, you obviously will need to join the discussion yourself. Perhaps it can take place at the dinner table.

The Lipman Approach Goes to College

Michael Sandel teaches one of the most popular courses at Harvard.[18] That may sound like he deals with pedagogical issues very different from what you face with your children, but let's consider his wise approach and what you can take from it. In many ways it is an extension of the approach that Matthew Lipman pioneered in the 1970s, only this time for college undergraduates.

Every year, nearly a thousand undergrads at the oldest university in the United States crowd into one of Professor Sandel's classes, and years later they tend to recall it as a transformative experience. So how does Sandel approach teaching?

If you examine his class as we did, you will find that he certainly pays attention to what's already on the minds of the people taking the course. But he doesn't stop there. He tries to find a way to provoke their interest in something new. "Above all," he argues, teaching is "about commanding attention and holding it."[19]

"Our task," he once told us, "is not unlike that of a commercial for a soft drink or any other product." The main difference, he went on to argue, is what teachers might do with that attention once they catch it. Listen to his account of what he does. You can use parts of it in your home. "For the most part" he explained, "we want to hold the attention of students for the sake of *changing* the things they are likely to pay attention to most of the time. We want to grasp students and direct their attention *someplace else*."[20]

But how do you do that best? Shout at them? Insist they listen to you? Inflict "hard-nosed" discipline that includes a warning about hell-fire and damnation? Threaten them with dire consequences if they are not paying attention? Shout louder?

Not if you want to become an award-winning teacher in Cambridge, Massachusetts. Fundamentally, Sandel asks intriguing questions, and we can all learn from how he frames them. You can stir your kids with your own provocative questions.

Sandel teaches a popular class called *Justice: What's the Right Thing to Do?* He begins on the first day with an intriguing puzzle. We could try to do justice to it here in prose, as we've attempted before.[21] But now that Harvard makes the course freely available online, you and your older children can experience it for yourselves.[22] The first session is entitled "The Moral Side of Murder." Now are you intrigued?

The murder question is a tough one and probably not well suited for an eight-year-old. For young people of greater maturity, including college students, it works like a charm to draw them into a deep moral conversation about how to define justice and decide on the right thing to do. But your mileage may vary. The major idea is to introduce your kids to fuzzy problems, matters that involve value judgments and can't be resolved with a simple response or by consulting the internet.

Sandel grounds his approach in the ideas of Socrates. The ancient Greek philosopher "began by attending to what people thought they knew, and then gradually and systematically to wrench them from their familiar place."[23]

We offer the Sandel example as a powerful way to spark curiosity if your kids are older. But this is advanced stuff for mature college students. Sandel warns at the end of the first episode that anyone who chooses to engage in this discussion can never undo what they have seen and heard. It is not for every high school student, let alone for kids in kindergarten.

YouTube allows you an alternative place to watch the first two episodes of Sandel's classes without any registration.[24] If you look at the more than seventeen thousand comments on that page, you can begin to appreciate the depth of interest such an approach invokes. Just consider these examples:

"I love how he doesn't make students feel right or wrong and encourages people of different perspective to speak."

"I took philosophy although not in Harvard. In over half a century living on this planet, I have never found an experience that was more painful and rewarding than beginning to learn how to think more thoroughly. The world would be vastly different if we all had exposure to philosophical thinking."

"What an incredible professor. Everyone should have an experience like this in their lives."

"I would never skip classes if my professor would be engaging like this."

"This is why Philosophy is the best. Every other subject will teach you what to think, offering you material to absorb and internalize. Philosophy, however, teaches you how to think. . . . No other discipline on campus, in my opinion, is more apt at giving you the tools, tricks, and abilities to work quickly and safely around any problem; giving you no answer, only justifiable means of generating one yourself."

If you watch this one- or two-lesson sample, notice how Sandel reacts to students' views, never judging any thought. He might say that something is "interesting" or "brave" but never "right" or "wrong." He maintains a strong sense of humor and an inviting, welcoming personality. It's an approach you can use in your family discussions.

FOUR

Fostering a Creative Mindset

REYNA GRANDE was born in a small village in central Mexico that was prone to flooding.[1] When she was two, her father left his family in Iguala, fled the poverty of his native land, and moved north to the United States, dodging immigration officers as he crossed the border.

Eight years later, he came back, collected his children, and took them north to California. By then Reyna's parents had divorced and remarried, and the little girl and her older brother and sister moved in with their dad and his new wife. Her father became increasingly depressed because of the poverty his small family endured. He worked in an economy that paid immigrants desperately low wages, especially undocumented immigrants who lived in constant fear of arrest.

You might expect that Reyna became another story of a child who did poorly in school and eventually gave up. But that's not the case. She graduated from the University of California Santa Cruz, published several highly acclaimed and popular novels, and now teaches creative writing at UCLA, living a highly productive and creative life.

What accounts for her success? How did she get more out of school while others didn't? Her story can help you stimulate a creative mindset in your family.

No one factor can explain everything. On one level, Reyna enjoyed a little luck. She had some good teachers, and her family encouraged her to mine the resources she found. Her father saw the value of a formal education and encouraged his three children to do well in school.

Yet a string of lucky developments cannot alone explain why and how she became a creative and successful writer. Nor can it form the basis of any recommendations to you. We can't just say, "Get lucky." Our analysis must look beyond any chance occurrences. It must offer approaches that you can adopt to take advantage of any good fortune that may come your way. After all, no one could seriously argue that, on balance, Reyna Grande enjoyed some special measure of good fortune relative to other people. Indeed, the exact opposite seems to be the case.

Perhaps most important, we will *not* argue that anyone can overcome enormous hurdles if they simply follow what we are about to offer. Life isn't that simple or fair. Nevertheless, we can all learn from what Reyna experienced. Reyna and her family did get their green cards, thanks to both a Republican president and a Democratic congress working together to find paths to citizenship for several million people, but even that luck alone can't explain what she eventually achieved.

The biggest single element that helped her overcome the challenges was how she developed what is known as a *creative mindset*. This is an approach to learning that can supercharge your children. It can help your kids get more out of school.

Let us remind you, however, that when we speak of learning to live a creative life, we're not focusing exclusively or even primarily on the arts or artists. All too often, we are confused about what creativity is. Reyna writes novels, but creativity is not confined to artistic endeavors. One can be creative in running a business, raising children, reacting to a crisis, solving problems, or repairing relationships. If your children learn to develop that same creative mindset, it can change how they get an education. It can reshape how they think about learning and what they get out of school, no matter what subjects and careers they may pursue. It can have a huge influence on how they live their lives.

THE BASICS

We first encountered the idea of fostering a creative mindset in the teachings of Paul Baker, an innovative educator and theater impresario from Texas.[2] In classes he taught from the 1930s through the 1990s, Baker created an environment where originality could flourish and be prioritized in school.[3]

We chose to use his thinking on creativity as the centerpiece of our approach for a variety of reasons. His ideas are less well known today than they were sixty or seventy years ago, yet they offer a full plate of rich concepts and practices that still deserve broad consideration.

Today, people are better acquainted with the thinking of Ken Robinson, the British educator whose TED Talk on nurturing creativity has, as of this writing, garnered more than seventy-eight million online views.[4] But the two educators had quite similar ideas, and the Texan outlined them first, offering a robust and detailed set of ideas with important implications for all of schooling.

Both men began their work in the theater, Robinson in London and Baker in Texas. We aren't aware, however, of whether Robinson even knew of Baker. Perhaps the ideas of the American had crossed the Atlantic and filtered into the stages of English theater without anyone's noticing. Charles Laughton, the acclaimed English actor, once described Baker as "Irritating, arrogant, nuts—and a genius.... one of the most important minds in the world theater today."[5] Perhaps both Baker and Robinson owe their thinking to some still earlier third party.

Baker had studied at Yale and then toured experimental drama venues across Europe and Asia before coming home to teach in Texas. His ideas are important because of the way they foreshadowed and complemented more recent concepts in psychology, like growth mindsets. Baker's ideas are both intriguingly simple and easy to understand. They are also lush in their implications and applications. First, we'll show you how his classes worked. Then we'll tell you how you can bring his ideas home to your family.

Some people will argue that you can't teach anyone to become innovative, but Baker demonstrated that one can design activities and create spaces where the natural tendency to act creatively blossoms and flourishes. This begins with a new definition of what it means to get an education.

For Baker, education wasn't primarily about memorizing information or procedures, as educators had long stressed. The point was not to learn dates and names, or even to acquire practical skills like the ability to repair a car or computer programming, crucial as these facts and skills might be. Nor did getting an education mean getting a degree from a prestigious school. It wasn't about the connections you could make and the reputation you could build with people you met. It didn't matter how many august and acclaimed positions you held or what kind of status you had.

For the Texas professor, a solid education meant something else: it meant learning to live a creative and innovative life. Innovation wasn't limited to the arts, although paying attention to how artists work and think could foster the development and growth of a creative mindset in all areas.

While we have written and talked about Paul Baker's ideas and teaching practices for years, we did not appreciate their full value at first. We make this confession because your children could have the same initial response, and that response could cause you to abandon his practices. That would be unfortunate.

Bringing the Message to Your Kids

Can you imagine talking with your children about what it means to learn and grow in school? That discussion could begin as a philosophical one. What is the purpose of getting an education? What does it mean to be creative? It could continue with an invitation to your children to take up a life of innovation, to expand their imaginations.

Consider how Baker's "Integration of Abilities" instruction did that (that's what Baker called his course). "This is a class in discovering your own creative ability, and all you will have to help you with your discovery is yourself and getting acquainted with the way you work," Baker liked to tell his students.[6] "Everything you create will come from inside you, so you must know yourself. You write to get it out." The thought of taking a class about themselves fascinated students. It can intrigue your children, too.

You can say to them, "Find out what excites you. Find a creative project that interests you. Study it. What did the artist do? How did she work? Probe an ingenious endeavor, seek its inner nature, and explore the possibilities it presents. Then find your own passion and let it drive you." As Baker warned, "If you are not capable of excitement, you will never produce anything."[7]

This is not the old "you are the smartest kid on the block" routine, the building of self-confidence by making your children feel superior to others. It's not even the "you are special" message that often drives gifted and talented programs. It isn't what psychologists call contingent self-worth, where someone's value and abilities depend on how they rank in comparison to other people—an idea that became popular among parents in the late twentieth century with sometimes disastrous consequences. It is simply the recognition that while "people are people," with common characteristics that make them human, nobody is like anyone else, and originality stems from that uniqueness.

As part of your message to your kids that everyone is unique, make sure you emphasize that their friends are all unique, too. "You are not *better* than someone else," you might explain. "You're just different. You have a certain combination of strengths and weaknesses, and the capacity to expand the former and overcome the latter."

We can all learn from one another, from all human experience. Great ideas and creative work emerge at crossroads where people can feed on the results of many perspectives. By the same token, individual creative growth blossoms when we bring a variety of outlooks together to nourish our minds. We're not suggesting that all ideas are equally good, but rather that everyone can contribute to the challenging task of engaging in careful, reflective judgments.

The second thing you should emphasize is the importance of learning to look outward—of feeding on the richness of human history and learning how to integrate the valuable thoughts and experiences of others into one's own ideas and perspectives. One might draw inspiration from many different people and groups. But filtered through one's own body and brain, these produce a mix that is unique.

Yes, there are still "facts" and ideas to learn, but they are now cast as part of the process of creativity. "There are insights that you encounter from learning to look around you, and listening to teachers, researchers, scientists, scholars, and others," you can explain to your kids. "The facts and ideas you gather will nourish your own creative growth." Calculus becomes the thinking of Newton, Shen Kuo, Leibniz, and the numerous mathematicians who contributed to its development. You can help your kids see great thinkers as a growing network of friends, a neighborhood full of people connecting in casual, front-stoop conversations and walks through the woods.

Early in this book, we quoted Einstein's great response to an interviewer: "I am enough of the artist to draw freely upon my imagination. Imagination is more important than knowledge. Knowledge is limited. Imagination encircles the world."[8] You can ask your children why Einstein would make such a statement. What does it mean? Do they agree with it? Are both imagination and knowledge valuable? What is the relationship between the two? Do we need to decide if one is more valuable than the other?

This is a whole new way of casting and thinking about what we've called "general education." In the new thinking that is emerging, your children will find opportunities rather than demands imposed on them. It is a chance for your kids to expand their own minds within the fertile soil of all of the ideas that have ever emerged. Say to them, "This is about *you*—about how you can learn about yourself and use that self-knowledge to grow as a highly creative individual."

When should you have the creativity conversation with your kids? It's your call. For some, it might be in grade school. For others, in high school or college. For that matter, it shouldn't be a one-shot-and-done topic—you can return to it multiple times. It's a discussion you can weave into a conversation about schooling and getting an education. It is an important ingredient in building a learning household.

A New Language for Creativity

Baker developed a new language to express this vision of creativity and built a new course to use that vocabulary, first at the college level and later for grade school kids, high schoolers, and graduate students. Over seven decades, the Texas impresario's course changed the lives of thousands. You can use it, too, to alter how your children think about themselves and their learning. We will devote some paragraphs to explaining that creativity course, and then help you understand how to bring it home to your children.

In Baker's framework, every creative act, regardless of the field, involves five elements: space, time (or rhythm), motion (direction or line), sound (or silence), and silhouette (or color). One of his former students, who became a city planner, once told us that ever since taking the course, "Those five elements have always been a part of my thinking on any project I do."[9] Another former student argued that every major concept can be expressed in terms of Baker's five elements, including Einstein's theory of relativity. Think about how that could be true. Then bring your kids into that conversation.

Engineers, business leaders, scientists, legal scholars, parents, and others learned to use Baker's language to build their own creative mindset. Imagination became an important ingredient in their education—the secret sauce that transformed how they experienced learning.

Unless you live in the Dallas area and enroll your kids in the Children's Theater program that Baker founded with his daughter, Robyn Flatt, or in the Booker T. Washington High School for the Performing and Visual Arts that Baker created in the 1970s, you won't have much of an opportunity to get your children into a modern version of the creativity class. That's why you need to engage your kids in this approach to learning at home.

No one else will do it for you. No two people will do it exactly the same way. No two families will come away with precisely the same results. But in taking this deep dive into a world where imaginations run wild, you and your children will begin to see school in ways you never imagined.

Think for a moment about how this approach speaks to one of the most persistent debates in education. On one side, people have argued that students need a broad education. Beginning in grade school and continuing into college, in most schools in the United States, your children will take courses in science, social science, history, language arts, humanities, and fine arts. That general education is considered a foundation for everything else that they might study. On the other side of this educational squabble, people argue that those general education courses are a waste of time, a distraction from the classes that prepare them for jobs. Our hope is that you and your kids can now see them as important to the growth of a creative life and mindset. Every class your children take, and everything they learn, can feed their creative growth.

Students coming out of the Integration of Abilities course begin to realize that every bit of knowledge acquisition they make is ultimately about them. It is about how they develop the dynamic powers of their minds. That's the message you should share with your children. Different exercises will play differently with each person. You have to find out what works best for your kids.

You must also believe in the power of this approach if you want your children to do likewise. Humans can read each other's attitudes with almost perfect clarity. If you don't trust the creativity approach, that attitude will show on your face. You have to convince yourself before you can expect to win over your child. Otherwise, they will probably not enjoy the full benefits of this kind of education. For the results to be maximized, all parents and caregivers should be singing the same song.

You cannot, however, make the transition to a creative mindset if you engage in these exercises without understanding the basic metaphors of schooling. In traditional conversations about schooling, we often talk about climbing a ladder, getting to the top, and doing so faster than anyone else. Some people will talk about "winning" in school, about being better than anyone else. In the ladder metaphor, students are graded and then ranked, producing winners and losers.

In the creative mindset approach, these notions of ladders to climb or competitions to win don't exist. Instead, we focus on how each person brings a unique perspective to a conversation and how everyone benefits from an exchange of ideas. The dominant metaphor is community, not competition. Everyone has something in common with everyone else. Students grow together, learning how to think, create, and contribute to the diversity of the whole. Everyone benefits from the village they have formed. One person is not better than another—they are only different in the experiences they have had and the unique perspectives they contribute.

Five Easy Pieces

The Integration of Abilities course invited students into a series of five core activities that Baker used to try to break down conventional ways of acting and thinking. In each one, participants engaged in a deep conversation with themselves about how they approached one or more of the basic elements—space, movement, time, color, and sound. In what follows, we will show you how you can adapt each of these five activities for use in your home.

Activity 1—For the initial activity, ask your kids and their friends to move through a space twice, each time conveying a different mood. The first time, their movements should express a sense of tragedy. The second time, comedy. After giving them these simple instructions, assure them that there is no right or wrong way to do it. As Baker put it to his students, "You will fail only if you do not use the exercise to learn something about yourself."[10]

Once they're done, invite them to examine their choices: Why they did do what they did? How did they use a space in each case? What alternatives did they consider, and why did they choose one over another? What do those choices say about who they are as individuals? What life experiences shaped and influenced how they used space on this occasion? They should use the experience to explore themselves, to examine their thinking, to find pieces of themselves that they had never noticed before or had long forgotten. If all goes well, your children will make good use of the chance to explore who they have become, ask why they have the attitudes and values that they do, and imagine how alternative attitudes and values might produce different results. In short, they will become more creative.

Activity 2—Invite your kids to have some fun with "automatic writing." Announce that you will say just a single word and their response should be to jot down, without taking any time to ponder the matter, whatever words or phrases pop into their head once they've heard it. Give them thirty to sixty seconds with each word. You might begin with a color or direction, a feeling or attitude, anything that comes to mind. Tell your kids to be just as free-ranging in their responses. As Baker would advise his classes, "You can write someone's name, a place you've been, a place you want to go, a color, a mood the word elicits, something silly or serious, whatever occurs to you."[11] Likewise, your kids don't need to follow any rules of writing. Say to them, "If a string of words come to mind, just jot it down. Start with a single word if you want, maybe because you like it, or think it's funny or sad. Don't worry about grammar or spelling. Let the words flow like water."

Next, do essentially the same thing in a visual mode. Hold up a line drawing and ask each kid to respond with a fast creation of their own, just as spontaneously. It could be a single, long mark twisting and turning across the page. It could be a simple cartoon of an animal or person. Anything that strikes their fancy.

When you finish both of these exercises, ask your children to mark the date on their papers. Collect and save them. Once they've played this game some number of times over the subsequent days, weeks, months, and years, you can display their creative responses side by side and prompt them to comment on what the differences say about them. In both of these exercises, you are letting their minds and muscles run wild and then asking them to study what comes out, to look at themselves from fresh angles.

Activity 3—Have your kids call some very familiar person to mind—someone they have had plenty of time to observe in action. Then ask them to think about the rhythms they associate with that person. What is the tempo of their walk, the cadence of their speech? As your kids begin recalling these rhythms, ask them to try playing them back—to clap the beats with their hands, tap them out on a table, or beat them on a drum. How does the person move through a crowded room, gesture in a conversation, settle into a chair? What changes when they are mad or happy? Do the rhythms of their movement seem to go with the way they dress—their choices of styles and colors?

Baker would remind his class that they had been studying rhythms all their lives. As infants, when someone lifted them from a crib, a big part of what made that person familiar (or not) was the past experience of their typical motions—their bends and bounces, their cadence, tempo, pace, lift, and sway. Baker would ask his students to use those insights to distill the rhythms of their friend and ultimately to reduce all of the information they collected into a single beat.[12]

"Don't rush through any part of this exercise," you can say. "Go back and do it over if your first attempt doesn't seem right. Let each version flow spontaneously, but always remember that you can do it again. You are drawing a picture with sound but without lines or words. You are combining your thoughts and feelings into a rhythm picture."

Ask your kids: "Where did your friend grow up? What do they value? What games do they play? How do they work? What are the beats of each part of their history and life, their culture, their likes and dislikes, the games they play? What do they fear? What do they dislike? Or love? Put all of that into a beat."

Your facial expressions, words, posture, tone of voice—and, yes, your rhythms—should encourage your kids to have fun, to feel free. Tell them that the real object isn't to arrive at the right final clap or drumbeat but to use the experience of this game to appreciate the role of rhythm, and learn something about themselves that might help them build the next version of who they are. Ask them to think about why they assigned a certain rhythm to one place or another, to a color, to an attitude, to a culture. What did their choices say about how they think?

If your children are already in school and taking a multitude of classes with various teachers, ask them which ones excite them most, which ones invoke their deepest learning, which ones they enjoy best. Next, ask them to think about the rhythms of each class. Do those rhythms help predict which classes will rank the highest? Could they change the tempo and cadence in their own mind to enjoy a class or subject more fruitfully?

Activity 4—Tell your kids to find a tree limb, a rock, part of a plant, a flower blossom, a leaf, or any other inanimate object you can locate outdoors that has lines they find fascinating, challenging, or beautiful. Have them look at their object from various angles. Then offer up some descriptive words about it. Color, size, rhythm, texture—whatever adjectives spring to mind.

Have them look at something like this early in the morning, then another intriguing object just before they go to bed, calling their attention to things when they are feeling either tired or full of energy, either bored or excited—in whatever different states of mind you can catch them. Notice how their thoughts and feelings vary with their moods and circumstances. Record the telltale words and phrases used at different times and under different conditions.

Now bring up rhythm again, and get them thinking about what kind of motion the object embodies and reflects. Ask them to imagine the object as a living being: What kind of character might embody all those attributes they have named? What actions would such a character take? What would it say? What scene would it act out? How would it move through a space?

Activity 5—Like the last one, this exercise begins with an object that has various fascinating dimensions to it. But this time, instead of describing those with words, ask your kids to draw them. Have them choose the aspects they like the best, however intangible, and try to put them down on the paper, letting their bodies guide the curves and sways, the stops and turns of their chosen lines. Find the words to advise them that they should let their minds escape the strictures of conventional or rational thought. As they continue to feel the movement of the lines, they should feel free to abandon some portions of a drawing to concentrate on others that interest them more, even repeating those portions, so that the drawing moves in the directions they find most pleasing. "Think with your body," you might tell them, "and notice how it feels to start a new line and then build a really satisfying curve or straightaway." Invite them to assign colors and sounds to the journey across the page and even to various parts of that line as it meanders and jots its way through this space.

Finally, say something like this: "In the coming weeks, how about making some time to produce a piece of art that takes the lines you like much further?" They might be more inclined to compose a tune than to paint, or to sculpt rather than write prose or poetry. But whatever they choose to do, you will plant the important thought that creative work grows and that paying attention to that growth helps them understand how their brain works and grows.

Young people have always drawn pictures, whether with crayons on paper or sticks dragged through wet sand. They have molded art out of clay and sung their own tunes. Baker's approach (and our adaptation of it) takes that artistic play and gives it fresh significance. With the creative mindset approach, young people learn that the important rewards of creative growth do not come in the form of awards or auction prices for paintings or sculptures, but rather in the form of more joyful lives. The conversations you have with them about space, time, lines, sound, and silhouettes will help them bring more creativity to whatever they do.

Students in Baker's course gradually learned to reject the prevailing notion that only people with special talents create anything significant. They instead embraced the liberating view that creative success comes to those who engage deeply with fundamental elements of human action, who reject the easy answers and work toward something fresh. Like Baker's students, your kids can come to see creativity as a process that is valuable in itself—and one that applies to every aspect of life.

KEEPING THE CREATIVITY FLOWING

We've described how you can bring some of the key activities that went on in Baker's classroom home to your kids. Now we will explore some ways to expand on this basic repertoire and help you envision how these creativity-enhancing games can be adapted as children grow older. The key is finding new ways to reinforce the same core messages:

- Everybody is unique, and anybody can create a work of genius by combining ideas from their own experiences and perspectives with the ideas of others.
- Diligence is the key to a creative life.
- Imagination and creativity are not innate talents bestowed on gifted individuals. Anyone can develop them through hard work.
- Your kids are in charge of their own learning.
- Learning begins in a conversation with oneself and grows as one expands the discussion to include other people and their ideas.
- Your kids must find ways to motivate themselves, to develop passion for the work they do, to push their bodies and minds, to overcome their resistance to work.[13]
- In conversations with themselves, students learn to appreciate the world and to stand in awe of it.

Below, we've compiled a list of exercises.[14] You can pick the right ones to use with your kids. They all contribute to the growth we are trying to foster. Choose the ones that will appeal to your children. But above all, be flexible. Don't treat these as a set of rigid drills. Prioritize understanding and empathize with your children. What's eating them on a droopy day? What excites them, what amazes them, what drives them? Make these activities fun and not forced.

- Ask your children to think about a singer, writer, actor, or other artist they admire. What seem to be that person's attitudes? What rituals does that artist follow?
- Suggest that your kids write an essay or poem or song about their resistance to work or how they muster their passion for creative growth.
- Ask kids about the first creative acts they recall. You can imagine raising this question as you and your kids sit around a bowl of popcorn. When we interviewed highly creative families, we found that they talk almost constantly to each other about moments of inspiration and innovation. Rather than sitting like couch potatoes immersed in television or computer games, they explore and share their creative lives, imaginations, and fantasies. The chatter about creativity fills work time as well as leisure, a constant banter about imaginative moments as they sweep the floor, gather trash, or dust the furniture. One woman we spoke to recalled how this happened in her home: "My mom would pose a question—a math problem or logic puzzle, or maybe about some creative moment—and my brother and sister and I would chomp away at her bait as we did other things."
- Invite your kids to share a fun or interesting idea they have had. What made this idea memorable? Why is it so special in their minds? These examples will grow and change over time.

- Ask your child to work with a parent or another kid to take turns writing down experiences from their earliest memories. As they practice retrieving items from their recollections, your kids will learn about their thought processes.
- Suggest that your kids imagine they are traveling through time and they see William Shakespeare watching a performance of one of his plays, or Harriet Tubman as she rescued people from slavery.
- Ask them to invent a different ending to some story they have read or that you have read to them.
- Ask your kid to write an autobiography of themselves. Repeat that request or suggestion from time to time as they grow older. If they share it with you, read it and marvel. If they want to keep it to themselves, respect their privacy.
- Have your kid compose an "un-essay," a device that one Dallas-area teacher we interviewed swears by.[15] It begins with a large sheet of butcher paper laid out on the floor. Your kid stretches out on the sheet while someone draws a rough outline around their body. In the days to come, your child fills the outline with segments cut out of old magazines—different scenes and colors, shapes, and even words that capture his or her rhythm and life—building an autobiographical collage. Maybe your kid draws the items rather than cuts them out of a magazine. Your child then creates a sign to place next to the drawing: "Why did I make the choices that I did?" As always, your children will talk to themselves about how they react to the experience. They can keep journals and record their thoughts, examining their thinking and discussing how they overcome their resistance to work to get something done. After looking back over their masterpiece a few days after it is

finished, they pretend they are travelers from Mars. What do they know about the person who created this scene? What is her rhythm? What lines and colors does he like?

When your kids try these exercises, you can pull back into the shadows. Let them devise and play on their own. Approach them in the same manner you would employ if you were unwrapping a box of chocolates or a popular board game for the first time. Perhaps you never want to use the word "class," but will want to call it the "creativity game." Whatever words speak excitement to them. And passion. Some families might want to create small groups or pairs of siblings while others may invite one or two of their children's friends.

Over the Years

You can invite your children to participate in these exercises in their early school years. But as they get older, as they learn more about themselves, and as their ideas become more sophisticated and more imaginative, the activities can become more sophisticated, too. Let these games unfold and mature with them.

These exercises should feel like an adventure in which students are exploring themselves and their sense of purpose. They should feel like games. The whole experience will become most memorable for your kids if they are laughing, if they feel free to explore, to move around, to make the whole tamale their own.

Take your kids to see works of art that address space and movement, or other elements of creation. These could be plays, paintings, sculptures, music, new buildings, or even shopping centers. Your kids can learn to read a building and how it treats space, movement, color, rhythm, and time. Help them become amazed at what humans have created.

Artists often like to talk about their own work. Tap into the local art community. Take your kids to performances and exhibits. You may be surprised at the diversity of people you will find working in the local theater. Find creative people in your town who do imaginative things and arrange for your kids to talk with them.

That creative artist might be a songwriter or a painter. But it could also be a political leader or someone who started their own business. It could be a parent or a person who collects the trash in an innovative way. The most creative people you know may be the people who find a way to endure the pains that wrack their body.

Show curiosity about what's going on in your child's mind. For example, if you're working with them on Baker's first exercise—expressing tragedy or comedy through movements—ask your kids how and why they came up with a particular movement to convey these feelings. You might get little reflection at first but be prepared to listen and act interested when they begin to talk about themselves and their creative work. One way you can encourage them is by modeling your own self reflections. You may need to do that multiple times before your kids join you. But you primarily need to stand back and let them express themselves. If you begin the process early in their lives, you will delight in how excited they can become. As your kids grow up, you'll see how truly transformational it can be.

The More You Look the More You Find

When we discussed Carol Dweck, we noted that she and her colleagues encountered the challenge of turning fixed mindsets into growth mindsets as children grow older. We know that this transition has enormous power, but the most successful experiments have been conducted with kids who are twelve and younger. Baker's course, on the other hand, was originally focused on much older students—even college undergraduates and graduate students—and, at least based on our own interviews, it was tremendously successful in helping these students find their creative selves. We think it holds great promise for solving the growth mindset limitation for kids at any age.

Jeff Hawkins, the Palm Pilot inventor we met earlier, certainly appreciated the power of a creative mindset. The computer scientist never met Paul Baker and did not take a creativity course from anyone. Yet when we talked with him, many aspects of his home life sounded like pages straight out of Baker's playbook. The idea of looking both inward and outward coursed through his thinking. Much of his childhood experience sparked imagination. He explored the idea of looking at ordinary matters in fresh new ways. This future giant in the computer industry became fascinated with why certain sounds and not others would intrigue people in a musical composition.

You can raise that question with your children. In doing so, you begin to cast ordinary experiences—like listening to music—in a whole new light. That will encourage your kids to look beyond the rigid categorizations we often apply to the world.

In the days and weeks leading up to Hawkins's invention of the first highly successful portable computing device, he was actually looking for a way to better understand the human brain. How does it acquire and store information?

We could add a thousand more stories about people who used the same approach to live creative lives in other fields. Some came out of the Integration of Abilities course. Others discovered the power of a creative mindset from their experience in medicine, science, politics, architecture, business, journalism, parenting, hairdressing, law enforcement, lawn maintenance, or elsewhere. The whole idea changed the way people thought about learning, their own growth and schooling.

CREATIVE DECISION-MAKING

We have argued that creativity can appear in multiple aspects of human life, not just in art and its creation. This becomes abundantly clear in what we call "creative decision-making," a process of bringing systematic steps—mixed with imagination—to the business of deciding what to do in difficult situations.

Let's say, for example, your family is faced with some tough choices. Should you buy a new house closer to work, or stay in a neighborhood everyone loves? If your children are young enough, you probably won't bring them into the discussion. Ken's parents didn't ask him if his father should take a new and better-paying job in the Midwest when he was a year old and living in a tiny Georgia town near the Alabama border. Nor did they ask his three-year-old sister. But they did include his seventeen-year-old brother in the conversation.

You must decide when and how your children can consider such matters. But you will help your kids mature into rational and creative people if you give them a chance to join a mature conversation as early as possible. That experience will pay off as they face difficult choices in school and life.

The creative and rational approach begins with brainstorming and lots of note-taking. What are some important questions that we must answer to make a good decision in this case? They are similar to the questions that an artist asks about what color to use, what lines to employ. What are some possible responses to each of the important questions that we can ask?

As your kids hover around a bowl of popcorn throwing ideas into the hopper, you continue to prompt speculation. If we go this direction, what could go wrong? Are we willing to pay the price in time and effort to overcome this possible outcome? How will our decision affect other people and our broader society? Are we using good evidence? Are we being influenced by ideology? Do we avoid saying something like "I wouldn't do that because I'm a conservative, or a liberal?" As you face complex dilemmas, even ones with conflicting values, how can you devise creative solutions that satisfy multiple needs and standards?

Such discussions can model calm and careful thinking that invites multiple perspectives, that encourages everyone to be tolerant of other people and their views. But they should also allow imaginations to run wild. Everyone should feel welcome to say silly things, even as they eventually return to more sober assessments.

Perhaps most important, such discussions should deliberately seek out people with whom you disagree. If you're engaged in highly political matters, for example, ask your kids to interview someone with whom they strongly disagree. Encourage them to look at problems and situations from completely new perspectives.

Elizabeth Emery, an English teacher from West Jordan, Utah, asks her students "to choose a sensitive topic with weighty consequences, find someone who disagrees soundly with their own opinion, and have a conversation with that person." She wants them to "ask questions and listen, taking notes." When they write up a "summary of the conversation," they explain "how it made them feel, and whether or not they changed their mind on the topic."[16] Imagine asking your kids to do something similar.

In a world that is warming all too rapidly, some families like Reyna's are facing almost stupefying choices about where to live, about what dangers are worth enduring or rivers worth crossing to reach a happier place. Yet the introduction of this creative decision-making need not involve something as monumental as pulling up roots and moving across country or to a new nation. You can help your children develop a tradition and method for creative decision-making on much smaller but still important matters. Each experience with this approach will enhance their ability to get more out of school and life, emphasizing that learning doesn't mean just remembering facts.

EXERCISE AND CREATIVITY

If you want to increase the influence of your work on creativity, get your kids to engage in physical exercise before, during, and even after your games. Baker certainly did this in his classes. If your kids are young and in good health, you won't find much resistance to such an activity. Your six-year-old, and maybe your teenager, will be eager to try out their arms and legs, tongues and lungs. You'll find them twisting and shouting with the best of them.

But here's the best part: a small but growing number of scientists are finding that physical activity enhances thinking.[17] Try it with your kids. Make systematic exercise a routine part of the learning household you are building. Make it fun. Turn it into a ritual.

Some kids love to move, and that appetite can lead teachers and parents to misdiagnose them as having attention deficit hyperactivity disorder (ADHD), when all they have is a desire to move and dance. We remember when our oldest grandson was three or four. He was taking Chinese classes every Saturday. We went with him one week, and for about forty-five minutes, he endured a mind-numbing parade of memory exercises. Finally, he jumped up and ran around the room three times before coming back and plopping down in his chair again.

Some people would have wanted to medicate him.

INTERLUDE

Life is full of decisions that have nothing to do with how we make our living. If we judge our schooling only by the salaries we make—as many contemporary observers do—we miss out on the rich potential of an education. Schooling should help our kids navigate both the promising rewards their education can provide and the tough decisions they must make in life.

Talia Lisa Brown understood that.[18] She had learned to plan ahead, to anticipate possible problems, and to find solutions for them before they created a crisis. She had learned to ask good questions and to probe deeply. It is not surprising, therefore, that during the pandemic she thought early about what her elderly parents should do if they tested positive for Covid-19. When she asked them to talk with their primary care physician to make a plan, the doctor responded with a fairly routine recommendation.

Talia might have accepted the advice without further action, but she didn't. Instead, knowing that her mom had a chronic medical condition, she wondered if the physician had taken it into consideration. She began poring over the medical literature on both her mom's chronic ailment and the evolving treatments of Covid, and learned that, in this case, the standard prescription did not make sense. Indeed, Talia found epidemiologists calling for something else entirely, because the normally recommended medication had potential to cause harm to people with her mother's condition. When she shared what she had discovered, her mother promptly took it to the primary care doctor and they agreed on a new plan.

Talia had no medical training, but she knew how to find scientific papers and had learned how to interpret what she read. She had a healthy respect for medical professionals, but she had also developed an equal devotion to evidence-based decisions in all areas of life—from medicine to child-rearing. She always asked herself, "What are the problems I would face if I believed this or that, and what is the evidence that such problems would arise?"

How and why did Talia develop these habits and abilities? She didn't take a course on how to react to a physician's prescription. What *did* she get out of school that fostered her advanced problem-solving ability and her healthy questioning? Much of the answer may be buried in a classic puzzle developed by the German psychologist Karl Duncker. The puzzle goes something like this: Imagine you are given a tea candle, a large box of matches, and a single thumbtack. How could you attach the candle to a wooden wall using only these items? This problem has a simple answer, but most people don't think of it: Dump out the matches, thumbtack the empty box to the wall, and stand up the candle inside the box. Then use one of the matches to light it. Those who are able to reach this conclusion tend to be more persistent and imaginative problem-solvers.[19]

Researchers who presented this puzzle to their subjects found that those who solved it quickly were more likely to have lived in a foreign country and to have adapted to the culture of that society (not just visited). That experience of living in a different kind of way had taught them to break down their own mental models and build new ones.

Talia had lived in both Bogotá, Colombia, and Valencia, Spain. She had traveled extensively, walking the Incan trail in Peru in the midst of a civil war. She had learned to adjust to a new place with a different culture, language, and political history. She had adapted to environments where everything from what people ate to how they greeted strangers was new and different. In short, by living abroad and learning other languages, she had faced a barrage of challenges to her conventional habits as she navigated through the common practices of everyday life. In the process, she had become more open to new models of thinking and more creative approaches to problem solving.

Katherine Phillips and other researchers discovered that just working with someone from a different social group or ethnicity can make you a better problem solver, even if you feel uncomfortable in doing so. Indeed, social discomfort may be a hidden boon, placing you in an environment that challenges your thinking. And, we might add, the same is true of exposure to people from different points on the political spectrum. Help your kids embrace problem solving rather than run away from it.[20]

Does this mean that your children must participate in study abroad programs? Not necessarily. But it might mean that they should study new languages and different cultures. Talia did study other languages and societies, and that challenged her as well. She often sought different kinds of friends and acquaintances. She did not take Paul Baker's Integration of Abilities course, because it wasn't offered where she went to school. But she did find his book on her own and work her way through the exercises.

In our current era, taking language courses, studying abroad, majoring in Latin American studies or other regional concentrations, or taking a course on creativity often receive low marks from parents. We've heard so many people say, "Don't study a foreign language; learn coding instead." That's unfortunate. If everything is measured by the kind of jobs it gets you, we lose sight of how an education can enrich your kids' lives and help them solve difficult problems. Even on the job.

Please don't get us wrong. Talia got good grades, graduated from a demanding university, and has had a dynamic and rewarding career. Yet it's her problem-solving abilities, both at home and on the job, along with her community of diverse friends, creative lifestyle, curiosity, broad knowledge, critical thinking abilities, and devotion to the common good, that suggest she got a lot out of school.

FIVE

Helping Your Kids Learn Deeply

IT IS POSSIBLE for your kids to acquire broad knowledge *while* practicing deep learning and critical thinking skills. We call the combination *smart learning*. Indeed, taking a deep approach to learning will enhance kids' ability to build an extensive library of information and ideas that they can use.

If your kids are too influenced by teachers who require students only to remember facts, they will not be prepared for life. As adults they will not have developed their abilities to think creatively and critically, and to operate as *adaptive experts*. It's a term we will define below, but for the moment, consider what the phrase might mean and how it might differ from routine expertise. In a world of conflicting claims, deep learning is what enables developing minds to make wise judgments as they encounter disputes about the truth.

Young people must also learn how to confront messy problems that can't be solved with simple or definitive responses. Such problems require reflective and wise judgment. What can you do to help your kids learn to make tough decisions wisely?

Many complex questions have multiple good answers, requiring sensitivity and discernment to choose the best among them. How can schools and parents help kids handle the barrage of claims coming at them and learn to think logically and carefully?

Deep learning is about living with uncertainty in general, making good decisions not just in academic settings but every day with friends and family. How can we help our kids develop the confidence to learn yet still recognize the limits of their knowledge in the face of fundamental uncertainty? We want our children to believe that they can learn deeply, but we don't want them to become blind to how much they don't know.

What can parents say or do that will help kids find a balance between confidence and blind, arrogant ignorance, to see missteps as an opportunity to grow, and to recognize the problems they face in believing whatever they may entertain? How can kids learn to disagree without getting mad, to keep exchanging thoughts with others, to respect each other, and to live with uncertainty? Perhaps most importantly, deep learning will help your kids enjoy life more.

As a parent, you face an unprecedented challenge that you must take on if you want your children to get more out of school. Much of what we must understand is embedded in how people define learning and how they promote it. That's where we will begin, but we will move toward specific recommendations about how your kids should read and study. If you don't already see the connection between how they learn and messy problems, you will before this section is over. We hope.

SURFACE AND DEEP LEARNING MINDSETS

Carol Jinkins and Sabato Crain were born a month apart, and lived the earliest years of their lives in the same apartment building.[1] Their parents became good friends. Even after Carol's family moved to a Philadelphia suburb, while Sabato's stayed in Newark, the two families often visited one another. "We grew up like we were brother and sister," Sabato explained. "Or at least cousins."

In school they had much in common. Both aced math and history. In high school, Carol took Spanish and played the violin in the orchestra. Sabato wielded a mean saxophone in the jazz band and took four years of Mandarin. They both won high marks for their efforts. But they also had very different intentions when they studied, and those differing aims changed nearly everything about what they got out of school.

Carol wanted to get the highest grades possible. That's it—there was nothing complicated about her ambitions. She thought only about how she could finish each assignment at a level that would be rewarded with an A. By contrast, Sabato wanted to understand the material as deeply as possible and to think about the implications, applications, and possibilities of everything he studied. The boy from Newark liked finding connections and common threads through the various subjects and topics presented to him.

Sabato's study tactics matched these aims. When he read something, Sabato paid attention to the argument being made and focused on the big ideas. He took careful stock of the evidence offered and the conclusions being drawn from it. He recognized when statements contained arguments and when they did not, and looked for additional meaning lying behind the page. He distinguished between cases where there was disagreement about facts and cases where parties looking at the same facts expressed different attitudes about them. When he studied math, he connected the problems in his homework to key concepts rather than just following that lesson's procedure for arriving at correct answers.

You might think that the difference between Carol's and Sabato's intentions would make little difference to their outcomes. But researchers have been probing that matter since at least the 1970s and have found that these different approaches to learning yield substantial variations in the results. You will want to know about this research. But fair warning: it's a bit complex. Stick with us.

From time to time in this book, we've used the phrase *deep learning*. That sounds quite positive, and it is, but it is not the same as having a growth (or creative) mindset, which we discussed earlier. If you want your kids to get the most out of school, you should promote the view that intelligence can grow and advocate for living a creative life. You should let their curiosity grow and create home environments where it will. But you must also foster deep learning. If your children don't get that last piece, they will miss out on something important to their future.

But what does deep learning mean, and how can you promote it in your children? A little history will help answer those questions. Fifty years ago, a group of educational psychologists at Gothenburg University in Sweden wanted to know more about how students study and learn. Ference Marton and Roger Säljö, two professors of educational psychology, found that intentions play a huge role in what kids get out of school.[2]

Recognizing Deep and Surface Learning

The Swedish scholars gave a group of students an article, telling them that after reading it they would be asked to respond to questions about its content. Some students sped through the selection. Others read more slowly. Yet the speed of their reading did not matter nearly as much as another factor that became clear to the researchers after they had interviewed each person in the room.

As they did, it became apparent that not everyone had taken (and *taken* is a key word here) the same approach to their reading. Some had seized on bits of information they could memorize quickly. They expected that some of the questions would go to these factual details, and they wanted to be prepared. These young people didn't focus on grasping the main ideas of the piece or considering broader applications or implications of its claims. Marton and Säljö called these folks *surface learners*.

We know from other studies that surface learners see their mission as getting credit for a course so they can move on to the next. In the language that many of them use, they are just "trying to get out of this class alive." They show little or no interest in the implications, applications, or possibilities of the material they encounter. For them, learning something means committing it to memory long enough to spit it back on a test or in a paper they write. Their education has little enduring or substantial influence on how they think, act, or feel, and it seldom occurs to them that it should.

By the 1980s, some researchers recognized that surface learners can have very different levels of ambition. Some just want to pass their courses, but others are seeking the highest possible grades.[3] We call the latter group *strategic learners*. They are not more interested in learning deeply than their less ambitious peers, but they want to enjoy the respect and other rewards that come with high academic achievement. For many of these students, a course's impact on their grade point average is the only thing motivating them to do well in it. But an excessive preoccupation with making the honor roll can set them up for lives of perfectionism and a host of psychological ills.

Strategic learners devote their energies to discovering what the teacher wants and how to ace the exam. If they learn something along the way that changes how they think, act, or feel, how they understand the world and themselves, it's largely by accident. They seldom set out to challenge their current understanding of a subject, much less change their lives. They simply want the recognition that comes from graduating with honors.

Problems with Strategic Learning

Because, by outward appearances, the Carols and the Sabatos of the world seem to have much in common, it can be easy to mistake them for the same type of student. If you are tempted to think that strategic learning is a satisfactory compromise—a difference only of degree and not really of kind—then you should pause to consider the many personal and social ills that can flow from it.

Let's say, for example, your daughter aspires to become a physician. She needs to learn buckets of gory details about the inner workings of the human body. She has to demonstrate that she can recall those facts, or at least recognize them on a multiple-choice quiz. If she takes a strategic approach and merely tries to remember as much as possible, with no attention to the implications and applications of what she is learning, she is not preparing herself to do the most essential part of the job she wants—namely, to perform the differential diagnoses that can tell her, for example, why someone is having splitting headaches and what treatment will most likely address the pain with least risk of stirring up new troubles.

After she graduates and starts practicing medicine, she might not make an essential connection between a particular fact she memorized back in school and the ailment of the patient now in front of her eyes. Strategic learners often cannot transfer information they learn in one context (like a classroom) to a new situation (such as a medical clinic). If your daughter faces an unusual case, with symptoms different than most others, she may not recognize those anomalies and be able to imagine how the treatment should be adapted. The same is true of bridge builders and corporate executives, refrigerator makers and gasoline chemists. Practitioners of every kind fall short if they have not learned their professions deeply. But if doctors in training never get past strategic learning, they can kill.

Over the last fifty years, many leading medical schools have recognized these problems and have changed the way they teach to foster deeper learning. In the most advanced versions they have fashioned marvelous learning environments.[4] You can benefit from what they have devised. No matter what your kids go on to do in life, they will do it better if they gain the ability to learn deeply rather than strategically.

Education, to the strategic and surface learners, is not an adventure to be relished in progress. They rarely take risks, lest some original or extra line of work end up not going as planned, messing up their grade point average. These students don't ride their curiosity and imagination in magical journeys through the unexplored wilderness of life. Most important, they don't learn much, no matter what kind of grades or SAT scores they get.[5]

Please don't get us wrong. Schools and parents do not foster surface or strategic learning because they want to torture children. Often their actions come out of a serious misunderstanding about learning. We must explore their conceptions if we hope to make any progress.

Deep Learning

Unlike surface learners, deep learners consciously look for views with which they disagree. Deep learners are interested in their own intellectual growth. They want to keep learning, to find new ways to use an idea or piece of information. They want to integrate everything they encounter, to see connections and differences between ideas. They are comfortable with the habit of thinking again, of constantly exploring the possibility that they might be wrong. In other words, they are a lot like Sabato.

As a result, deep learners act in their own unique ways when they encounter new and difficult problems. Most important, they talk to other people (and themselves), grappling with fresh ways to understand a situation, to find a solution, to make appropriate analogies, to develop new ideas, to understand the intellectual flaws of the ideas and beliefs they may hold. They recognize the immediate and long-term consequences of their decisions.

They like to take ideas apart, to look for arguments in what they read, and to distinguish between conclusions and the evidence that supposedly supports them. They also like to synthesize—to pull the deconstructed parts of an idea back together, creating a new whole, a new argument with a fresh contention. Finally, they like to theorize, gathering evidence to support and validate their contentions. These are the people who really do well in life and are happy with themselves. They contribute to the well-being of their families and communities. They live innovative and creative lives.

These versatile problem-solvers are aware of important concepts in a field and understand its underlying ideas. When they employ a standard procedure in, say, math, it isn't because they have blindly memorized a series of steps. They are endlessly curious and not afraid to make mistakes. They are willing to build new models to understand the world.

Yet they also exercise a healthy respect for the wisdom of old ideas and ways of thinking and living. Like a longtime homeowner cleaning out the attic, they can take up an older idea, fondly examine it, and discover a new use for it, while also recognizing that some cobwebs and clutter must be swept out to clear space for new ideas. They ask questions—lots of them—and stand in awe of how much more there is to learn.

Indeed, one of the key markers of deep learners is that they are acutely aware of how much they don't know and are never reluctant to show their own ignorance by asking a question. "I don't care if anyone thinks I'm dumb," we heard from more than one deep learner we interviewed. "If there's something I don't understand, I know I must ask questions about it."

When Does Deep Learning Happen?

If you look carefully at the research and theoretical literature on deep learning, a simple picture emerges: If you want your kid to engage in deep learning, you need to give them a problem that strikes them as significant, interesting, or beautiful. If your kid also thinks of it as fun, then, *bingo,* you've got a winner. The key is to present them with a genuine problem, something that will challenge them to reconsider their assumptions and reexamine their basic models of reality. This is how people learn—not by doing rote exercises, but by sinking their teeth into authentic tasks.

You can help support that environment. Pose questions that will puzzle, intrigue, delight and sometimes frustrate your children. Remember our earlier discussion of philosophy for children. That's a gold mine.

Listen to their questions. Welcome their inquiries. Share your own. Let them see that you, too, grapple with some big mysteries of life. Avoid the impression that every question can be answered by an internet search. Expose them to diverse views. Let them hear controversy. Take them to public lectures and debates, and not just to hear people with whom you agree.

How to Promote Deep Learning

If you foster growth and creative mindsets, you will produce a rich soil where deep learning can grow. Yet that often isn't enough. To help your children surface ways of reading, you must understand more and ask why some kids, like Sabato, become deep learners while others, like Carol, pursue a strategic or surface approach. Do those distinctions come out of anything that we might call intelligence? Are deep learners just smarter?

No, it isn't a result of intelligence, no matter how we define that trait. The answer is both simple and enormously complex.[6] Let's start with a single word: *conditioning.* People are conditioned to pursue surface or strategic approaches and to avoid deep ones. It isn't part of their DNA or some unchangeable facet of their personality. It isn't due to physical characteristics they have inherited from their ancestors along with their blue eyes, dark skin, or abundant sweat glands. It isn't because they are tall or short, over- or underweight, muscular or slight. It is a result of conditioning.

Some strategic learners have quick minds. They seem to remember easily. Yet they have been conditioned to go after surface and strategic goals.

But where does that conditioning process take place? It happens everywhere, and that's what makes overcoming it so complex. It happens at the breakfast table, around town, in the movie theater, in front of the television, in the newspaper, on social media, and certainly in the classroom. It happens throughout our culture and society.

Students are too often judged by what and how much they can memorize and regurgitate on exams or in papers they write. Seldom does anyone ask, "Can you connect what you are doing with something you learned last week? Can you transfer and generalize this concept to another area of learning? Can you propose and test new theories based on what you are hearing or reading now?"

When young people hear constantly that they must strive for high grades so they can get into good colleges and make lots of money, they begin to think that school exists solely to provide career preparation. In their minds, education is simply job training. Rather than expanding their fascination with the world with new ideas and problems, conditioning shapes their brains to ask only one question: How will this learning help me make money? This narrow focus is particularly unfortunate given that researchers have been unable to find any clear link between making money and doing well in school. Note the many major innovators whose GPAs were not high.[7]

When you talk to your kids about school, don't emphasize what's called *careerism*. Stress how learning can change their lives, provide exciting adventures, lead to new insights, and answer questions. There's nothing wrong with preparing for a job, as well—but if that's all your kids get out of school, they'll miss out on a lot. As the essayist Jonathan Malesic put it, "You're a worker for only part of your life; you're a human being, a creature with a powerful brain, throughout it."[8]

If children believe that some people are smart and others are dumb, they may try to prove to themselves and others that they have what it takes. "I don't want anybody to know that I don't know something," they may say to themselves. They won't ask questions because that would expose their ignorance.

We've heard parents advise children to just keep their mouths shut; that way, no one will know when they don't know something. Instead they should be urging kids to ask the questions that will spark critical thinking and deep learning. Philosopher and physicist Arnold Arons, in a classic text on teaching introductory physics, lists ten basic processes that underlie all thoughtful analysis and suggests ways for teachers to help students build these reasoning capacities.[9] Arons's practices raise probing questions to ask yourself, and encourage your kids to ask, on approaching any subject of inquiry:

1. What do we know about the given subject? How do we know what is true? What evidence do we have? Why do we accept that evidence?
2. What information is missing? Can we recognize when we don't really have sufficient data or evidence to say something is true? Can we tolerate that uncertainty?
3. Can we recognize when we have *observed* something versus when we have *inferred* it?
4. Do we understand the difference between the *words* we use to stand in for ideas and the *ideas* themselves? For a new concept to be critically examined, it must be explained using prior words with commonly understood meanings. Are we learning

to parrot technical jargon without first mastering the "operational definition" behind the concept in question?
5. On what assumptions does an assertion rely? What does it imply should be taken as a given, while not spelling that out explicitly?
6. How can we determine if inferences from data, observations, or other evidence really support inferences being made and conclusions being drawn? Are any alternative explanations or interpretations equally valid?
7. Do we understand the principles and constraints governing a system well enough to be able to engage in hypothetico-deductive reasoning—to imagine, that is, how certain interventions would result in different outcomes?
8. Do we understand the differences between structural problems with an argument and what logicians (people who study logic) call informal fallacies?
9. Can we discriminate between inductive and deductive reasoning? Are we aware when an argument is proceeding from the particular to the general, as opposed to from the general to the particular?
10. Is our own line of reasoning internally consistent? How can we tell? How, with practice, could we learn to test our own thinking and become intellectually self-reliant?[10]

UNDERSTANDING DEEP LEARNING MORE DEEPLY

The two of us have a video that we filmed and edited years ago. It shows a very young child, just twenty-two months old, sitting on a couch and playing with a toy. While the boy fiddles with his trinket, an adult voice off-camera says in a sing-song fashion, "two times three is . . . ," and the toddler looks up and says "six." The grownup voice continues with "six times three is...," and the young kid responds, "eighteen." Then comes the final prompt, "and the eighteenth letter of the alphabet is...," to which the toddler calls out, "R."

We've shown that clip—recorded in early 2006—to hundreds of educators since then. We always ask, "Is this deep learning?" And always, the overwhelming majority answer is a resounding "no." That's when we point out that what the toddler just showed—his ability to give correct answers to factual questions—is often all they know about their own students. "If your students are learning deeply," we ask, "how can you tell? For that matter, how could a parent know?" These questions provoke a lot of smiles and, better, "aha" looks on many faces.

The educators are right. What was shown in the video was not deep learning. It's a parlor trick a mother taught her son. Whenever she was driving around town with the child tucked into his safety seat, she would play some educational fare like *Schoolhouse Rock* songs on the car stereo. Soon enough, she discovered that her little boy had learned the lyrics to the simpler tunes. If she sang the first part of a line herself, he would pick up the cue and chime in with the rest.

When, however, someone stated the math prompt to him slightly differently—"What is two times three?"—and in a normal speaking voice, he would not respond. He did not understand the question, let alone the meaning of the answer. Likewise, flipping the prompt to "three times two" got no answer or sign of interest as the boy continued to play with his toy truck.

How do we define deep learning, and how do we promote it? You can't do much to improve what kids get out of school unless you define what it means to progress. We need a more systematic definition of the concept. Luckily, several researchers and educational theorists have given us one. Let's start with the ideas of John Biggs—a Tasmanian-born educational psychologist who, along with his colleagues in the 1980s, developed a process for thinking about thinking.[11]

These days, Biggs has a full head of wavy, white hair and has turned his talents to writing novels and nonfiction works. Back then, he spent his time dreaming up ways to find out more about how people learned and thinking about what it meant to do so. Most notably, he developed a list of five levels of learning, each level better than the one before it. Yes, *better*. You see, Biggs was concerned not just with how much students learned (that is, how many facts they could repeat from memory), but with the quality of their thinking. He was part of a generation of teachers who dared to ask what real *value* kids were getting out of their schooling. Teachers had been giving their young charges scores for their work in the classroom for at least a century, and parents had pored over those report cards like they were the be-all and end-all of schooling. But few people had stopped to ask: Are the kids really learning to *think*?

In most American classrooms, if you could reproduce a list of key facts perfectly, you got an A. If you could remember only eighty-nine percent of them, you got a B. And so forth. In other parts of the world, educators dished out numbers instead of letters. Neither system concerned itself with quality. If you asked a teacher how they gauged the quality of a student's thinking, and whether one way was better than another, they might cite some vague criteria. We've actually run into instructors and parents of adolescents who believed, "you can just tell from the handwriting." What does that mean? We have no idea.

Others we've interviewed have said that good thinking is, in the words of one teacher, "well-organized, coherent, factually accurate, and comprehensive." But, again, what does that really mean? When does a work become comprehensive? Or well-organized? When it mentions more than 50 percent of the facts the reader was expecting? Or 75 percent? Biggs wanted a better way to describe quality. Biggs put people who had no idea what something meant in the first level of his classification system (called a *taxonomy*—a word borrowed from biologists and botanists who put plants and animals into meaningful groups).

He called this level of knowing *prestructural*. (We warned you that psychologists love to use new words and phrases they have coined.) When the parent sang "two times three is" to the twenty-two-month-old, he would chime in with "six." That was prestructural.

In the second level, your kid knows and can repeat one isolated fact but probably hasn't thought about what it means or how it is connected to anything else. For example, imagine that your child is learning about cows.[12] In the prestructural level, they wouldn't have the faintest idea what a "cow" is. In the second level, however, they might know that "a cow is an animal for milking." People at this level can identify, recite, or even carry out a single procedure. Biggs called their thinking "unistructural."

In the third level, students can understand several aspects of a subject. They can list and even put some things together. "Cows give us milk and when slaughtered, they give us oil, meat, fat, bone and leather." But they fail to understand significance or how these items are connected to bigger ideas, questions, or problems. They may be able to recite facts about bovines until (sorry about this) the cows come home, but they won't ask where these creatures came from or how they changed economies, diets, landscapes, atmospheres, or health. They won't ask new questions. Biggs called this a "multistructural" level.

In the fourth level, called the "relational" level, your child will grasp how each part of a subject relates to the whole—how calculus and moral philosophy, for example, are important in life's journey. They can connect concepts and ideas and see the relationship between matters that are seemingly distant from one another. They are able to see the implications and applications of diverse subjects—from history to surgery, from cutting the grass to figuring out how human life can survive on this planet. Here we have entered the terrain of deep learning.

In the fifth and highest level—Biggs named it the "extended abstract" level—kids can combine ideas and understand why one thought contributes to others to form a structure of knowledge.[13] "Cattle are large, domesticated, cloven-hoofed herbivores, which means they eat plants. They have four legs, and horns growing out of their heads. They live in places around the globe."

But these highest-level thinkers can do more than tell you information. They can also find the assumptions that are made in an argument, or abstract ideas rather than concrete observations. They can recognize when people are disagreeing about the facts and when they are battling over attitudes. Deep learners can pinpoint the central ideas around which other notions are distributed and how the various parts are related to each other. People who think on this level can form new theories, understand the implications and applications of such theories, and even envision how their theories can be tested. You could say they are highly creative. "It seems to me that humans must have played an important role in cows' evolution," they might say, "because they were selected for different genetic characteristics like milk, meat, size, coloring, and behavior, to name a few."

As we think through these levels, let's keep in mind why students might think deeply in the first place. On the most basic level, it's because they care. They are exercising a fundamental human need to know, to understand. It's not because someone threatened them with a low grade.

That process begins early and continues through years of study. To make that journey, your kids will need to study with deep intentions. If someone doesn't want to learn deeply, it seems highly unlikely that they ever will. (Intentions alone don't mean that they will know how to learn deeply, but more on that idea a little later.)

You could throw up your hands and give up on your children, saying something like "I just want my kids to get good grades. All this mumbo jumbo about deep learning is too complicated for my children and me." That would be too bad, because you and your kids can do better. Don't sell yourself or your kids short. It takes time and hard work to learn deeply. It requires talking with yourself and with other people.

Lots of people had given up on the MindDrive students in Kansas City, and they had given up on themselves—until, that is, Steve Rees came along and helped them find their passion and enjoy a kind of success that fed new interests. Some people had given up on Carol Greider because of her reading problems. Let those students become your models and inspirations to ask what you can do to foster your children's deep learning.

Stop harping on grades. Start raising interesting questions instead. Make those questions open-ended rather than ones with fixed answers that someone could memorize. And don't tie everything to career ambitions. Help your kids see how deep approaches to learning will enhance their lives and work, no matter what jobs they do.

HOW TO STUDY DEEPLY

One Saturday morning we went to get bagels at the coffee shop where we had met with Charlotte and Michael. We heard three kids discussing an upcoming exam. They were sitting around the same table where we had talked about the meaning of education. The only available spot was right next to them. We slid into those seats with as little fanfare as possible.

It became evident that they were preparing for an exam only two days away and that they had made limited progress in their studying. Often kids wait until the last minute, and even if they don't, they sometimes have little idea how to study. The three young people decided they would read aloud to each other for five hours a day over the next two days.

"If we go through this three or four times," one girl announced, "we should remember enough to ace the exam."

She had an ambitious plan but not a deep one. Still, her two male friends eagerly followed along. "I'll read first," one of them volunteered quickly. He launched into reading every word of the first chapter of an introductory physics textbook out loud. Their teacher had said the test would be on that section of the book, and the young people intended to buzz through those pages. It was a strategic approach to learning.

After a few minutes, they all looked bored and sometimes scribbled something in their notebooks, often underlining a passage or simply writing a big question mark in the margins. One of them had an array of highlighter colors. He put this collection in the middle of the table so everyone could reach them.

We gathered up our bagels after a while and headed down the street. When we saw them a few weeks later, we asked, "How long did you read?" They responded, "At least four hours the first day, and more than three the second." And how did they do on the exam? "Not so well. We're just not good at science."

Those kids believed that if they read something over and over again, they could burn it into their brains. They thought they could stoke the fire if they highlighted with multiple colors. But human minds don't work that way. Research shows that people who study by repeatedly rehearsing often remember little come test time.[14]

Even if they manage to pass the exam, these students quickly forget everything.[15] No long-term memory. They don't become adaptive experts or understand deeply enough to solve anybody's problems. Typically, their method doesn't spark new questions, stimulate their imaginations, or help them see connections between what they are reading and other ideas or problems. It doesn't produce deep learning.

As we walked down the street, it occurred to us that some kids don't learn deeply because they just weren't taught to read in that manner. The last time many high schoolers had any formal instruction in reading, they were exploring the lives of Sally, Dick, and Jane, or some equivalent elementary school literature. Now they are asked to read and make use of textbooks, novels, scholarly articles, historical documents, and research reports.

You can help them. Yes, schools should tackle these issues, and they often do, but not always, and seldom with methods that have strong support from research on how people learn. When Ken was teaching advanced courses in history at Vanderbilt, NYU, and Northwestern, he spent a fair amount of time helping students learn to read both historical documents and secondary sources, but none of his colleagues did the same. Indeed, some of the best-known professors simply read material to the class in much the same fashion that the high schoolers read to each other.[16]

Below, we share a series of research-based principles for reading and studying that will help your kids read deeply. You can share these ideas and practices with them. While these insights will become increasingly important as your child progresses through school, they are relevant all the way through.

Relate, Relate, Relate, Understand, Understand, Understand

Your kids have two interrelated tasks on their path to deep learning: They will need to understand information and ideas, and they will need to remember what they supposedly understand. While some people still insist that you must first "know" material (meaning memorize it, we guess) before you can begin to understand it, you can help your children appreciate that studying should go the other way around. It is much easier to remember something you understand than it is to stuff isolated bits and pieces in your brain and expect to pull them out later.

That's because when you understand something, you have connected it to other ideas and information, seeing both differences and similarities. You have built an extensive web in your brain in which you have compared and contrasted, noticed how one item is a product or cause of another, observed that something conflicts with something else, engaged in far transfer (that is, thought about how two seemingly unrelated items are connected), built some new concept or theory around two or more observations or inferences, and perhaps made some value judgments. The more connections you make, the easier it will be to retrieve information and use it.

Understanding can help you remember, but raw memory doesn't improve understanding. Try to remember, for example, the following digits: 149162536496481. That's easy if you understand that they are the squares of the numbers 1 to 9. One times one is one. Two times two is four. Three times three is nine. Four times four is sixteen, and so forth. Understanding makes remembering easier. You can help your kids understand that deep learning will help them remember, but memorizing will not, by itself, help them think deeply.

Question and Test

When you read something new, ask yourself what the evidence and reasoning is that supports it. What does it imply? How is it connected to something you encountered last week or year?

Speculate, Speculate, Speculate

Rather than flooding kids with memory exercises, pose questions—big questions—then coax the kids to suggest possible answers. Let's say the assignment is to calculate the height of a flagpole. Get them to invent possible ways to do so, even before they consult their math books.

Passion, Passion, Passion

Remember the MindDrive kids. They learned a lot of details about how cars are constructed, how it takes energy to get objects moving, how they could reduce the load of the cars they built, and so forth. In short, they learned a lot of physics and engineering. Yet all of those achievements came from their fascination with cars.

You should help your kids experience the power and joy of being passionate about something so that they can become enthusiastic about anything they try to learn. They must know what passion feels like before they can muster it for something completely new. Without passion, any one of the study techniques we've introduced here will seem more difficult and tiring to them. With passion, they will push themselves to work harder and even feel more satisfied with their work. Once they learn how to become passionately interested in anything—from Pokémon to pogo sticks—you can help them figure out how to apply that same kind of energy to topics in which they have little initial interest.

Retrieve Rather than Rehearse

The students at the coffee shop spent hours cramming their brains with material, and no time retrieving it as they would need to do on the upcoming test.

So what should they have done? Our suggestion comes from a wonderful book called *Make It Stick,* written by the novelist Peter Brown and two cognitive psychologists at Washington University, Henry Roediger and Mark McDaniel. Brown brought his knack for telling a good story, and the Washington University professors contributed years of research on human learning.

Here's what Brown and his coauthors would suggest. After the three students got their textbooks and started taking notes in class, they should have met for about thirty minutes every day to ask one another questions and answer them. They might have connected by phone or on Zoom or met at one of their homes. In short, they could have spread the seven hours they eventually spent over about fourteen days. Had they used this method of "spaced repetition," they would have spent the same amount of total time and done far better on the examination.[17] They also would have learned deeply.

Make It Stick suggests that in study sessions, students stop reading every few minutes, close their books, and ask themselves questions: "What are the key ideas? What terms or ideas are new to me? How would I define them? How do the ideas relate to what I already know?"[18]

They might write their responses down and then share them with one another. They might also raise questions that many textbooks put at the ends of chapters. Or they could pretend they are teaching the class and asking students what the most important points in this section are.

They could then check with the textbook and class notes to see if they were right. Every few days, they could remind themselves of the key ideas they had already reviewed. This quizzing, spread out over many days, helps students practice retrieving information and ideas. It also helps them assess whether they understand the material. It's called "retrieval practice."[19]

No need for marathon study sessions right before the exam. Teach this different approach to your children as early in their lives as possible and keep asking them about it from time to time. "How are you using retrieval practice in this class?" Remember, too, that all of these suggestions will work best if your kids take a deep approach to their learning. Intentions matter. Foster curiosity. Don't think about school as simply job training.

Space It Out

Building comprehension and memory requires time. The research that Roediger, McDaniel, and others have done demonstrates that it is best to do a little retrieval practice every day rather than spending long hours doing so on one night (say, right before the test). Some people may think doing it close to the exam will keep it fresh in students' minds. But research strongly suggests that spaced repetition will make the knowledge stick and produce much deeper understanding.

Mix up Different Ideas and Tasks (Interleave)

If students need to learn, say, three different ideas or procedures, they often focus on one at a time, only moving to the second once they feel comfortable with first. Then they go on to the next item. In other words, they approach what they wish to learn in blocks.

Imagine a baseball player who takes that approach in batting practice, starting with fast balls and, only after developing real skill at knocking these zingers out of the park, finally switching to curve balls. Many practice sessions later, it's time to take on a sinker. But in real games, pitchers mix up the throws so the batter can't guess what is coming next. A batter who has tried to achieve mastery in this way won't have developed the reflexes to spot and respond to the variety, and may not even have worked on some pitches before the season is well underway. Should I hack at this pitch or let it pass? If I swing, do I prepare to hit a curve ball or a spinning slider? Only when they don't know what's coming do players gain practice in making quick decisions about how to respond.[20]

When a physics student faces a set of problems that all require the same formula to solve them, the student isn't required to understand deeply. They just plug the right number into the proper formula. If, however, they are confronted with sets of disparate problems, they must refer to a deeper understanding of the key principles to know which formula to use to solve each one. A study session that mixes it up is more likely to foster that deep learning.

In our description, we've talked about a small group of kids working together. In many cases, they can employ these approaches alone just as well or even better than when they are working in a group. But with some material (like physics problems, for example), a group effort can be more effective, especially if each student brings different strengths and weaknesses to the sessions.

The kid with a strong background will benefit from explaining an idea to someone who is struggling, or asking a question that offers some insight into the material. Someone with a weak grasp will benefit from asking questions and hearing responses from someone close to their level. Everybody wins.

Use Mindful Learning

Our brains can, at times, operate on automatic. Everyone has experienced that. You drive down a familiar street without thinking about every little part of the journey, every stop and turn. You fix your morning coffee without paying close attention to each step in the process or how one step is different from or similar to another. You turn on the kitchen light without pausing to notice how your hand slides over the switch.

By contrast, a *mindful* brain focuses on everything: the choice you make to have coffee rather than water, how the flavor compares to a cup you had last week, and so forth. You turn your actions one way and then another, looking for new ways to go through your morning routines. You examine the objects you use to carry out those activities and consider why you have chosen to use them rather than other objects.

Think back to the exercises from Paul Baker's creativity course. Why does one way of crossing a space convey comedy while another conveys tragedy? What are the rhythms of your friend's personality? Why do your muscles like a particular movement? Why do you consider some sounds (as in music) uplifting, and others scary or alarming? In each of these activities, you played with the novelty of taking something, exploring its lines, expanding that into a rhythm, and eventually creating a character and a dialogue, all the while being mindful. You were paying attention to each line, each movement, each sound, letting nothing slip by unnoticed. You might have even been paying attention to the fact that you were paying attention—being mindful of your own mindfulness.

So what does all of this have to do with learning how to learn deeply? The answer lies in a famous experiment by the Harvard psychologist Ellen Langer and her colleague Alison Piper.[21] In the experiment, they handed one group of students a rubbery object they described as "a dog's chew toy." They then gave a second group the same object but told them it "could be a dog's chew toy." Their hypothesis was that turning an absolute statement ("this is") into a conditional one ("this could be") would make students more flexible, and therefore more mindful. The second group would have the power to decide what the object was and adjust their definitions if the circumstances changed.

Sound like nonsense? Wait until you hear what happened. As part of the design of the experiment, all of the participants reached a point when they needed an eraser. Many of the people who had heard the rubber object referred to equivocally ("could be") realized they could use it to do the job, while those who heard it definitely identified never considered that possibility. In several experiments, changing the language caused students to be more mindful, and mindful learning prompted better understanding, greater enjoyment, and more imaginative problem-solving. If children contemplated deep philosophical questions surrounding the information and ideas they were learning, they were more likely to remember and use their learning in multiple ways.[22] In short, Langer showed how deeply language shapes people's thinking. Once children realize this, they can imagine alternative worlds, and in the process, their thinking and behavior change. Creativity flourishes. Life blossoms with excitement.

We can, for example, think of any number of ways to reframe studying. Think of it as a game. The game can still be difficult and challenging, and indeed, if it is, then so much the better. If you have to struggle to recall information, then you will make stronger connections in your brain that will allow you to retrieve it more easily later. No strain, no gain. Help your kids appreciate this principle. Struggling transforms learning, and students will say later that they enjoyed the process. If you help your children learn how to transform their attitudes toward struggling, they will get more out of school.

Let's return to our students in the coffee shop and consider how they might have approached physics if they were using techniques of mindful learning. Before they did anything, they could have told themselves and each other, "We're going to play a game in which we are astronauts preparing for a journey to Mars. Before we go, we need to understand how sound waves work. Will we be able to hear in space? We need to know why planets revolve around the sun, and other things about the workings of the universe. That way, if our spaceship gets into trouble, we'll be better prepared to find a solution." If they had done this, they would have had more fun and probably done better on their exam.

PUTTING IT ALL TOGETHER

We have shown you some study techniques that will save your kids time and help them to learn deeply. That means that they will remember longer, and understand how their new knowledge is similar to and different from what they already knew. They will use what they learn to solve problems, develop new ideas, and raise fresh questions that will lead to even more learning down the road. They will think about the implications of what they've learned—even in distant areas—and how the principles can be applied broadly. In short, these techniques will change how your children act, how they use their brains to think, and how they feel—not just for an hour or day, but for a long time to come.

Let's bring all of these ideas together. We'll stick with learning physics for our example, but the same approach can inform any studying. We've borrowed a real example that has been used for several years. You can help your kids apply it to any level.

In a traditional approach to schooling, a teacher might simply ask students to read a section of a textbook. Some might complete the assignment, but many won't, or they will simply run their eyes over the pages. An alternative is to start with a question. A whole program, like Steve Rees's MindDrive for example, can be launched with a question to students like *How could we build a car that would use relatively little energy?* In this example, we begin with the question of how a child could help others, perhaps by focusing on poor children living in some impoverished place in another part of the world.

There is a lot of evidence that human beings naturally enjoy helping other people. That feeling arises at a young age. We even have a name for it. It's called *altruism* (or charity). If an adult in a room drops something near a toddler playing nearby, that child will most likely retrieve the object and deliver it back to the adult. In our physics example, Eric Mazur, the award-winning Harvard professor, appeals to that sense of altruism by telling students about the late José Antonio Abreu, a Venezuelan conductor and economist, who created a charity to help poor children around the world.

As Mazur tells the story, Abreu thought of a classical orchestra as a kind of ideal society, and a special educational opportunity that could help disadvantaged children break out of the cycle of poverty and change their lives forever. So, in 1975 he founded El Sistema, a classical music education program that would be open to any child willing and able to devote several hours a week to instruction and rehearsal, regardless of their ability to pay. Within a few years, the model had spread to many countries and more than half a million kids had enrolled.

These avid music students were, however, so poor that many could not afford to buy real instruments to play. These children used cardboard models of violins, horns, and woodwinds to practice the right moves, but those facsimile instruments didn't really make any sounds. This was intensely frustrating to Abreu, who had envisioned the children's music-making stirring their souls.

"I now invite you," Mazur writes to his students, "to design new kinds of musical instruments made from parts that other people have thrown into a junkyard. How will you do that? Music is made of sounds and sounds are waves. You have studied waves in your physics class. You can find junk that will vibrate and use it to fashion your new musical instruments." Then, after providing links to a couple of videos and other materials that would help students understand some of the basic science behind sound and waves, he lets them loose.

"Have fun!"

Don't think this would work? The story of Maestro Abreu and his children's orchestra has actually been used in Mazur's college physics course for over ten years.[23] We could cite other examples from a growing list of project-based courses.[24] Recall Trinity Marshall and her flowers. She became excited about learning botany on her way to using flowers to create beauty.

Our point is that your children can learn most deeply when they are trying to solve a problem (helping poor children get musical instruments, for example), and when they can try and fail, get feedback and try again, and do all of that without threat of penalty. That environment involves invitations and help, not assignments and requirements. Your children will engage in this deep learning because they want to do so.

Involve all your children in project-based learning at home, regardless of their varying ages or other differences. You can do something like the physics project, but you can also explore your family history, conduct a sociological study in your neighborhood, or become involved in any number of other pursuits.

Getting Project-Based Learning into Your Schools

Many schools already have good case-based or project-based learning programs. If your child's school does not, you can help organize support for such programs. Form a book club with an education theme and use that group to introduce the concept of project-based learning to school leaders and to school board members and candidates. You might use some of the examples and evidence in this book to make your case.

Our previous book on project and problem-based learning, *Super Courses,* may also be valuable. In it, we present nearly twenty case studies. One of our favorites is the story of the "DIY Girls" extracurricular project pursued by high-schoolers in Los Angeles. They learned engineering principles by entering a national contest for STEM students, choosing to build solar-powered tents that would be especially beneficial to homeless people who would otherwise lack heat and light.[25] You may like other examples. One way or another, if you and your kids can rally other families around a compelling project-based learning opportunity, everyone in your neighborhood stands to get more out of school.

INTERLUDE

On a pleasant morning in Charlottesville, Virginia, about fifteen years ago, Ken had breakfast with cognitive scientist Daniel Willingham. Both of us have long respected his work, so this early morning meeting with the University of Virginia professor was a real treat. As Willingham responded to question after question, Ken sat in awe of his broad and deep understanding of human learning.

A prompt for the breakfast invitation had been the recent publication of Willingham's 2009 book, *Why Don't Students Like School?* Ken had learned of it just a short while before his planned visit to Virginia, so he wasn't yet ready to delve into its content that day. But if he had traveled a bit later, he would surely have zeroed in on a line in Willingham's book that would soon spark a firestorm of controversy among some education experts and draw admiration from others. It's a five-word pronouncement that sounds like a truism to many. To others, it's blithering nonsense. Here's what he wrote: "factual knowledge must precede skill."[26]

To this day, we're not sure what all Willingham was saying in that line. When some people quote it, the point they want to make is that you must first commit much about a subject to memory before you can think deeply about it. Most of these people will say *learn* rather than *memorize*, but if you pay attention to their words and actions, it becomes clear that they equate learning something with being able to recall it. Among these people is British politician Michael Gove, who as secretary of education advocated for stricter standardized testing of memorized information, arguing in part that it would make students more creative. (We're not making this up.) In a 2012 speech, Gove cited Willingham's book as scientific justification for his claim that "Only when facts and concepts are committed securely to the working memory—so that it is no effort to recall them and no effort is required to work things out from first principles—do we really have a secure hold on knowledge."[27]

Late one night, Willingham was alerted to Gove's citation of his work by a friend's post on social media, which linked to a critical article in *The Guardian*. As he told an interviewer some months later, his first reaction was *uh-oh,* because "I'd never spoken with him or anyone from his office, and the headline said that he was calling for 'rote' learning, which is not what I say at all." How embarrassing.[28]

What Comes First In Learning?

So what should come first in learning—the facts or thinking about them? Actually, neither. To undo this twisted mess, we must turn to what we have called a *natural critical learning environment*. That is, we must remember how and why human beings ever began to learn anything.[29]

How did *Homo sapiens* start to learn and how did our brains emerge to engage in that process? (Hint: doing well in school had nothing to do with it.) Our brains emerged to answer questions—solve problems—that humans have faced in living on earth. Often messy problems that have no simple answers. Some questions are about food or fulfilling some desire. Others are about power or morality, or about any of a million details of life.

Learning emerged to solve whatever mystery intrigued or bothered us. If we want to spark learning, we must begin, not with facts (because that would be like answering questions that no one has raised or cares about) but with questions.

We should raise problems in a way that will cause students to *want* to answer or solve them. If they then receive information, ideas, or procedures that will help them with that process, they will gladly devour whatever relevant material is provided by you or a teacher. They will no longer face tasks as assignments and requirements, but rather see them as challenges, opportunities, and resources.

Again, think about the MindDrive kids. They learned many details about how cars are constructed, how those vehicles use energy to move from rest to motion, how to reduce the weight of an automobile, and so forth. In short, they came to understand a lot of physics and mechanical engineering. Yet all of those achievements stemmed from their passion for cars rather than from sitting in a corner somewhere, trying to rehearse physics facts.

Once they understood the value of building lighter cars that run on electricity generated by natural forces, they wanted to communicate their new discoveries to others (a new problem). That led them to embrace communication skills—thinking and writing and editing their thoughts, or making oral and visual presentations.

In the old days, as we noted earlier, much of schooling was devoted to just memorizing stuff. Teaching often consisted of drills and quizzes, and delivering information and ideas that kids were supposed to commit to memory on their own. But in the last fifty years or so, many schools have made enormous progress toward introducing deep learning into the curriculum (and some began that transition even earlier).

In the best programs, kids learn logic (how to think about ideas and information), how to identify arguments, how to separate evidence from conclusions, how to make good judgments and use careful reasoning, and how to distinguish between facts and opinions.

Some people still worry that too many kids don't *know* the key facts. By that, they mean students cannot remember enough. Many of these people still believe that the best way to learn about a subject is through blind repetition. But in deep learning, you start with a problem and you read or do exercises to solve it. You don't learn a fact simply because someone has assigned you some homework. You don't digest a lot of facts first with hopes that you will understand their significance later. You grapple with beautiful, important, and intriguing questions and encounter lots of information, concepts, and procedures as you do so. That grappling is what allows you to remember.

In short, rote memorization isn't a necessary first step to learning deeply. To be sure, making lots of connections and understanding how one idea or piece of information is connected to other ideas and information helps everyone remember better. But simply cramming material into one's brain through rote memorization will not, by itself, enable anyone to learn deeply.

SIX

Preparing Your Children for the Slings and Arrows of School

YOUR CHILDREN will face a variety of challenges as they go through school. In particular focus here are three social threats that can interfere with academic success. These currents can sweep through your kid's life, sometimes disrupting all of their educational plans. To understand how to help your children get more out of school, you must appreciate the force of these currents and the speed with which they can swell up within the gullies of life, bursting out of their banks and flooding everything.

Most important, we will demonstrate that the answers to your questions about getting more from school do not center on test scores and other measures of academic success. Our children play many roles as they move from preschool to high school and beyond. In each of those roles, they encounter complex assortments of pressures and expectations that influence how and what they learn and what kind of people they become.

As you learn here how to look for signs of trouble, and to mount the defenses that can make your kids safer and happier, it may strike you that they differ from suggestions you have heard before about supporting kids' schoolwork. Some of those popular tactics actually aggravate the dangers.

Your kids may or may not face the dangers we are about to explore. But even if you expect they won't, this discussion should prove quite valuable—both because you may be underestimating the threats to your family, and because it offers generally useful insights into how you can help your child develop intangible qualities they'll need outside of school, like grit, determination, character, compassion, decency, and curiosity.

PERFECTIONISM

In recent years, psychologists have noticed a growing pattern of perfectionism among young people, from kindergarten through graduate school.[1] The symptoms of it include growing anxiety, depression, anorexia and other eating disorders, and even self-harm.[2] Perfectionist kids can become overwhelmed with feelings of failure and guilt, shame and low self-esteem. If these young people fall even an inch short of the goals imposed upon them, they can face multiple psychological problems.

They can become indecisive and procrastinate easily, failing to do the work necessary to achieve their goals. As one of Ken's former editors put it, "they let the perfect become the enemy of the good." Overanxious parents can contribute to a nasty cycle with enough momentum to run through multiple generations. Attempts to create learning households can unwittingly establish conditions for perfectionist environments, and you should be aware of that danger.

To understand this problem, we must comprehend what social scientists mean by perfectionism, how it contrasts with more healthy ambitions, and why it can interfere with a vibrant learning household. Jennifer Wallace, a journalist, offers the best definition we've seen. "While healthy achievers enjoy striving for excellence and cope well with setbacks," she writes, "perfectionists are motivated by a fear of failure and reach for high goals in an effort to prove their worth to others."[3]

Some people find joy and fulfillment in trying to do their best in everything they tackle. They think about what they can learn from their mistakes and their failures. These aren't the people we're talking about. Rather, our focus is those who feel ashamed if they make even the smallest mistakes, who live in constant fear that if they don't do everything perfectly they will be shamed, blamed, and judged. If you understand perfectionism, you can begin to comprehend the thin line between that destructive tendency and a healthy home that fosters deep learning.

In school, the most serious problems arise when doing well is defined by how students score on exams testing mastery of content presented in courses—but this should be recognized as a rather arbitrary academic game invented in the nineteenth century. The students most invested in that game are the strategic learners, and too many of them become perfectionists. We should emphasize an earlier point: while not all kids who take a strategic approach become perfectionists, a growing percentage of them do.

Kids engaged in that highly competitive contest aren't primarily interested in how much they come to understand, or in how it relates to their efforts to lead creative and fulfilling lives. The game they want to win is all about achieving higher scores than other students. They seek that achievement to feel important, get a job, or win admission to a school that some ranking system has declared to be top-notch. In that game, kids often feel like complete failures, even when the mistakes they make are small ones, and especially if they believe their parents' love depends on the grades they bring home from school.

We realize that many readers did not immediately think about competition for high grades when we first used the word *game*, but that's precisely what we mean. Back in the Prelude to this book, we contended that focusing on raising someone's GPA could end up fertilizing weed patches. Perfectionism might be the crabgrass in this analogy—the hardest invasive to weed out of the academic garden.

Parents can impose perfectionism on their children, insisting that they make the honor roll or the varsity team, play piano concertos with flying-fingers perfection, or get jobs that will make them rich and famous. Feeling the pressures of a society that defines excellence in terms of standardized test scores, grades, fame, and salaries, parents can spend an inordinate amount of time and energy curating the right set of experiences and credentials for their children rather than thinking about what it means for them to be well educated and to develop as creative and compassionate critical thinkers. Kids begin to think that their parents will not love them as much if they don't meet the family expectations. As a result, they start to act like perfectionists, and to experience all of perfectionism's negative side effects.

For parents and kids trapped in this vicious cycle, it is often difficult to recognize that grades will take care of themselves if both sides focus on deep learning, growth mindsets, and the keys to living a creative, compassionate, critically thinking, well-informed life. It is also difficult to accept that making mistakes is a necessary part of learning deeply.

In the last thirty years (at least), more and more Americans have worried about getting their children into the "right" schools. Some have even risked prison terms to secure spots for their children in universities they perceive as prestigious. A US Department of Justice investigation that became public in 2019—code-named Operation Varsity Blues—exposed a corrupt network by which hundreds of wealthy parents had collectively paid millions of dollars to obtain the fraudulent college admission test scores and other credentials that would get their children accepted to highly selective schools.[4]

Perhaps the greatest irony of the Varsity Blues scandal is that it emerged at a time when the opportunities to get a superior education had broadened considerably. Drawing on decades of research on human learning, teaching centers around the country were helping universities and individual professors develop excellent deep-learning environments for their students.

University quality was once gauged by attributes like the size of campus libraries, but with the appearance of electronic collections and the internet, far more schools can now offer learning resources superior to anything even the best of institutions could muster fifty years ago. Now excellence comes from staff and programs that help students tap into the vast body of knowledge that humans have amassed. To say that the increased competition to get into a handful of "top schools" is silly and counterproductive would be an understatement.

Yet that form of perfectionist competition seems to have intensified since at least the 1980s, and so have the problems that stem from it. We can imagine that when people try to impose ideal standards on others they become more critical and treat those who don't measure up with greater hostility and disdain.[5] Communities and nations become more divided, more aggressive toward each other, and more vindictive toward those who don't meet the standards of the perfectionists. Charity and trust evaporate.

As gaps between rich and poor widen in the English-speaking world (and elsewhere), the pressure to perform at the highest levels only increases. Parents push their children to excel so they will land amongst the few who get the big prizes, not so they will make wise choices as they pursue their own interests and build fulfilling and meaningful lives. These parents are mainly responding to social and economic pressures. As raising children becomes more anxiety-inducing, parents become more controlling.

Parents are more likely to monitor their children closely, offering admonishments like, "Your father and I worked very hard to get where we are today, and I'm not going to let you throw it all away with all your lazy ways. Go to your room and get your homework done." But it doesn't have to be that way, and this is certainly not what we mean by a learning household. We'll show you practices that will work far better.

To help children avoid falling into perfectionist traps, it's important to recognize that perfectionism doesn't usually come from any evil intent. It stems instead from the most positive and noble ambitions. Many of these counterproductive practices emerge because parents love their children and want the best for them. Yet that positive origin is one of the chief reasons it is so easy to fall into dysfunctional perfectionism, and so difficult to extract ourselves from it.

Spending More or Less Time with Your Kids

We can begin to see the problems in something that sounds entirely positive: the growing amount of time that some parents spend with their children. If you look at any large studies of how much time parents spend helping their kids with schoolwork, you might get the wrong impression and think that's what we mean by a learning household. On average, adults in the English-speaking world now spend twice as much time with their kids as they did fifty years ago, with much of the difference devoted to boosting academic achievement. More privileged families often devote even more hours to the cause. In 1970, differences didn't show up along socioeconomic lines—everyone devoted about the same portion of their waking hours regardless of their incomes or educational backgrounds. Fifty years later, parents with college or graduate degrees are spending substantially more time with their kids on homework and other school activities.[6]

But here's the rub. This isn't necessarily the learning household, either. Building a learning household is not about the *quantity* of time spent on learning but about the *quality*. You could spend time fostering curiosity and helping kids find their passions. You could also give them space and time to daydream, to explore, to play with other children, and to make decisions and live creative lives. You could help your kids understand that making mistakes provides wonderful opportunities to learn.

Or you could use the extra time to beat the drums for higher grades. You could stress the importance of being number one and becoming perfect. You could spend the precious time you have with your kids pushing them toward fields they dislike simply because those fields will bring them money and conventional markers of success. This would be a terrible mistake. If your children conclude that you will not love them as much if they do not clear the bar you have set, you have created the conditions for perfectionism and all the psychological problems it brings.

How Did the Pandemic Affect Perfectionism?

During the Covid-19 pandemic, the pressure on children grew in many parts of the world. One survey of over ten thousand American students conducted in late 2020 showed that kids experienced even more pressure and stress related to academics than they did before school closures and remote learning disrupted their lives. Meanwhile, parent pressure did not ease up for most of them, and for just over a third, stress related to "meeting my parents'/guardians' expectations" increased.[7]

In the early twenty-first century, parental fear and anxiety had a detrimental effect—even as threats of violence actually declined for most children in the United States and many other countries. While many cities reported lower violent crime rates, parents in the English-speaking world became increasingly unwilling even to let their kids travel to school alone. In 1971, 90 percent of British kids went to school without adult escorts. By 2010, barely 20 percent were allowed to do so.[8] In many cases, increased parental anxiety and fear—not elevation of the actual threat—had the greatest negative effect. Perhaps, to quote Franklin Roosevelt, the greatest thing families had to fear was fear itself.

When you add those fears to the increased drive to become perfect, you begin to see the full scope of the undesirable consequences. Thomas Curran, a psychologist at the University of Bath in England, has sounded the alarm about growing mental illness. "Parental expectations have a high cost when they're perceived as excessive," Curran writes. "Young people internalize those expectations and depend on them for their self-esteem. And when they fail to meet them, as they invariably will, they'll be critical of themselves for not matching up." This is especially true when meeting expectations is defined as earning a higher score rather than achieving creative and cognitive growth and learning deeply. "To compensate, they strive to be perfect," observes Curran. And that leads to all of the problems we've discussed here.[9]

High Standards without Perfectionism

Can parents set high standards and still avoid perfectionism? That depends on whether they establish warm and loving relationships with their children, so that the help they offer doesn't feel controlling. Instead, their close attention to their kids' achievements is interpreted as avid support of activity the kids agree will benefit them and objectives they want to meet. Parents need to offer clear and rational explanations for why anyone would want to meet a high performance standard in a given area, and encourage and allow their kids to ask questions and express their own ideas and views. Remember: don't make those standards about grades.

Create an atmosphere of belief that "everyone can improve and grow." If your kid comes home with a D in a subject, remember Marton and how his mother reacted with curiosity and understanding rather than anger and shame. Treat failure as an opportunity to learn something new. No one can avoid all mistakes, but if parents help their kids see the value of, say, working on their assignments before dinner time—without hysteria and threats of punishment—the kids can become more diligent students.

Avoid tying their achievements to school honors and grades. Don't emphasize that nineteenth-century game we mentioned earlier, in which students just try to outperform their peers. Appeal to their passions, curiosity, and sense of uniqueness rather than a misplaced drive to win some competition called schooling. Ten years from now, no one will remember who won or lost that contest.

"Consider me your coach," we've heard successful parents say. "I'm here to encourage your best effort and give you some valuable secrets to successful learning." Keep smiling. Make sure they know you love them unconditionally.

Most of all, avoid extremes. Eschew the permissive style of parenting that says, "I'm afraid I'll lose your love if I confront you over some ill-advised behavior, so I'll just let you do whatever you want." But also steer clear of the highly authoritarian approach that attempts to turn the family into a military regiment. (The 1979 film *The Great Santini* offers a powerful indictment of this approach. You can watch it with your teenagers and let it stimulate a good philosophical discussion.)[10]

When younger kids get out of line, provide a firm but loving explanation of why their actions are unacceptable as well as, perhaps, that time-out in their room. As your kids go through adolescence, gradually grant them more autonomy. Help them find their passions, and notice when they do. Give them support, even if the subject that excites them doesn't align with the interests you might have anticipated or preferred. Remember the MindDrive students' resolve to build a car, and Trinity Marshall's passion for flowers.

Every part of your being—your body language, tone of voice, words, and attitude—should say, "I love you, and I want to share with you an approach (or behavior) that could serve you well." Avoid displaying anger or disappointment, let alone shouting or resorting to physical punishment. The evidence from rigorous research more than supports the style we are urging here.[11] Yes, we know that parenting can produce its moments of intense frustration, and most people will occasionally fall short of their own standards. But short of pushing *you* toward a counterproductive perfectionism, which could cause undue stress to yourself and your children, we urge you to keep those standards high.

BULLYING

Kids play rough mental and physical games with themselves and each other, especially once they become teenagers. At the extreme end, bullying can become expensive and even deadly. Most Americans are aware of a growing incidence of mass shootings and other violent attacks in schools. Research has shown that an alarming percentage of the perpetrators of such violence were victims of bullying themselves.[12] In addition to the hundreds of deaths from these shootings over the past couple decades, thousands of kids suffer from increased fears of becoming statistics with the next rampage.

Thankfully, the odds of your child encountering an active shooter remain remote. As much as these terrible events grab headlines and capture the imaginations of concerned parents, students, and activists, the problem of bullying runs far deeper than the fear or reality of violence. Your child is far more likely to encounter a milder form of aggression—which, however, is still quite harmful. When kids are incessantly mocked, for instance, it can take a serious psychic toll without any bloodshed. In the early grades, it can create increased risks of self-harm and an assortment of mental illnesses, including depression.[13] People who were bullied as children are more likely to be overweight as young adults.[14] Exclusion and ridicule from their classmates can seriously undermine children's learning. When young people feel they do not belong, that they have few friends, they get less out of school. With growing numbers of kids reporting that they have been bullied or excluded socially, that takes a heavy toll across society, as many parents seem to understand.

What Can Parents and Schools Do?

Some interventions have reduced conflicts among younger kids in elementary school. Yet similar kinds of interventions applied to other populations have had only modest success. Examples include schoolwide programs aimed at teaching conflict management to high school students, and targeted therapeutic interventions for students who have had problems with aggressive behavior. The mixed results generally imply that many interventions work better for younger kids than adolescents.[15]

To think about broader solutions, let's think first about the large number of children who experienced bullying in school but do not become depressed, or think about harming themselves, or gain excessive weight as they grew older. We might say that those people are more resilient in the face of bullying. Can we learn something from their experiences?

Psychologist Lucy Bowes and her colleagues certainly thought so. In a 2010 study, Bowes and her team looked at a huge sample of people who had experienced bullying but managed to escape the long-term damage that plagued others. They found interesting correlations. Those who had survived a childhood of bullying largely unscathed were far less likely to have had anyone in their immediate family commit or attempt suicide. Unlike most of the long-term sufferers, they had not been physically mistreated by an adult. Their parents were warm and loving. Their brothers and sisters were affectionate with each other, and everyone tended to be emotionally supportive of others. Their households were generally clean and organized, with parents often displaying the kids' artwork. Parents expressed sympathy and empathy for the children, and kids did the same for one another.[16]

Those findings are useful to know because they suggest some goals to achieve at home. Yet a much deeper intervention comes from psychologists who apply the concepts of fixed and frozen mindsets to the study of personalities.[17] Researchers find that a fixed view of personality—the idea that aggressive personality traits are "hardwired" into some people and cannot be changed—can be intimately connected with bullying. Such a view is related to the fixed mindset regarding intelligence we discussed earlier, but nonetheless distinct enough to deserve special consideration here.

When kids think of themselves as having permanent personality traits that they can't change, they tend to view other kids the same way. Brian Shea certainly did. The shy, young boy from Little Rock sometimes imagined that someday he would have the social abilities of Kirby Williams, the most popular kid in school.[18] But then his mom, trying to console him, would say, "You don't want to be like that scoundrel. He's a bad person. You're not." For Brian and his mom, some people were just born "bold and mean," and some others were naturally "meek and shy." While she wished her son could have more self-confidence, she often told him that, if she had to pick between him and Kirby, she would much prefer her own child because of his basic goodness.

Kirby had bullied Brian mercilessly since the early days of grade school, giving him the nickname Loser O'Grady. Other kids had picked up on the insulting nickname, and Brian felt the sting of exclusion and humiliation.

For weeks, Kirby battered Brian with demands that he pay up on a "debt" that Kirby had simply made up to torment him. The young boy had forked over part of his lunch money to help settle the matter. That story spread, and Brian heard the shadows of those rumors rippling down the hallway—whispers followed by laughter or, at best, glances of pity. Brian felt alone and depressed.

That's not an unusual response for many young people. Here is how one student in a psychological study described his experience of making the transition to high school: "Some people in school began treating their friends, including me, in a way that showed we weren't as close or not important anymore." For that young person, the social signals had changed. "This morning I was walking by and all [my former friend] could do was act as if I weren't there. Seeing them look at me in the face without a 'hi' or smile makes me feel invisible."[19]

For thousands of children, maybe millions, teasing, physical aggression, and exclusion from social interaction have become all too common. In response, many school communities have combined anti-bullying campaigns with harsh and rigid disciplinary measures for the brash offenders. In general, these efforts haven't worked.[20] Bullies continue to harass. Kids form cliques and exclude those who've been condemned as losers. Rival gangs form in some schools, creating battlegrounds where those in the middle are constantly afraid of becoming victims. Even if kids survive unharmed, it often costs them enormous amounts of mental energy—some of it devoted to psychologically warping fantasies of visiting revenge on the bullies of the world. Learning suffers. Deep learning can evaporate entirely. Resentments build.

Kids become double victims. They first suffer the abuse of those who ridicule or isolate them, keeping them out of the "in crowd," but then they often isolate themselves. On a subconscious level, they become highly aware that many people could hurt them. These kids focus on staying out of the way or, potentially even worse, they start imagining how they could harm the "bad kids" they regard as their mortal enemies. Not only do they have few friends, but their learning also suffers. They don't get as much out of school.

We know what some readers are already telling themselves. "None of this relates to me. My children have lots of friends, and they don't bully anyone." Wonderful. Yet you should still become aware of the many forms this problem can take. We're not trying to make you worried, but we do hope this account will help you understand the complex challenges that your kid might face now or later, and how you can help them—without becoming an overzealous parent who makes matters worse.

We recently had a conversation with Peter Felten, who told us about a young woman he'd interviewed. Felten is a historian and teaching and learning expert, and with Leo Lambert wrote the wonderful bestseller *Relationship-Rich Education*.[21] The young college student he mentioned said she could not stand to associate with other students. When she entered a class, she looked for a chair in the back corner of the room, hoping that isolation would save her from talking with anyone. If her teacher asked students to turn to a neighbor and exchange some thoughts, as many instructors increasingly do, she could escape having to do so because no one was sitting near her. She was, of course, missing out on all the benefits of classroom interaction.

Such people have long been written off as naturally shy. We now understand that the causes are more complex than that—but also that the solution is more readily available.

Social Psychologists to the Rescue

We've always known that some kids learn to handle abusive behavior and overcome feelings of shyness with great skill. They have a big dose of what is called *resilience*. That's often defined as the ability to handle life's difficulties—and determination to push forward when life becomes especially rough. Your kids can develop that quality, and you can help them to do so with the assistance of some powerful research. This will come in handy whether your kids are wallflowers or center-stagers, whether they're ruthlessly bullied or effortlessly float above the fray.

If you want your kids to become more resilient, the best place to start is with the research done in recent years by a small group of enterprising social psychologists who began to think differently about the matter. These scholars, who include Carol Dweck, David Yeager, Kali Trzesniewski, and several collaborators, have found ways to help kids handle and even change the abusive behaviors of bullies who take their lunch money, exclude, and ridicule them. They have found ways, too, for kids to conquer their own shyness, timidity, and fear. Everything hinges on whether kids view themselves and the people who torment them as having fixed personality traits or more flexible ones.

When kids like Brian think to themselves, "I'm just a loser," or "Kirby is just a bad person, a brute who can't be changed," their focus tends to be on wishing they could punish their tormenters, rather than imagining what they might do to cause those people to think and act differently. This doesn't usually mean they fantasize about getting their hands on an assault weapon and opening fire in their school hallways (although sometimes it does). For most people, it means experiencing intense frustration—and it blocks any progress in defusing the situation, stopping the exclusion and ridicule, curing their own shyness, or solving any of the other problems in their lives.

What if the victims of exclusion and bullying were able to change the way they looked at themselves and their tormentors? Would that alter the whole social structure? Yes, it really could help to create an alternative culture in which social exclusion, harassment, and bullying would not take place, or at least take place less frequently.

Sound fanciful? Let's look at an experiment the results of which hold great promise for every family, whether they have been victims of mistreatment or not. It took place in a high school a decade ago. We'll call it Bay City High School.

Yeager, Trzesniewski, and Dweck went into Bay City High to find out what could be done about a persistent bullying problem. They already knew that members of this age group generally didn't believe that personalities could be changed and were more pessimistic about the possibility of change than were kids four or five years younger. The researchers were also familiar with prior studies suggesting that, when high schoolers with fixed views of personalities encounter aggressive classmates, they usually want to "retaliate aggressively."[22]

These researchers believed that merely teaching kids "social coping skills" would not reduce aggression. But they also believed that children, if they were shown how personalities could evolve, could gain a "new framework for understanding the social world" that would lessen their desire for revenge. To test those views, they created three comparable groups of students and subjected each to varying treatments. They did nothing for the first group, simply collecting data on the experience of those students. They provided the second group with six weeks of special classes to equip them with "new strategies for thinking positively following conflicts or setbacks and new ways to resolve conflicts productively."[23] (That approach had worked well with ten- and eleven-year-olds.) Only the third group got something brand new—and pay attention to this approach, because it's the one that worked best for high schoolers, the age level where conflicts are likely to turn most violent.

The psychologists did not want their subjects to worry that they had been singled out for treatment because of bad behavior, so they told everyone that the purpose of the program was to train them to help new students the following year. (Recall that people like to assist each other.) Equally important, they didn't promise any easy miracle cures—they were clear that, while it was certainly possible to change a person's disposition, it would take a long time. Kids on both sides of the school's conflicts, however, could alter their personalities. The bullies could gradually become less abusive, while the victims of bullying could give up desires for revenge and focus on ways to change their adversaries and convert them into friends.

At the heart of this change was a better understanding of how the brain works. As students lounged around a classroom, some paying more attention than others, they heard the psychologists say, "Scientists have discovered that people do things mainly because of the thoughts and feelings that they have—thoughts and feelings that live in the brain and that can be changed." These young people learned about neurons and pathways between cells, and how the organization of human brains could change with certain experiences. "When you have a thought or a feeling," the psychologists explained "the pathways in your brain send signals to other parts of your head that lead you to do one thing or another."[24]

It was a revolutionary message for some of these children that, by consciously changing their brain's pathways or their thoughts and feelings, people can actually change and improve how they behave after challenges and setbacks. Think of the sense of power such a message must have conveyed. Imagine, too, how your kids will feel hearing from you that they (and all their peers) have the power to make themselves over, and you can give them the keys to that makeover machine. So it's not that some people are "rejects" or that other people are "bad," as the psychologists put it. "Everyone's brain is a 'work in progress.'"[25]

To put the icing on the cake, the research team gave these teenagers a new vocabulary that summarized what they were learning about the brain. People who thought personalities didn't change much had an *entity theory* of human traits. Those who were beginning to see that they could reshape themselves were shifting to an *incremental theory*.[26]

As we pointed out earlier, social psychologists love giving special labels to their ideas, but that's not just a whimsical impulse. They realize, no doubt, that once something gets a name, it becomes more real to everyone. A name reminds you that something exists and makes it easier to keep it in mind. In this case, Yeager, Trzesniewski, and Dweck used the same basic terms they had previously applied to theories about intelligence.[27] In that realm, the entity people believe IQ doesn't change while the incremental crowd knows that it can.

Yet this approach did not involve teaching the students concrete methods for resolving problems. There was no explicit instruction telling students how they could create healthy relationships with their peers, no step-by-step directions for deescalating a bullying situation. The psychologists never said, "Don't use violence to solve problems." Instead, they sought only to change the way kids understood themselves and other people, in hopes that such a transformation would lead to a shift from entity views to incremental ones, and would in turn alter behavior.

Active Learning

During their sessions with the psychologists, the students of Bay City High were invited to participate in active learning exercises. You can use this approach with your children on any topic you might imagine. It's a way of teaching that has become more popular over the last fifty years. If your children have some teachers they really love because those people helped them to learn deeply, there's a good chance they have encountered active learning pedagogy.

You may have run into active learning in your own journey through school. But thousands of people still haven't. Or they're unaware that there are many good models of this innovative approach. We saw a bit of active learning earlier in these pages, in Michael Sandel's classroom, but there are models out there that are even more "active."

Let's begin to understand active learning by contrasting it with the old-fashioned method of instruction that was so dominant in our youth—and is still the norm for too many kids. In that old-school version, students listen to lectures, maybe take notes, then go home and read through their written records. Or they ignore them completely.

Passive lectures can be terribly boring, but even when they are exciting, funny, and captivating, relying on this format fosters, at best, the accumulation of information. Research suggests that passively listening to lectures doesn't usually help learners understand complex ideas or learn to engage in complex problem-solving.[28]

In active learning, they encounter information and ideas while doing something else—solving a problem, playing a game, talking with other students, going on a scavenger hunt, writing and acting out a script, or engaging in one of myriad other activities. (We've already explored an ingenious program where students learned a whole host of important subjects and big lessons about themselves while devising new kinds of cars they were excited to build.)

The psychologists at Bay City High, for example, invited kids to remember "one time when you felt left out, rejected, or upset by an acquaintance at school," and to write about it. "Imagine that the same event . . . happened to another student just like you," they further prompted. What could the student say to help that imagined person "understand that they can change and that the things that are happening to them could change?"[29] You can invite your children to play out the same scenario after you have introduced the idea of personality mindsets to them and discussed the advantage of holding an incremental view.

How old must your kids be before they engage in such exercises? That's something only you can determine, maybe through trial and error with them. Kids mature at different rates, and you know your children better than anyone. All of the examples discussed here took place in high school, but your kids might be ready in middle school, or even earlier.

At another point, the researchers created pairs of students and assigned them roles to play. Role-playing is a common exercise in active learning. "You are an alien from the planet of the entity theory," they told one member of each pair—someone who had never heard of incremental theory. The earthling counterparts of the "aliens" then tried to help them understand incremental theory and how it can change a person's thinking and actions. The students were then invited to switch roles so that everyone had the chance to explain the basic ideas.[30]

These prompts gave students a chance to take control of their own education. You can invent similar active learning exercises that will appeal to your kids. What if you have only one child? Then get ready to star as an alien from the entity planet and let your kid try to change you.

Did these interventions change anyone? They sure did. It was well established that students who faced bullying were more likely to miss class or show up late. The kids who went through the incremental mindset training were far less likely to follow that pattern. Surveys also found them, on average, to be less in favor of retaliating against classmates who excluded them, and having far fewer episodes of depression, than kids who continued to live with entity views of the world.[31]

We can't say that problems as complex and deep-rooted as aggression, depression, and exclusion will always disappear when someone tells kids that "bullies can change." And nurturing a growth mindset does not mean your kid will turn into a completely different person overnight.[32] Still, getting students to believe that personalities do change is a powerful way to alter learning environments. It isn't easy to foster those new mindsets. But if you weave that optimistic message into numerous conversations with your kids, if you show them the evidence for how brains work, if you make brain education a key element of their learning at home, you have a wonderful opportunity to help your kids get the best education from school.[33] When kids realize that they can change, that they really are works in progress, they develop greater resilience. The work on changing mindsets has demonstrated that growth is possible. Kids can escape both the small irritations and the large nightmares that would otherwise interfere with their lives. Children who get that message become free to become deep learners. And any parent can contribute to that process.

When we were writing this section, we showed it to numerous people to get their reactions. A few reviewers could not get behind the idea of encouraging high schoolers to try to change the behaviors and thinking of dedicated bullies. "This places too much responsibility on the victims," one reader protested, "and generally will not work." In fact, this reviewer seemed convinced that the only solution kids would ever find effective was violent retaliation.

Yet researchers have collected evidence that a growth-mindset approach really can work and is far more successful than sanctioning your child's impulse to punish an adversary. The latter is a recipe for many wasted hours contemplating revenge, and potentially a nightmare cycle of violence and ill will, fueling even more ferocity.

If your kids associate the evil enemy with a particular "race" of humans, their frozen categories may be especially difficult to melt. When you foster a growth mindset you may help dislodge that iceberg and begin to melt it. Below, we will help you begin to address the stereotypes and prejudices that our cultures have given us.

Ken remembers an incident and how it played out when he was in the eighth grade. Larry Pea set off a firecracker in the stairwell. Their mutual friend Benny Klain saw him do so and reported it to the principal. Larry, a big guy with far more muscle than Benny, wasn't happy about that and made it clear that Benny was "dead meat."

Benny must have had an incremental theory of personality because he began working on the much larger Larry right away. "What good will that do?" he asked. "That will only get you into more trouble." And besides, he persisted, "I can be your friend and I can help you out." For days and weeks, the slight kid kept up the message, and in the end it worked. Larry and Benny became the best of friends in high school and learned to laugh about the "firecracker incident."

Empty Promises of Zero Tolerance

Let us ask you something. If you feared your kid might become a bully, would you be tempted to declare a zero-tolerance policy in your household? Would you say something like, "If you violate this cardinal rule even once, you will be severely punished"?

Many parents make such strict rules part of their household code. Schools do, too. They are understandable when kids need to be protected from serious dangers. But does it work to say "one strike and you're out"? Or does it create its own problems that would be better avoided?

When a school imposes a zero-tolerance policy, it is sending a strong message that "bad kids" can't change. If Bay City High School had issued such a mandate in the midst of its experiment, that edict might have undercut their efforts to foster incremental views of human traits. That worried the social scientists who designed the intervention. It has long worried many psychologists.

The American Psychological Association created a Zero Tolerance Task Force in 2005 to examine the matter. While conceding that research had so far not produced direct evidence of the effectiveness or ineffectiveness of zero tolerance, that group suggested many reasons that policies of kicking kids out of school for various infractions might not result in safer learning environments. Meanwhile, they might even be counterproductive, especially if they fell most heavily on children of color. The panel pointed out that there was no evidence that rates of violence or disruption were higher among African American students, but they were more likely to get the boot than other children. Perhaps, the task force suggested, "African American students may be disciplined more severely for less serious or more subjective reasons." This seemed to be happening regardless of how much money their families had.[34]

As you contemplate these findings and consider what to do for your children, think back to the MindDrive kids we discussed earlier. Many of them had been kicked out of public schools for behavior problems. Yet the program that Steve Rees and Linda Buchner created helped them find their passion. It changed both their behavior and their academic performance. If you want to help your kids get the most out of school, you must help them believe that problems can be overcome.

It might be that your children have never faced bullies and never will. Regardless, having a growth mindset, a deep understanding of how and why everything from personality to intelligence can change, and the ability to forgive will help your kids live happier and more productive lives. But there is more that you can do. In the next section we'll put additional pieces together to help you address other lingering issues.

Counting Your Blessings

For centuries, religious leaders around the world have spoken about the power of being grateful. Followers of Buddha as well as billions of Hindus, Christians, Jews, and others have counted their blessings and urged the faithful to do likewise. The Psalmists wrote, "This is the day that the Lord has made; let us rejoice and be glad in it."[35] The idea that humans should live lives of thanks flows through countless sacred texts. Christians stressed that even in challenging times the faithful should not fail to be appreciative. "Give thanks in all circumstances," wrote Paul the Apostle to the Thessalonians facing persecution.[36]

Do people feel better when they give thanks? When humans count their blessings, do they experience less anxiety and depression? Are they better able to corral the demons that rumble through their minds? Could that ancient practice of noticing good things and saying thanks—to nature, to God, to random chance—improve mental and physical health?

Certainly many people think so. When a major polling company asked teens and adults in the United States about such matters, a whopping 90 percent of them said that when they gave thanks, they felt "extremely happy" or "somewhat happy."[37]

About twenty years ago, two psychologists decided to see if they could collect evidence to support such views. Robert A. Emmons, who teaches at the University of California at Davis, and Michael E. McCullough, who now teaches at the University California at San Diego, sat up a grand experiment to test these waters.

Having scoured the existing literature, they already knew that many great thinkers believed that "the ability to notice, appreciate, and savor the elements of one's life" was a key to living well.[38] But Emmons and McCullough wanted stronger evidence, not just opinions and religious views. When they asked people to write down, once a week, "up to five things in your life that you are grateful or thankful for," the benefits grew. When other participants were asked instead to write down five "hassles" they had recently faced, those people didn't enjoy the same positive results.[39]

The gratitude folks reported fewer health issues. Everything from headaches, dizziness, and acne to irritable bowels and sore muscles diminished among those who wrote about their blessings. They also reported exercising more, nearly ninety minutes more per week on average.

In a later study, the researchers asked participants to write down their blessings every day, rather than just once a week. Once again, participants reaped the benefits of the exercise. People even displayed greater sympathy and empathy. Those who wrote about their blessings daily were more likely to "report having helped someone with a personal problem or offered emotional support" to someone else. They also got more and better sleep.[40]

Since these studies, researchers have found a link between gratitude and how kids react to bullying. Among adolescent victims of bullying, especially girls, practicing gratitude lowered the risk of suicide.[41]

So what can you do to foster gratitude? Starting when your kids are young, ask them to write down their blessings every day. Join them in doing so. If your kids are older when you read these lines, start today. It could be an activity at the evening dinner table. Or maybe at bedtime. Think deeply about how and when to introduce this routine to your kids.

Ask them to keep a diary of the good things that happened to them. But, as with everything else we have suggested, respect their list. And help them steer clear of comparing their experience to that of anyone less fortunate, indulging in what social scientists call *downward social comparison*.[42] There is little benefit to be gained from saying, "at least I'm better off than *that* poor friend."

PREJUDICE

Bobbi Wilson encountered prejudices in a rather odd way. The nine-year-old girl in Caldwell, New Jersey, embarked on what seemed like a noble and innocent science project. She had become concerned with the spotted lantern flies damaging the plants around her home. Bobbi heard about efforts to collect and kill the invasive bugs and followed a recipe she saw on social media. The enterprising young girl mixed up a concoction of water, dish soap, and apple cider vinegar, poured it in a hand sprayer, and set out to do battle with the speckled varmints.

That's when a neighbor called the police. "There is a little Black women [yes, he actually said *woman*] walking around spraying stuff on the sidewalks and trees.... I don't know what the hell she's doing. Scares me, though."[43]

Fortunately, the police officer who responded to the call quickly saw the reality of the situation. A few months later, Yale University even rewarded Bobbie for collecting the insects. The Ivy League school invited the little girl and her older sister to visit their campus. A newspaper ran a smiling picture of the child with her assortment of lantern flies mounted under glass, ready for display at Yale's Peabody Museum.[44]

Yet the whole affair troubled her mother, and with good reason. She thought about how, "in a country perpetually plagued by police killing unarmed Black and brown children," as one news outlet put it, her neighbor's phone call could have endangered her daughter.[45] Perhaps the story of six-year-old Kaia Rolle, from Orlando, Florida, was fresh in her memory. In 2020, the first-grader had had a tantrum at school which culminated in her kicking and punching three school employees. The adults called the police. That's right, not a counselor, but the police. By the time a cop arrived, the child had calmed down. But he was there to make an arrest. The officer bound the six-year-old's wrists behind her back with zip tie and ushered the child into his cruiser as she sobbed and begged to be set free.[46]

Bobbi Wilson's episode turned out far better than Kaia Rolle's, but it still captured the attention of many experts on children and inequality, who saw both cases as part of a larger pattern of little Black girls being treated as though they were bigger. A 2017 survey by the

Georgetown Law Center on Poverty and Inequality, for example, found respondents answering questions quite differently depending on whether they were being asked to make generalizations about white girls or about Black girls. In particular, the survey revealed a pattern of "adultification" by which Black girls were judged to be markedly "less innocent and more adult-like than their white peers."[47]

Earlier studies had also found that "Black boys are more likely than their white peers to be misperceived as older, [to be] viewed as guilty of suspected crimes, and [to] face police violence if accused of a crime."[48] But in recent years, the problem has been especially acute for Black girls. Compared to white girls, "Black girls are over five times more likely to be suspended at least once from school, seven times more likely to receive multiple out-of-school suspensions . . . and three times more likely to receive referrals to law enforcement," reported the *New York Times* in 2020. This was higher than the disproportionality between Black and white boys. Yet research had produced no evidence that their actual misbehavior was worse than white children's or that it justified such a level of police involvement.[49]

To be sure, many schools rely on police to deal with children in situations where interventions by counselors and teachers might suffice or be more effective. Scared by the threat of school shootings, they have diverted funds away from educating to policing.[50] In the midst of this transition, kids from some minority populations have faced far more frequent encounters with the law than have white children.

Such prejudice is damaging to people in general—whether they are the victims or the perpetrators of discrimination. We are now discovering that students who hold racist views do not learn as deeply as those who shed their prejudices. Furthermore, when it comes time to look for jobs, the kids with strong biases find fewer opportunities than students who have learned to work with diverse groups.[51]

Why? The largest corporations are doing business around the world, trying to appeal to largely nonwhite populations. They want leaders who can work with everyone. The most innovative companies have found that employees who believe on some level that certain "races" are superior to others do not work well with colleagues or clients of diverse backgrounds. Planning and problem-solving committees become less creative with such prejudice, and organizations suffer.[52]

We've focused on racism because it is the most disruptive and brutally cruel form of prejudice in our country and many other places in the world. Victims of racial discrimination have suffered unspeakable horrors that we must recognize, but there are other ways prejudice can manifest itself. We turn now to a form of prejudice and discrimination that affects the victims of racism but can also strike the lives of people who face no racial discrimination or prejudice. It illuminates one of the most complex ways the devil of bigotry can appear in our lives.

Think for a moment about a human habit that at first may seem as if it has nothing to do with prejudices or getting the most out of school. We speak here about how we and our children form our identities. If someone asked the two of us to describe ourselves, we might say something like "we are writers." We would identify ourselves as members of a group (writers). That group would become a part of who we are in our own minds.

Yet if anyone identifies with something that has become the target of an ugly stereotype, they can feel devalued and fearful that others will think of them in terms of that negative image. They can become intensely anxious that something they do or say will confirm the popular image of people like them. Their very identities begin to feel shaky and sometimes even worthless. On a subconscious level, those wounds can fester, and in high-pressure situations, like test day, they can create floods of anxiety, fear, and even panic.

We suspect that most people have experienced these feelings, which psychologists Claude Steele and Joshua Aronson summed up with the term *stereotype threat*.[53] We certainly have. As we write these lines in the fall of 2024, for example, Ken is approaching eighty-three years old, and Marsha is celebrating her eightieth birthday. Each time one of us fails to instantly recall some detail of a memory we've had for years, we are reminded that many people think old geezers like us are senile. Our memories grow worse when we fear we will confirm the stereotype that elderly people can't think straight, which causes us to think less well.[54]

But age is not the only source of stereotype vulnerability. Far from it. Over the last thirty years, researchers have found it in a multitude of areas.[55] We even know what can happen in our bodies when stereotype threats arise. A small portion of the human brain can trigger a chain reaction in the face of danger, real or imagined. The amygdala signals our adrenal gland to squirt cortisol throughout our bodies. Blood pressure can go up and so can breathing rates. With those physical changes, it becomes more difficult to remember and make use of many skills that are needed in school and life.[56]

That can happen to your child in the face of racism, homophobia, sexism, or any other prejudice. It can happen to males who buy into the emerging stereotype that school is for girls and that men and boys get jobs and make money.[57] It can also happen to economically impoverished kids of any skin color who realize that our culture has long taught that poor people are not as smart as the wealthy.[58] (An old saying expresses that stereotype clearly: "If you're so smart, why aren't you rich?") It can happen to student athletes who get pegged as dumb jocks.[59] It can happen to a kid who comes to a school having grown up in a different part of the country.[60]

Stereotype threat has many faces. If a popular image says that people like you can't do math very well, for example, and you accept that stereotype as true, then you probably won't be able to do math very well. It becomes a self-fulfilling prophecy. Yet you don't even have to accept the negative image of "your kind" for it to influence you. If you know there is a popular belief that says that people like you can't do something, and you want to do well in that area, it may simply bother you on some level that other people think of you in terms of this negative image. It may bother you so much that it becomes a huge distraction that can hurt performance.

Ken and his siblings were born to a southern white couple from the Sand Mountains of northern Alabama. His family came out of a culture of poverty and racism at the southern tip of Appalachia. Only later did Ken learn about the negative stereotypes associated with "hillbillies." Economic deprivation made him and his family question themselves, to dream of less ambitious goals. Yet he also enjoyed privileges that many others did not receive. One day in 1919, his grandfather, enjoying the rewards of a bumper cotton crop that year, hitched up his mule to a wagon and took his daughter (who would later be Ken's mother but was then just fourteen) down off Sand Mountain and enrolled her and her sister in a Presbyterian Seminary, where she learned to teach. Two of her children eventually received doctorates.

Marsha grew up in a tiny Texas town just south of the border with Oklahoma. She attended local schools, and her father sat on the school board, but the people of her community didn't have the economic advantages that many in Dallas, Fort Worth, and Houston did. Her parents encouraged her to learn in school, but when she was seventeen her father died of a sudden cerebral hemorrhage, deeply affecting her life and illustrating how chance events can reshape someone's future. The racism in her community that severely harmed Black and brown people didn't leave white racists untouched, either. In an event in the 1930s that symbolizes how racism can harm the racists, a white mob bent on capturing and killing a certain black man accused of a crime burned the new local courthouse and jail to the ground. Both Ken's and Marsha's families used education to try to escape the legacy of racism, but they could not break away entirely until they examined their own heritage.

What to Do?

Whether your children are targets of prejudice or have their own prejudices, you might begin with an approach used in the University of Colorado physics department.[61] There was an old stereotype that women couldn't excel in physics. And guess what? As a group, they didn't.

To help everyone do better and eliminate the gap between genders, the department leaders did something in an introductory course that sounds a little odd but makes perfect sense in light of all that we've been discussing. They asked some students—both men and women—to write for fifteen minutes about something they valued most in life. Not about physics or science, but about something they valued. That happened just twice during the semester. Many chose to write about relationships with friends and family.

The exercise was designed to give students a chance to celebrate and appreciate who they were and the special qualities and experiences they brought. And it worked. Both male and female students did better, but the latter group—long the target of negative stereotypes about their potential—improved the most. On average, their scores rose by a whole letter grade. Those gains wiped out the gap that had traditionally existed between genders.

Did anyone fall back? The professors asked all of the students to note their level of agreement with the statement that women could not perform in physics as well as men. Male students who held that prejudice performed worse in the class. It's another example of bigotry harming the bigoted. If you want your kids to get the most out of school, help them avoid common prejudices. Imagine the benefit your kids will receive if you ask them to spend just fifteen minutes now and again writing about themselves and what they value. Imagine how your kids will prosper if you purge your own mind and language and actions of prejudices. Instead, stress that people are people—regardless of their gender, wealth, religion, sexual orientation, or hometown—and everybody deserves decent treatment and a good chance in life.

Talk to your children about how we all benefit from the diversity that comes from new and different groups. It doesn't matter if someone's family comes from Europe or Africa, Asia or the Americas. An egalitarian approach to life that appreciates what each group will contribute can help your kids get more out of school.

But don't just talk about it. Live it. Diversify your community of friends. We all derive our unique and valuable perspectives on life from the lives we live and the cultures we absorb. We benefit when ideas and experiences mix, when we recognize the value of what other people bring to the table. Great civilizations arise at the crossroads of the human experience. Creative people emerge from exchanging insights, rhythms, colors, lines, and spaces. The key is to understand who we are—to look inward—but also to look outward to other people with empathy, appreciation, and even admiration. You can help your kids do that.

Multiple parts of this book can assist you. Go back and look at the section on fostering creativity. Help your kids explore their own uniqueness and how they can mine their unique experiences to create something new and valuable. You can help them to take pride in who they are.

You can help your kids appreciate how their life paths have been shaped by their immediate and extended families, to take pride in historical examples of achievement while taking stock of historical injustice. In an earlier section on creativity, we discussed the power of looking inward. That process might include a family tree exercise in which your kids explore their own relatives and how they have dealt with discrimination, either as victims or perpetrators. Riana Elyse Anderson, a psychologist at the University of Michigan, argues that such an experience need not be confined to blood relatives but can include a broader community of people who have fought racism and triumphed.[62] The aim is to open up a space where children can feel comfortable asking about, say, racist patterns they see in the news.

Our earlier section on growth mindsets can bolster faith in everyone's potential to grow. The targets of prejudices can develop the perseverance and resilience to overcome prejudices. Those who discriminate can change, too. A growth mindset says we need not let someone else's prejudices define us. Look again at the Bay City High School experiment and how it reduced bullying and desires for violent revenge. Could something similar address racist discrimination?

On its website, Philosophy for Children (P4C) offers a rich assortment of books that encourage inclusion of everyone.[63] You can use Matthew Lipman's pedagogy to explore with your kids, even the littlest of them, the philosophical issues of friendship, beauty, and prejudices. Literature for very young kids can be particularly influential. We've put in the notes some additional examples of excellent children's books that foster inclusivity.[64] You can help your kids explore their own heritage and use it to live innovative lives, but they will not reap the greatest benefits until they have shed the remnants of any racism toward themselves or other people.

One of the most important things you can help your kids understand is that the whole notion of race is a historical fiction.[65] It is just a way of thinking about other people, of lumping them into largely useless categories. Humans invented the notion. The historian Ed Simon, for example, tried to find the earliest usage of the English phrase "white people." He found it was on October 29, 1613, when a new play opened in London.[66]

Race is not a distinction recognized in nature.[67] We are all *Homo sapiens,* capable of having children together and sharing love, and we are all related through common ancestors. Every one of us descends from families on the African continent of many thousands of years ago. Help your kids understand that the idea of dividing people into "races" defined by biologically inherited characteristics—like skin color, hair texture, and shape of eyes—is a fairly recent invention. Human beings have long divided one another into different groups and noticed that their fellow humans came in different shades and sizes. But for most of history, they didn't hand out privileges on the basis of these attributes or act as if they were the most important components of identity. Ancient Greeks and Roman societies had many social hierarchies, but race was not one of them.[68] Likewise, classical Chinese culture had no notion of race.[69] The idea didn't emerge until about four hundred years ago, when enslavers created it to justify who could be put in bondage.[70]

When your kids come to comprehend how and why the concept of race emerged, they will become better able to understand that there is nothing natural and inevitable about the notion that humans come in different races. That can help them throw off the yoke of racist thinking. They can also understand that, while a few people created the idea of race to benefit themselves, many people who hold racist views are themselves victims of prejudice. They, too, can escape the influence of that way of thinking. The two of us have spent our entire adult lives trying to do so.

You can also—and this is extremely important—help your kids appreciate that while the concept of race is a fiction, the practice of racial discrimination is not. The victims of prejudice are real people who have suffered and sometimes died because of the treatment they received. Racism—the practices and policies of treating people differently because of their supposed race—has hurt and killed flesh-and-blood human beings. Your kids need to recognize that harm. Depending on the age of your kids, you can create a family- and even community-wide reading group that begins to explore and understand some important books on these matters. We've put some great possibilities in the notes.[71]

We are all the same and all different, bringing together a rich assortment of experiences and cultures. As we said earlier, live out that creed. Bring all sorts of people into your social and professional circle. Let your actions—not just your words—say to your children that everyone is valued. One study found that "[white] children whose mothers had a higher percentage of non–European American friends showed lower levels of racial biases than those children whose mothers had a lower percentage of non–European American friends."[72] When you create the discussion groups we've suggested, try to make them diverse no matter what biologically inherited physical characteristics you possess.

A Mother's Tale

Ken's grandmother died giving birth to her youngest daughter. A hundred years ago, pregnancy and childbirth were the leading cause of death for young women. She lived in one of the poorest counties in an industrialized country. No access to birth control. No hospitals. Few doctors.

New Deal policies helped change that. Deaths from childbirth declined rapidly in the United States across the twentieth century. Yet they are rising again, especially among families of color. Today, the rates of maternal death due to complications from childbirth in the United States are the highest among the forty richest countries.[73]

You might think that such statistics reflect higher poverty rates among minority families. Poverty does play a small role, but it is not the only factor. As one researcher put it, "even the wealthiest Black women and their newborns experience worse outcomes than those from the lowest-income white families."[74] Yet you can't argue that women of color are somehow genetically inclined to die early at higher rates than other females. Black mothers in other rich countries outside of the United States do not face the same statistics.

Think about what that means. Racism—or any other form of prejudice—doesn't occur only because bad people discriminate. If you could get everyone in the country to cleanse their minds of all racist thoughts, differences would still persist because of past racist policies and attitudes and the social and political structures and habits they have created. Scholars who study this phenomenon call this *institutional* or *systemic* racism.

If these outcomes bother you, then learn more about them and help your children to join the conversation about how best to address them. Remember: guilt and vengefulness do not solve anything. Take positive action, guided by a deep understanding of the social and historical forces that shaped your world. Your children will benefit, in school and for the rest of their lives.

What does this have to do with helping your kids get more out of school? If you bring this topic into your home, you can build a stronger learning community for both white households and families of color, where kids become good thinkers and problem-solvers. You can use it as an opportunity to help your children learn important skills of calm self-reflection and civil exchange of ideas, crucial ingredients in building a learning household. Invite your kids to look at some of the literature we have recommended, selecting age-appropriate items. Invite your kids to ask questions. If you come from a highly racist culture, as we did, you can have a candid discussion about that with your children. Ask your kids how your family can learn to reject the idea of race. Avoid calling anyone a name like *racist* or *bigot*. Treat yourself and your children as works in progress, always capable of growth.

SEVEN

Helping Your Kids Get a Higher Education They Can Use

BY THE TIME kids finish high school, parents have had years of experience offering advice about schooling. The temptation can be strong to continue handing out nonstop guidance right into college and even graduate or professional school. Some parents want to pick where their sons and daughters go to school, what they study, and even who teaches them.

But something has changed by the time young people reach this point in their lives, and you must recognize that change if you want to help them. They are no longer children. They have entered adulthood, and are ready to take the driver's seat in their educations. If you don't let them get behind the wheel, you can impede their intellectual and emotional development—not to mention cause conflicts within the family.

You can still be a resource and sounding board ready to help them if they ask, to listen to their ideas and to respond with good questions. But don't hover over them, micromanaging every step along the way. Give them the chance to think, to make decisions, and even to make mistakes. We hear too often from undergraduates that parents are interfering in their course selection, sometimes agreeing to financial support only if students choose certain majors, like business or computer science.

With the rising cost of higher education, such parental reactions are understandable. It's expensive to go to college, art school, or trade school, and parents tend to hope for the best return on their investment. Kids do, too, for that matter. With no national policy of strong financial assistance for the expenses of higher education in the United States, no one wants to emerge out of school deeply in debt. (We remember finally managing to pay off our own school debts just as our own kids were entering college.)

We interviewed a few parents who sought to play an outsized role in their kid's college experience even though they had plenty of financial resources. With a kind of "this is my last chance to make an imprint" mentality, they sought to dictate every major decision. That, of course, has at least two potential problems. Parents may be wrong about their choices, and their attempt to impose them may harm the otherwise healthy maturation process that young adults need to enjoy.

Don't bring preconceived notions to your child's advanced education. Perhaps you're sure that majoring in business is better than concentrating in gender studies, but listen to your children with an open mind. Don't assume that you know what the outcome of an educational choice will be.

We want to help you appreciate the great advantage of letting your kids pursue their passions and share ways for you to do that. Let's begin with a closer look at some popular beliefs that often distort the world your children will inherit.

JUST FOUR LETTERS?

Over the last fifty years or more, a growing number of parents have offered their kids simple advice as they head off to college: study whatever will lead to the highest-paying job offers. To many people that means majoring in computer science, business, or some related field. We are going to show you that such guidance is far from adequate.

Morris Baker received plenty of that counsel as he approached his high school graduation and started making plans for college.[1] He recalls, as early as the eighth grade, family members and friends urging him to study something that would make him rich. "When you get to college, don't major in history or English," they warned. "Philosophy is a useless waste of time and money. And certainly don't study the arts, unless you want to starve."

"The liberal arts are dead, or will be soon," his Uncle Rupert was fond of saying. "The only four letters you need to know are S-T-E-M." But should your kid follow Uncle Rupert's advice? Or, assuming they agreed with him, *could* they even follow it? Oh, if only life were that simple.

Before we discuss anything else, it's important to note that the question of money is a lot more complex than you might imagine. In what follows, we'll draw from a massive study that Harvard economist David Deming and his colleague Kadeem Noray carried out in 2019.[2] Deming and Noray discovered something that would knock the socks off Uncle Rupert.

If you treat your education as an investment in job training and nothing more, you may make more money *immediately* after graduation than someone who approached college as a time of open-ended intellectual exploration. But will that still be the case ten or fifteen years down the line? Who will make the highest average pay over their lifetime?

When engineering and computer science students first get out of school, they usually make more than, say, history majors. In 2017, recent college graduates with degrees in those technical fields, on average, earned a little more than sixty thousand dollars, while their classmates in the social sciences and history averaged more than fifteen thousand dollars less.³ But the liberal arts students quickly caught up with much higher annual raises. Why did this happen?

Many applied STEM majors devoted their undergraduate years to learning specific technology-related skills that happened to be hot when they were barely out of their teens. But technical fields changed rapidly over the next ten years, creating demand for expertise that they had not acquired in school. Many couldn't keep up because, in opting for a narrow and highly specialized path they had not gained the capacities for lifelong learning they might have developed in the course of a broader education.

Younger workers, just out of school, arrived in their workplaces every year with fresher skills training and lower salary expectations. Any older hands who did not keep pace with evolving technology could easily be replaced. Short of losing their jobs, they could see their annual raises shrink from year to year, and their incomes stagnate. In a work world that changes faster than ever, parents should recognize that what will benefit their children most is an education that makes them more curious, hardworking, and adaptable.

At age forty, both groups—the techies and the "fuzzies" (as some people began calling the more generally educated folks)—had at least doubled their incomes. But guess which group got the biggest boost over time? Those with the broader educations—the history, psychology, political science, sociology, and economics students—and by a large margin.

Men with broader educations took home, on average, nearly seven thousand dollars more each year than men in applied STEM fields, and the differences continued to grow. For women, the pattern was the same, although not quite as stark.⁴ By age forty, the wage gap between women in STEM fields and the huminites had narrowed.

(Women in general still make less in income than male counterparts with the same education and experience working in the same field.)

People in the social sciences, humanities, and even the arts have often received broad liberal arts educations that allowed them to be more flexible in the job market. A deep education teaches students to think, make decisions, develop a creative mindset, question themselves, and even learn more rapidly. "A liberal arts education fosters valuable 'soft skills' like problem-solving, critical thinking and adaptability," Deming wrote in the *New York Times*. "Such skills are hard to quantify, and they don't create clean pathways to high-paying first jobs. But they have long-run value in a wide variety of careers."[5]

Yes, you want your kids to be prepared to earn a living, but if they don't also get a broad education, they will miss out on something valuable. This doesn't mean that no one should study computer science. And, yes, computer science majors can get broad educations too if they take courses in other areas. It just means that life isn't as simple as Uncle Rupert thought. Those people who rank schools and majors by how much money graduates receive in their first job may be misleading young people and their families. To make a decision that's right for them, your kids will need to consider other factors.

That's actually good news because it means your children will have much greater freedom and more choices. Let them exercise those opportunities. In general, it means that your kids should pursue what intrigues them, but you can also help them see that taking something new and different can challenge them in a good way and even spark a new passion. More than one student has grudgingly shuffled into a required course only to discover that they actually loved the field, usually with the help of a brilliant college teacher who puts the subject in a fresh light.

Most important, you can help your kids understand that a broad education will help them learn to think critically and creatively, ask strong questions, make good decisions, constantly question what they believe, and enjoy life more richly. Many of the people we interviewed found a combination of highly technical job training and a broad liberal arts education best served their needs on multiple levels.

Then there's this. If everyone funnels their kids into the highest paid fields, that will drain talent from areas that, for a variety of reasons, do not make high incomes yet are extremely valuable to society. That includes everyone from teachers and nurses to journalists and librarians. Many of these occupations provide extremely satisfying lives that wonderful young people enter because they want to. As a parent, the best way to help your kids is to respect their choices and understand that every important decision, including what kind of work they will do, doesn't depend on money alone.

How does anyone decide what to study? One theme will run through our advice, and it isn't money. It's fascination and thinking. What course of study will intrigue your kids and help them become better thinkers, able to make good decisions on any matter, *including the question of what they should study?* What kind of curriculum will foster the most logical, creative, and compassionate thought? What line of study will bring the most beauty and foster creative lives? How can parents support that line of study without backseat driving? What subjects will help your kids protect themselves from the hucksters and the hoaxes that float through the internet, ensnaring children and adults?

Before we go on, we want to recommend that your children read a book Ken published in 2012: *What the Best College Students Do*. Since then, thousands of students from higher education institutions around the world have read it in multiple languages. Some schools have assigned it to all first-year students. While the book you are reading is aimed at parents, *What the Best Students Do* is for students, too. It might make a valuable graduation present for your high school senior. But the timing is your call.

GOING BROAD AND DEEP

We've used the term *liberal arts* several times, but what does that really mean? It comes from the Latin for free (*liber*) and it was the kind of education that free children (as opposed to enslaved kids) often enjoyed in the ancient world. In the United States today and in many other countries, it means that students explore a wide variety of disciplines, from the natural sciences to the social sciences and arts, tackling important questions that necessitate exposure to such disciplines. Most important, it means learning to think and create in multiple ways.

In many colleges, students will begin with a rich gumbo of "general education" courses. Quite frankly, you probably won't have much influence over what your eighteen-year-old decides to study, but if you want to assist your kids in getting more out of school, you can encourage them to understand how those offerings can benefit them. You want them to see that all those prerequisite classes will help them enjoy life, learn to think critically, become innovative and creative, and yes, gain the "soft skills" that large and highly successful corporations increasingly value.

Every year the National Association of Colleges and Employers polls corporations, asking them what qualities they most want in their new hires.[6] Those surveys list critical thinking and problem solving among the highest-rated abilities that employers seek. They also want employees who can work well in diverse teams, have a strong work ethic, and can write and speak well, all absolutely essential qualities. A broad background can help your children develop those attributes, and they need to understand that reality.

By the time your children are young adults the best thing you can do is to avoid negative messages about getting a broad education. Don't ever say to them something like "I don't know why schools require you to take this. I've been in this field for years, and I've never had to use something from this course in . . ." Pick any example you want. Ask them about all of their studies and show interest in everything. Don't try to force them in any direction by using your power over the purse strings. To help your kids get the most out of school, you will *not* want to play your family's version of Uncle Rupert or any other negative relative.

Embrace the multitude of blessings that a wide-ranging education can bestow upon your children. It can enrich every moment of their existence. It cannot wash away all of life's challenges, but knowledge and ability can help children dance and swoon, enjoying each moment more deeply. It will do more than prepare them with ways to make money—although it will do that as well. A life of learning and thought can prepare them to act in many capacities: as citizens of the world, as parents and family members, as connoisseurs of the unique pleasures of humanity.

A HIDDEN BONUS IN HIGHER EDUCATION THAT MOST PEOPLE FAIL TO RECOGNIZE

Many students miss out on one of the best learning opportunities that higher education offers. In large research institutions, and even some small ones, professors will have two jobs at once. They are expected to help students learn but they are also expected or encouraged to continue their own learning. Indeed, in many places they are supposed to learn something new that no one has ever learned before. That means doing original research.

Critics of higher education often bemoan the amount of time professors spend doing and supervising research projects and their graduate students. But those enterprises can often give undergraduates a golden opportunity that few of them recognize. Remember the advice that Carol Grieder received when she first went to college. Knock on doors and look for a job in someone's research lab, even if you don't get course credit for it. For Grieder, this was the first step toward eventually becoming a Nobel Laureate.

HOW TO CHOOSE THE BEST TEACHERS AND COURSES IN COLLEGE

Learning to think well does depend on what your kids study, but it is also influenced by who designs and conducts the classes they take. In the early years of schooling, you and your kids have little influence on who their teachers will be, but by the time they reach higher education, the choices grow enormously.

This point bears repeating: you must let your kids lead the way and choose their own professors when they go to college. But you can begin at a much earlier age to help them think about such choices. How can you help your kids select the best teachers in college and beyond? With so much bad advice floating through society, it is easy to make less than ideal decisions. We have no surefire formula, but we can guarantee you that most schools have always offered some exceptional educators if you know how to find them. Today, with all that we have learned about human learning and how to foster it, the chances that you will strike gold are far better than they were when we went to school.

The study of human learning in recent years has produced powerful insights that teachers at all levels are using to foster smarter learning. But picking the right teachers, who are familiar with these insights, is still important—from preschool to a PhD. You can help your kids get more out of school by learning how to make good choices once they strike out on their own.

Choosing the Best Teachers and Courses

Here we will share some suggestions drawn from our work in higher education over the last fifty years. We hope that you and your children will find ideas here that work for them. Please don't regard any of what follows as hardnosed dictates. If you share any suggestion we make, please assure your kids that they are in charge of their own learning and lives.

Most importantly, your children should consider whether a course will help them become more passionate learners, think critically, learn deeply, and develop a growth mindset. They should also ask whether it will help them recognize the importance of making mistakes and avoid the problems of perfectionism, bullying, and racism. That's a tall order, but kids can fill it better if their parents let them lead the way, waiting to respond to their questions with researched advice, and only occasionally raising their own questions to spark thought.

We think one of the most powerful questions everyone can ask is, will students have the same learning environment professors usually enjoy and expect? That is, will they have the chance to demonstrate what they think they understand, come up short, get feedback, and try again before anyone puts a grade on their work?

If a professor is working on some research project and develops some tentative ideas, she might take her thoughts down the hall and share them with a colleague. She would expect the colleague to offer suggestions on how to improve her work and would be terribly insulted if that colleague simply looked her in the eye and said something like, "You're making a C thus far." That's how schools often treat their students.

We've been advocating changes in that practice for years and some people have adopted our suggestions, but frankly the number of converts is small. If your child finds someone who has made this shift, they should carefully consider taking that professor's class if other things check out. At a minimum, your kids can at least ask how they will get feedback on their thinking.

Choose courses with teachers who emphasize learning to think well and who stress opportunities for students to learn by thinking and doing. Deliberately search for project-based offerings, where students learn by doing something for their community. We've already offered you some examples of this type of course. For another great model, look at Andrew Kaufman's "Books Behind Bars" course at the University of Virginia, where students learn literature and a host of other disciplines by helping prison inmates change their lives. We cover this in our book *Super Courses*.[7]

Here are some questions you can encourage your kid to ask other students. Does the course and teacher help people learn to think, to judge, to ask questions, to create? Are the classes interactive and lively or sleepy and boring? You probably will want to know if the teacher has a sense of humor and keeps things lively, but avoid like the plague those who ridicule members of the class for the sake of a good laugh, or offer little more than entertainment.

Yet you don't want to make all judgments based on how entertaining a potential teacher is. Ken once had a professor in graduate school who bored even himself with his monotonous voice and shyness. Yet this scholar also had developed a deep understanding of American political history and had selected readings and organized discussions that allowed his students to grow into deep and creative learners.

Pick people who know a lot but also care deeply about the learning and development of their students. Don't choose someone simply because they are a famous scholar. Professors who concentrate only on their own research and publications don't always prioritize helping their students learn deeply, or know enough about human learning and motivation or how to assess someone else's learning.

Avoid professors who are concerned with oceans of minutiae rather than deep understanding. Ken once had a history professor who awarded high grades in a Greek history course based on who could name all the parts of the Parthenon frieze, the five-hundred-foot marble relief sculpture that decorates the famous temple sitting on a hill in Athens. It did not matter whether someone understood the major changes that emerged in ancient Greek culture and society. Nor did it matter whether anything students committed to memory had any influence on how they subsequently thought about that history. Ken can't say he remembers any of the parts of the frieze today.

Select offerings that encourage people to challenge their existing knowledge: "Why do I believe what I think I know? What's the evidence? What's the reasoning behind this line of thought? What are the problems I face in believing whatever I regard as truth?" Look for classes that stimulate creativity, even if they are completely outside of a chosen area of concentration.

Avoid teachers who seem to favor some types of students over others (whether based on gender, social class, ethnicity, being an athlete or not, or any other such criteria). Take classes from teachers who seem to believe that everyone can learn to learn with a growth mindset and lots of the right kind of assistance. Avoid any who subscribe to a genius theory of learning that says only the "gifted and talented" are prepared to conquer their courses.

These are suggestions you can make to your kids. They are not intended to be demands you make about their behavior. As we keep saying, remember that you must give your young adult children the keys to their educational lives. They should be in charge. Nothing about your language, posture, attitude, or tone should suggest that you are making demands.

Where Can They Find the Evidence to Make Good Judgments?

Help your kids to understand that they can learn a great deal about teachers and their courses from looking at a course syllabus before signing up. It might be available online or from someone who took the course from the same instructor in the past. If it is a new course, students can ask the professor for a copy, or look at other syllabi that teacher has created. Does that syllabus *invite* students into a stimulating learning environment (rather than just setting requirements and demands)? Does it begin with the big questions that the course will help you address? Does it give you some sense of what you will be able to do intellectually, physically, professionally, or emotionally as a result of taking the course?

An increasing number of good teachers will craft what we call a promising or invitational syllabus.[8] This is a document that talks about what the course promises students (sometimes called learning objectives). Or what it invites students to achieve. Most of all, it should discuss what kinds of conversations the students will be able to join, and with whom, as a result of taking the class. Who will be their partners in learning—other students, teachers, artists, policy makers, business or political or cultural leaders? Or someone else?

How can you encourage your kids to look at those documents without sounding like you are insulting them? Or taking over their lives? Just ask them if they have had a chance to look at the syllabus in each of the courses they plan to take. We don't think you'll receive much resistance if you approach all we've mentioned in this section with a sense of care rather than hard-nosed demands.

What do you say if your son or daughter says that the courses they are considering do not provide much information in advance, let alone a good invitational syllabus? To fill in the gap, students will need to talk directly with their professors. You could suggest that it is perfectly acceptable to make an appointment with the professor to ask questions before they even register for a class, but certainly as early after registration as possible. You might also suggest that it is equally reasonable to organize other students into a group that will make an appointment together. That way, the professor will not need to answer an important question so many times.

But what if you suspect your kids are too shy to knock on somebody's door and ask them questions? Please don't humiliate them or try to force them. If all has gone well, you will have taken the advice that we began offering in the prelude of this book, and will have already spent years helping your kids learn to talk to adults. But if they can't, that's not going to sink their educational boat.

Preparing for the Changes Ahead

Most higher education institutions will offer your kids an opportunity for a rich, multidisciplinary education, but we couldn't write a book about parents helping their children get the most out of school without tackling this important question: What can parents do to make their children's schools even better?

We realize most parents won't have the time or the resources to do a lot, and perhaps we should focus on small efforts, but as we near the end of our journey together, we want to make you aware of a big idea that is already changing some schools and may soon alter many others. Support from families like yours can bring some crucial aid to this potentially transformative movement, but even if you cannot lend much support to the effort, you and your children can benefit from knowing what may be coming down the pike.

But what is it?

A small but growing number of schools around the world have gone further than simply sprinkling a variety of disciplines into the curriculum. They have developed a broad, integrated and question-based curriculum for their students. Every course begins with a powerful question—a problem—that students will find important and interesting. To answer that question, students must pull ideas from a variety of thinkers. They work in small teams of four or five people, and those teams have the assistance of faculty from a multitude of departments.

Some of the big questions invite students to contemplate moral issues, while others encourage them to grapple with how to resolve physical and emotional challenges. They all help learners pull from many areas of study.

Most of the disciplines—from business to information science—emerged in the nineteenth, twentieth, and twenty-first centuries. The movement of which we speak is trying to break down the walls between subject areas to focus on questions and problems. Students engage in a project because they find the investigation important, intriguing, and rewarding. They develop problem-solving and creativity skills, improve their ability to communicate, collaborate, and think critically.

We first encountered this approach to schooling in southwestern China with the help of three amazing educators: Li Hao, Fan Yihong, and Zhou Bei, all at Southwest Jiaotong University in Chengdu. But you can also see it in the reforms that Pasi Sahlberg and others have engineered in Finland. You can find it in the work of Steve Rees and the MindDrive people.

From Kansas City to Scandinavia to China, educators have created multidisciplinary learning opportunities that begin with a problem, whether it's changing the way people get from place to place (cars) or creating beauty. As students struggle in small groups with the challenge, they learn a variety of subjects and come to see how all knowledge is connected. The movement toward problem-based learning is growing and if you join that effort, you can encourage your children to take up the cause. Ask for their advice. Bring your friends and neighbors into this conversation and go talk with teachers, school leaders, and board members from grade schools to colleges and universities. You may find that you must lead this movement, or that you can give encouragement and support to those who are already flexing these muscles.

As your children grow up, you can set an example of direct action to bring these possibilities to the attention of educators. Remain calm and civil yet persistent. Gather the evidence about what kind of courses schools can offer. Remember our book, *Super Courses,* as mentioned earlier.

In this new world, kids don't take chemistry to fulfill a prerequisite but to tackle how humans can survive and unravel the deep mysteries of nature. Their goal is not to ace an exam but to stand in awe of how the universe speaks to us in many dialects and to use our dialogues with the physical and social world to solve the problems we face.

How can we address global warming and climate change? How can we understand our own time and compare it to other eras? How can we keep in mind not just the immediate consequences of our actions but the long-term results? Let your kids know what you are trying to do so they will join those efforts as they approach high school and college.

If you have planted the seeds for this kind of effort with the suggestions we made in their earlier years, you'll be likely find your kids are receptive to these ideas. But remember, your kids must lead these efforts. You can only show them ideas and voice your support if they begin moving in this new direction. It's the foundation of a rich conversation that can enrich your home but also allow your kids to assume the leadership of this effort.

GRADES AS IMPORTANT FEEDBACK

Throughout this book we have repeatedly warned that when students focus on grades, they can suffer. Parents should pay attention to those dangers. But there is a way to think about the scoring system in school that can be quite positive. Adriana Butler understood that and used that approach to great benefit.[9]

The young woman from St. Louis made good marks in school and used them to win admission to a top ranked university. We'll call it SoapSuds U, just for fun. During her freshman year, she nearly tripped over an academic hurdle that often floors college freshmen. The university required all undergraduates to take a course in writing, and the grading policy in that program nearly ensnared her. Like so many others, Adriana had come out of secondary education thinking she could write well, only to arrive at college and face new, higher standards that made her question her confidence in her writing skills.

Some freshman composition programs still use a list of cardinal sins that young writers cannot violate if they expect to get credit for a required weed-out class in writing. Even schools that have no such list still impose tough standards that few freshmen can meet at first. In an engineering school or premed program, the equivalent might be a tough math requirement or organic chemistry.

At SoapSuds U, the high-flying recruits often received a D or F on their first freshman paper. "It was a wake-up call," Adriana admitted years later. "College was going to be a lot tougher than anything I'd taken before. I had to buckle down to keep from being washed out of school."

Adriana could have responded to this challenge in either of two ways. The grade or score could have become her only concern—and her chief motivation to work harder. Her parents, however, helped her take a different approach that kept her from becoming an obsessive grade grubber and perfectionist.

With coaching from her mom in particular, she began to say to herself, "I *want* to meet the higher standards of writing and thinking that I'm facing. They will help me think more clearly, to communicate my ideas to myself and to other people." Along with this came a revised priority: "I don't care about the grade. Ten years from now, no one will even know what marks I made, but I and everyone else will know how well I can think and write."

In that latter way of thinking, what is important is not the grade but the opportunity to grow as a thinker and writer, as a creative and critically thinking person. Adriana began to see that she could view the marks she received as golden messages, keys to a more productive and happier life. She was no longer playing an academic game focused only on how many points she could amass or awards she could ring up. Rather than reacting to a low mark as some curse, she delighted in the writing lessons she learned. That shift in thinking liberated the young woman. She would not become a slave to an extrinsic reward, letting someone else take control of her learning. Instead, she became a highly successful writer and editor.

Parents can play a large role in reframing how kids view grades. So can schools. One of the many workshops Ken has conducted for university professors over the years begins with a simple question and often ends in a new policy that dramatically improves student learning: "What does the grade represent in your class? Does it represent what students can do by the end of their time with you, or a compilation of what they have done at different times in the term?" Think about the difference.

Ken also often asks what it should be. In polls of college professors he has conducted since 1986, more than ninety percent have said that grades should tell society what students can do by the time they finish a course, not compile what they have done over a four-month semester. Yet many of those educators will continue to average grades earned throughout the semester, often allowing work done in the first few weeks of a college class to pull down final grades for the course. This tends to benefit those who've been lucky enough to have superior high school teachers while leaving behind many who, like Adriana, have the potential to become truly great writers.

A few professors will defend that old system by arguing that the new suggestions of giving people multiple opportunities to try, fail, receive feedback, and try again lowers standards. Yet the opposite is true. Such a policy shift allows schools to *raise* standards. When the grade represents what students can do by the end of the course, a writing or math teacher can insist that kids learn more deeply, do excellent work, and learn to benefit from their mistakes.

As we pointed out earlier, it also embodies the kind of environment scholars and scientists expect for their own learning in doing research: the opportunity to try repeatedly, fail, receive feedback, and try again. Should students petition schools to implement such an approach? Why not? It's one of the best and easiest ways for parents to help their kids get more out of school.

When Grades Become a Nightmare

Many of the pitfalls of grades became visible in what happened recently at New York University. Maitland Jones Jr., an organic chemistry professor, had been teaching for nearly fifty years when he retired from an Ivy League school and took another post in the Big Apple, but this time without a permanent appointment or the protection of tenure. Jones was passionate about organic chemistry, but he was an unforgiving grader who rarely offered students the chance to try again if they failed. Many of his students did not do well with his style of teaching. They became disgruntled with the low marks Professor Jones dished out. The undergraduates petitioned the university to dismiss him. As the outcry mushroomed, leaders of the school decided to fire the chemist.[10]

Think how different that story might have been if a learning center or parents had helped the students learn how to benefit from all the mistakes they were making. Or if the school had supported a well-funded teaching center to show the professor how everyone benefits when people have a chance to try, fail, receive feedback and try again before a teacher smacks a final grade on their work.[11]

The professor reported that he did everything he could to help students learn, but his chief example reveals a troublesome line of thinking. Professor Jones said he spent over five thousand dollars recording special lectures for students and could not understand why they didn't learn. Yet a considerable body of research questions whether passive lectures are the best way to stimulate deep learning.

His university had no well-funded teaching center or any other way for him to explore alternative means to foster learning, and no strong tradition of faculty seeking help with the design and execution of their courses. We know that because Ken founded the new Center for Teaching Excellence at NYU in 1986. But the history of that enterprise reveals much about what universities can do, but don't always.

NYU had recruited Ken to come to New York from Northwestern University with lavish promises of facilities and staffing. The university was, however, in a transition from one president to another, facing financial troubles, and facing pressures to cut anything that might seem frivolous. Ken still regrets that he didn't create a way for parents to bolster administrative support for the center and its ongoing struggle to bring research insights into learning and teaching. The promised new facilities and staffing never materialized. Within a few short years, he was moved from one inadequate single office to another. The school initially allowed him to hire one other person to help assist with course planning but cut that position in a budget crunch. It did not house the center in a central location that could signal to faculty an increased emphasis on evidence-based approaches to education.

So what does all of this about teaching centers have to do with what parents can do to help their kids get the best out of school? For one, when kids visit campuses to pick where they will apply for college, they often fail to ask some key questions. Do you have a teaching center? How is it staffed? What is its budget? Is there a strong tradition of faculty seeking help with the design of their classes?

After Professor Jones was fired, one of his former students, who now teaches psychology at the University of Southern California and holds a PhD in her field, wrote about her experience in his organic chemistry class years ago.[12] When Leslie Berntsen got her first test back in that class, she reported, Jones announced the highest score and the lowest. He didn't put any names on those marks, but Berntsen knew she had the bottom grade. "Even if other students didn't know he was talking about me, I knew," she recalls, "and that was more than enough." As Jones addressed the class from the front of the room, he began to mock her low grades, while some students laughed at his quips.

It was a humiliating and devastating experience. Berntsen gave up her dream of becoming a psychiatrist who worked with Doctors Without Borders to serve the needs of vulnerable people around the world. The silver lining is that Berntsen now tells all of her own students that story. "I want them to know that it is normal to experience academic setbacks. They do not define you, serve as a negative reflection of your character, or indicate that you are destined for perpetual failure," she wrote recently. "Rather, they are a universal part of the human experience and often serve as valuable learning opportunities."[13]

Jones may have never learned about the damage he did because learning chemistry deeply—which he did—does not mean that a professor knows anything about human motivation and learning. Or maybe he did. It took years for those chickens to come home to roost.

A LAST INTERLUDE

Going to college has long been associated with power and privilege. In the eighteenth, nineteenth, and early twentieth centuries, it was mainly something that the male children of white elites did as part of their birthright and to cement their social position. That changed slowly, as more people gained the chance to participate. In the United States in the 1830s, Oberlin College in Ohio began allowing women to attend. Lincoln's land grant program put a research university in every state (at first for males only). Roosevelt's GI Bill gave millions of ex-soldiers a crack at higher learning.

By the 1960s, the barriers to students of color pursuing higher education in the United States were coming down. Some super-rich folks (like the Rockefellers) championed the growth of public colleges and universities, with support from both Republicans and Democrats. Growing community college systems offered accessible two-year programs for all students over the age of eighteen. All of those steps began to democratize and diversify higher education. Something similar happened around the world.

Yet a major problem still loomed over the American system. While public schools, from kindergarten through high school, offered free classes to nearly everyone, students in the United States generally had to pay beyond that point. In the 1970s Senator Claiborne Pell managed to secure Congressional authorization for federal grants for lower income families to help pay for college, and many state legislatures subsidized public universities to keep tuition fees low. In 1986, when our son entered the University of Texas at Austin, he paid only about $50 in tuition each semester.

Unfortunately, the federal government's financial aid to schools and students in the 1960s and 1970s made some people angry and nervous, and some of them sought to reduce the national investments that allowed the children of Italian immigrants and Alabama farm families and millions of others to partake in higher education. Some wealthy folks wanted to keep that privilege for their own children and families. Thus, they began to cut public support for colleges and universities (and often for public education on every level). That made it increasingly difficult for average and lower income families to provide financial support for their children's education.

As legislatures slashed the money they provided for public universities, schools started raising tuition to make up for the cuts. At the same time, operating costs continued to climb. Microsoft and a few other companies got schools into a frenzy trying to keep up with each other on the purchase of new computers and software. To blunt the impact of rising costs and declining state support, schools, banks, and other institutions offered easy loans to students and their families. Many private schools, and even some public ones, tried to pacify students with lots of country club amenities like sports arenas and teams, and other forms of entertainment. Students' debts continued to grow.

Europe and Asia Go the Other Way

As legislatures made these cuts, enrollment in US colleges declined.[14] Meanwhile, higher education in Europe, Japan, and other countries moved in the opposite direction. By 2022 Great Britain had 12 percent more undergraduates than they did in 2016.[15] Even ten years ago, countries as diverse as Canada, Japan, and Israel had higher rates of college attainment than did the United States. Since then, the US rate has grown more slowly than in many other industrialized nations and the gap between America and its peer countries has widened.[16]

As educational writer and researcher Paul Tough informed *New York Times* readers in 2023, "On average, countries in the Organization for Economic Cooperation and Development have increased their college-degree attainment rate among young adults by more than 20 percentage points since 2000."[17] In the United States, growth has been slow by comparison. While American rates of attainment are still higher than most OECD countries, these rates are expanding more slowly than the OECD average.[18] At the same time, American leaders from both major political parties have put less emphasis on improving the quality of teaching and learning.

In 2014, as we were preparing to spend the first of two months in China exchanging ideas about faculty development and improved student learning, a US undersecretary of education admonished us not to "help them too much" and expressed serious doubt that US schools could learn anything from these interactions. But as Tough would write nearly a decade later, "Americans have turned away from college at the same time that students in the rest of the world have been flocking to campus."

Why Pursue a Higher Education?

We've known for a long time that both individuals and society benefit when most people go to school beyond the age of eighteen.[19] That adventure can take various forms, from art schools to liberal arts studies to trade schools, but we can make several observations that are common to most educational experiences after high school.

Not everyone who walks away with a degree gets the kind of education we advocate in this book. That is, they do not all learn to live creative, curious, critically reasoning, constantly questioning, competent (well informed), compassionate, confident, collaborative, contented, and communicative lives no matter what job or career they might follow. But if we look at people who graduated, we can get a pretty good measure of the benefits. They are substantial.

What is true of the whole of anything is not, of course, necessarily true of every part of the whole, yet on average, college graduates make substantially more money across their lifespans than do non-graduates. But success isn't just about money, and a constant emphasis on financial rewards obscures many other benefits. Research has found that higher education students become better problem-solvers, exhibit more imagination in cracking challenges, and are less likely to believe in conspiracy theories.[20] They also pass on to their children and subsequent generations the substantial advantages of their education.[21] When you think about the potential gains for your kids, keep in mind these follow-on rewards for your grandchildren, their kids, and the society around them.

You could quibble with some of these reported advantages, pointing out that they are subject to subjective judgments, but you can't deny this one: on average, college graduates live longer than people who don't finish or even go. In the United States, the current difference in life expectancy is about seven years.[22] That's a huge gap.

Does all of this mean that everyone should pursue a higher degree? Do some kids simply lack something—call it intelligence, interest, talent, perseverance, preparation, or whatever—that keeps them from becoming "college material?" Maybe, sometimes. But we would argue that, given our society's history, we are far more likely to exclude a qualified person or weed them out before we realize their potential than we are to send the wrong person to postsecondary education. When it comes to rates of educational attainment, as mentioned above, the United States is falling behind its peers. Furthermore, those rates in the United States vary considerably from state to state, with averages in some regions falling far below even the American norm. For the last few years, the percentage of recent high school graduates who went on to enroll in institutions of higher learning in the United States has been declining.[23] All of these statistics suggest that money and preparation in earlier years largely determine who gets an advanced education, not some native ability. Everyone in the society benefits when more people get the chance to pursue an education into their twenties.

It is true that right now, interest in going to college is declining in the United States. Yet that's not surprising. Public policy has made the financial costs prohibitive for many. Furthermore, powerful voices in our culture have bombarded our kids with an anti-education message for ten years or more. The emphasis has been on whether extra schooling will get you more money, rather than whether it will help you become a better thinker, problem solver, and ethical or creative human. Seldom does anyone explore and explain the rich advantages we have emphasized in this book. By overemphasizing money, Americans are priming themselves for disappointment. Those who pursue advanced learning opportunities but don't land high-paying jobs often come off as failures, even though this kind of education offers substantial advantages to both individuals and society.

What Can Parents Do?

If you want to help your kids get more out of school, push socially and politically for our society to provide stronger financial support for all of education at all levels. Organize for increased public financing, not only to lower tuition expenses for individual students and their families, but also to shoulder the costs of bringing the insights of research on human learning to every classroom. Over the last fifty years, we've made enormous progress in adopting an evidence-based approach to teaching and learning, but that revolution is incomplete.

Parents and their children can be a powerful force in advancing the agenda of lowering the financial costs of higher learning and guaranteeing everyone an opportunity to pursue it in ways that the research supports and their personal needs demand.

It's been nearly twenty years since Derek Bok, the former president of Harvard, wrote *Our Underachieving Colleges*. In that 2006 book, he argued that while most universities value and support research in nearly every area, they don't extend that respect to findings about human learning and how best to foster it. For generations, many professors have created their classes and taught them using methods that follow tradition rather than the insights from research on human learning, motivation, and evaluation.[24]

With support from teaching centers and student success programs, that world is changing. But it hasn't shifted completely. Far too many classes in college continue to use old-fashioned methods to encourage and support student learning rather than employing the insights born out of research on human learning and how best to foster it. We need to make higher education better, to use research to turn every class into a Super Course experience, and we need to make it affordable to everyone. At some schools, administrators have actually cut budgets for evidenced-based programs that might otherwise improve learning environments for their students and underfunded teaching centers.[25] Imagine a world in which parents and their adult children stopped that regression in its tracks. You can help your kids to understand what needs to be done, and do it. Don't fire the Professor Joneses of the world, but provide them with the support needed to create better learning environments.

Should Nearly All Students Go On to Higher Education?

In the course of researching and writing this book, we raised the question used to title this section with hundreds of parents. Most replied that the answer depended in part on how you defined *higher education*. "No one size or kind of education will fit all people" was the typical reply. Some will want the broad education of a liberal arts environment; others might want to concentrate on the arts; still others will focus on building cars, or programming a computer, or learning some other trade, from repairing appliances to mending human bodies. But all of those examples involve substantial schooling beyond the age of eighteen.

We then began to ask if higher education should have any central goals that typically require twenty years or more of schooling to achieve, and if so, what were they? Is there something that schools should strive to help everyone achieve, regardless of concentration? Something where the goal couldn't be reached for most people until they were in their early twenties, even if work on that achievement began at an earlier age?

We collected a variety of responses and selected the three that appeared most frequently. We then gave them to people as examples of the kind of suggestions they might consider, while still inviting other responses they might want to offer. We thought our examples would lead to a multitude of possibilities. They didn't. Instead, the overwhelming majority of people chose one of our examples, and virtually everyone picked the same one: helping students recognize misinformation.

Several people offered the same illustration. As one man from Birmingham put it as we rode an Amtrak train together from Metro Park, New Jersey, to Washington, DC, in 2020, "I come from five generations of Republicans, but in our democracy, we must try to make sure that no one is left with the anguish of an Edgar Maddison Welch."

We didn't recognized that name when we first heard it that day, but we've looked it up since. There's an actor and playwright with that name but that's not the person our friend on the train was referencing. His "Maddison," as friends called him, was a young man from North Carolina who had read on the internet that Hillary Clinton and other prominent Democrats were kidnapping children and chaining them in the basement of a pizza parlor in northwest Washington, DC.

There was absolutely no evidence for such a suspicion. But Maddison became so convinced that it was all going on that he drove to the nation's capital one night in 2016 with his AR-15 style rifle. He stormed the pizza shop the next morning, firing three shots before the police quelled him. In subsequent months, similar theories drove others to take similar action.[26]

Can an education help people exercise better judgment when they are tempted to accept false rumors? Such a goal has nothing to do with making lots of money, but it could very well save lives. Our world has become so fractured and troubled that addressing the proliferation of fake news has become central to our ideas about the purpose of an education.

NOTES

ACKNOWLEDGMENTS

INDEX

Notes

PRELUDE

1. Peter Gray, "The Decline of Play and the Rise of Psychopathology in Children and Adolescents," *American Journal of Play* 3, no. 4 (2011): 443–444.
2. We assign pseudonyms and use composite figures to protect privacy.
3. Nearly a decade ago, psychologist Angela Duckworth added *grit* to the list of big qualities more important than grades. We welcome that suggestion, even as we admit some reservations about it. See Angela Duckworth, *Grit: The Power of Passion and Perseverance* (New York: Scribner, 2016).
4. The recognition that one must update one's skills and knowledge continually to remain employable in a fast-changing world is now so widespread that it is easy to forget that it wasn't always so. A decade ago, Ken served for two years as the provost of a small public university in Washington, DC, a land-grant school and historically black college. In his capacity as chief academic officer, he met frequently with local leaders, and discussions often centered on the kind of education the school should offer. Nearly always, the advice for serving this (largely poor, black) student population was simply to "train them to hold down a good job." Yet the limited conception of a good job these leaders had in mind did not insist on ongoing growth or change. This is a discussion and debate dating back at least to the early twentieth century, when W. E. B. Du Bois's advocacy of broad education that could prepare students for positions of leadership stood in contrast to Booker T. Washington's calls for job training.
5. On the subject of children's education, parents tend to be woefully ill-informed. Too many books talk down to them or ignore them completely. Some well-publicized studies seem designed to stoke irrational fears, while other advice reflects only the writer's personal whims. Parents have largely lacked access to

what serious research has revealed about human learning. Part of our aim with this book is to remedy that.

6. Ken Bain, *What the Best College Teachers Do* (Cambridge, MA: Harvard University Press, 2004); Ken Bain, *What the Best College Students Do* (Cambridge, MA: Belknap Press of Harvard University Press, 2012); Ken Bain with Marsha Marshall Bain, *Super Courses: The Future of Teaching and Learning* (Princeton, NJ: Princeton University Press, 2021).

7. Baker in his renowned "Integration of Abilities" course outlined four levels at which people pursue personal growth and urged his students to be part of "group four"—those happy few for whom "growth is the discovery of a dynamic power of the mind." Paul Baker, *Integration of Abilities: Exercises for Creative Growth* (San Antonio, TX: Trinity University Press, 1972), 17. Much more will be said about Baker's approach to cultivating creativity later in this book.

8. Founded by renowned inventor Jerome Lemelson and his wife, Dorothy, the Lemelson-MIT Program at the Massachusetts Institute of Technology has, since 1994, worked to equip diverse groups of children with "the knowledge, skills and mindset needed to invent technological solutions to real-world problems." Read about the program at https://lemelson.mit.edu/forging-pathway-invention-education.

9. Giyoo Hatano and Kayoko Inagaki, "Two Courses of Expertise," in *Research and Clinical Center for Child Development Annual Report, 1982–1983*, ed. Kazuo Miyaki (Sapporo, Japan: Hokkaido University Faculty of Education, 1984): 27–36.

10. Jonny Beyer et al., "Environmental Effects of the Deepwater Horizon Oil Spill: A Review," *Marine Pollution Bulletin* 110, no. 1 (2016): 28–51; Mace G. Barron, "Ecological Impacts of the Deepwater Horizon Oil Spill: Implications for Immunotoxicity," *Toxicologic Pathology* 40, no. 2 (2012): 315–320; Thomas G. Safford, Jessica D. Ulrich, and Lawrence C. Hamilton, "Public Perceptions of the Response to the Deepwater Horizon Oil Spill: Personal Experiences, Information Sources, and Social Context," *Journal of Environmental Management* 113 (2012): 31–39.

11. George Sylvester Viereck, "What Life Means to Einstein," *Saturday Evening Post*, October 26, 1929, 117.

12. Children are naturally curious creatures and usually enter their first classrooms excited about learning, but they often lose that self-drive within a few short

years. Even in highly regarded schools, that childhood spark can become a rapidly dying ember.
13. Let's move away from the old notion that some kids are smart and some are not. Research has demonstrated that addressing this single objective—helping a child learn to rebound and grow from failure—will change school and life for your son or daughter more positively than any other single step you might take.
14. This can be tricky. You will want to avoid helicopter parenting that hovers over children constantly, smothering them, but you also don't want to abandon them and their learning.
15. In an era of rapid change how can you help your children learn to live creative and inventive lives? To flourish they cannot just memorize solutions to problems that may not be so important anymore or prepare for jobs that will soon disappear. How can they learn to imagine new worlds and invent fresh approaches? Parents, regardless of their own educational backgrounds, can help foster the creative and imaginative life.
16. Some children don't learn well or deeply because they don't know how, or even understand what it means to do so. We can help you change that. Back in the day, even the student stars used methods of learning that did not always work well, leaving holes in retention and deep understanding. A century of research has challenged those old methods and taught us a new way of thinking. Perhaps most important: How can our kids learn to think, to make wise decisions, to use the ideas and information they will encounter?
17. What should they study? Should your kids strive for a broad education or simply prepare themselves for a particular job, or line of work? Can they or should they simply follow the money and prepare for a career where the pay is highest? Our society seems caught between these alternatives, unable to decide. Pressure grows every year to do the latter, especially for families with little money. Is that the best choice, or even a realistic one?
18. Steven Johnson, "The Man Who Broke the World," *New York Times Magazine,* March 19, 2023, 38.
19. For more on Thomas Midgley and the dangers of lead exposure, see Herbert L. Needleman, "The Removal of Lead from Gasoline: Historical and Personal Reflections," *Environmental Research* 84, no. 1 (September 1, 2000): 20–35; Kat Eschner, "Leaded Gas Was a Known Poison the Day It Was Invented," *Smithsonian Magazine,* December 9, 2016; Kat Eschner, "One Man Invented

Two of the Deadliest Substances of the 20th Century," *Smithsonian Magazine,* May 18, 2017; David C. Bellinger, Karen M. Stiles, and Herbert L. Needleman, "Low-Level Lead Exposure, Intelligence and Academic Achievement: A Long-Term Follow-up Study," *Pediatrics* 90, no. 6 (December 1, 1992): 855–861; Bruce P. Lanphear et al., "Low-Level Environmental Lead Exposure and Children's Intellectual Function: An International Pooled Analysis," *Environmental Health Perspectives* 113, no. 7 (July 2005): 894–899; Howard W. Mielke and Sammy Zahran, "The Urban Rise and Fall of Air Lead (Pb) and the Latent Surge and Retreat of Societal Violence," *Environment International* 43 (August 1, 2012): 48–55; J. R. McNeill, *Something New Under the Sun: An Environmental History of the Twentieth-Century World* (New York: Norton, 2000), 111–114; Steven Johnson, "The Brilliant Inventor Who Made Two of History's Biggest Mistakes," *New York Times Magazine,* March 15, 2023.
20. Adam Grant, *Think Again: The Power of Knowing What You Don't Know* (New York: Penguin, 2021), 25.

ONE: SPARKING CURIOSITY

1. Scott Hershovitz, "How to Do Philosophy with Kids," *Psyche,* December 21, 2022, https://psyche.co/guides/how-to-talk-about-philosophy-with-kids-so-you-think-together.
2. Michelle M. Chouinard, "Children's Questions: A Mechanism for Cognitive Development," *Monographs of the Society for Research in Child Development* 72, no. 1 (2007): i–129.
3. Richard M. Ryan and Edward L. Deci, "Intrinsic and Extrinsic Motivations: Classic Definitions and New Directions," *Contemporary Educational Psychology* 25, no. 1 (2000): 54–67.
4. Ken Bain, *What the Best College Teachers Do* (Cambridge, MA: Harvard University Press, 2004): 32–36.
5. Richard M. Ryan and Edward L. Deci, "Self-Determination Theory and the Facilitation of Intrinsic Motivation, Social Development, and Well-Being," *American Psychologist* 55, no. 3 (2000): 68–78.
6. Wealthy families have long had the advantage of early tutors and schooling. In the 1960s, the Johnson administration created Head Start for poor families and the Carter administration expanded it in the late 1970s.

7. For other suggestions of thought-provoking movies, see Julian Baggini et al., "I Watch Therefore I Am: Seven Movies that Teach Us Key Philosophy Lessons," *The Guardian,* April 14, 2015. Choose according to your child's age and select others as they grow older.
8. For Charles Darwin's notebooks, see "Darwin's Notebooks and Reading Lists," Darwin Online, https://darwin-online.org.uk/EditorialIntroductions/vanWyhe_notebooks.html; for Marie Curie's, see Marie Curie, "Notebook," Wellcome Collection, https://wellcomecollection.org/works/cywqefw4/items?canvas=9.
9. "Philosophy and Children's Literature," PLATO—Philosophy Learning and Teaching Organization, https://www.plato-philosophy.org/childrens-literature/.
10. See Bob Hirshon, "These DIY Science Projects Let You Help Real-World Research," *Discover,* updated July 9, 2020, https://www.discovermagazine.com/the-sciences/these-diy-science-projects-let-you-help-real-world-research.
11. Quoted in Donald Sheff, "'Izzy, Did You Ask a Good Question Today?'" letter to the editor, *New York Times,* January 19, 1988, A26.
12. Dan Rothstein and Luz Santana, *Make Just One Change: Teach Students to Ask Their Own Questions* (Cambridge, MA: Harvard Education Press, 2011).
13. Rothstein and Santana, *Make Just One Change,* 27.
14. Thanks to Belmont University math professor Mike Pinter for both of these suggestions.
15. "Compare the States," *Chronicle of Higher Education,* August 2, 2024, https://www.chronicle.com/article/almanac-states.
16. For analysis of the spring 2020 and fall 2020 semesters, see Wan-Lae Cheng, Jonathan Law, and Duwain Pinder, "COVID-19 Crisis Pushes US Students into an Uncertain Job Market," McKinsey & Company, July 7, 2021, https://www.mckinsey.com/featured-insights/sustainable-inclusive-growth/future-of-america/covid-19-crisis-pushes-us-students-into-an-uncertain-job-market.
17. Molly Woodworth, quoted in Emily Hanford, "At a Loss for Words: How a Flawed Idea Is Teaching Millions of Kids to Be Poor Readers," *APM Reports,* April 22, 2019.
18. Hanford, "At a Loss for Words."
19. "NAEP Report Card: Reading," The Nation's Report Card, accessed April 5, 2024, https://www.nationsreportcard.gov/reading/nation/achievement/?grade=4.
20. Emily Hanford, *Sold a Story,* podcast, https://features.apmreports.org/sold-a-story/.

21. "Word of the Day App," accessed April 5, 2024, https://wordwordapp.com/.
22. The Starfall Learn to Read app is free to download wherever apps are available. Starfall also offers educational material on reading and the alphabet at www.starfall.com. It used to be entirely free but now some of it is behind a paywall. The free part is still valuable. For other resources, see Bonnie Terry, "Best Practices for Teaching Phonics," Scholar Within, February 23, 2022, https://scholarwithin.com/best-practices-for-teaching-phonics; Louisa Smith, "10 of the Best Phonics Books to Help Your Child Read," A Dime Saved, September 4, 2023, https://adimesaved.com/best-phonics-books.

TWO: HELPING YOUR KIDS DEAL WITH FAILURE (AND SUCCESS)

1. Herschbach quoted in Ken Bain, *What the Best College Students Do* (Cambridge, MA: Belknap Press of Harvard University Press, 2012), 57.
2. See Ken Bain with Marsha Marshall Bain, *Super Courses: The Future of Teaching and Learning* (Princeton, NJ: Princeton University Press, 2021), 25–26.
3. J. M. Barrie, *Peter Pan in Kensington Gardens* (New York: Charles Scribner's, 1916), 27.
4. Albert Bandura, "Self-Efficacy: Toward a Unifying Theory of Behavioral Change," *Psychological Review* 84, no 2 (1977): 191–215.
5. See Carol S. Dweck, *Mindset: The New Psychology of Success* (New York: Ballantine, 2006). Some readers will already have a deep understanding of this territory, others will merely think they do, and still others will encounter these ideas for the first time. Our hope with this brief summary is that many will find in it at least some element they have not explored. Certainly, your children stand to benefit enormously from Dweck's ideas and research.
6. Carol I. Diener and Carol S. Dweck, "An Analysis of Learned Helplessness: Continuous Changes in Performance, Strategy, and Achievement Cognitions Following Failure," *Journal of Personality and Social Psychology* 36, no. 5 (1978): 451–462. We first discussed this experiment in an earlier work and, at the risk of offending the gods who protect high standards in academia, we have leaned on that account to construct this one. For that earlier and longer version, see Ken Bain, *What the Best College Students Do* (Cambridge, MA: Belknap Press of Harvard University Press, 2012), 104–111.

7. Melissa L. Kamins and Carol S. Dweck, "Person Versus Process Praise and Criticism: Implications for Contingent Self-Worth and Coping," *Developmental Psychology* 35, no. 3 (1999): 835–847.
8. Jamie Amemiya and Ming-Te Wang, "Why Effort Praise Can Backfire in Adolescence," *Child Development Perspectives* 12, no. 3 (September 2018): 199–203. What the authors call "effort praise" we here also call "task praise."
9. Geoffrey L. Cohen, Claude M. Steele, and Lee D. Ross, "The Mentor's Dilemma: Providing Critical Feedback across the Racial Divide," *Personality and Social Psychology Bulletin* 25, no. 10 (1999): 1302–1318.
10. Claude M. Steele, "Thin Ice: Stereotype Threat and Black College Students," *The Atlantic,* August 1999: 44-54. Among those who responded so affirmatively to that third approach were African American students who had suffered through tons of stereotype threats,
11. Another reason some people can't replicate these findings or the studies of fixed and growth mindsets is that they use grades as a measure of change. But grades are notoriously inexact. Later we will relate the memory of a history professor who awarded high grades in a Greek history course only to those who could name the parts of the Parthenon's frieze—the marble sculptures, that is, ringing the big temple sitting on a hill in Athens. It did not matter whether someone understood the major changes that emerged in old Greek culture and society. Nor did it matter whether anything students committed to memory had any influence on how they subsequently thought about that history.
12. Kyla Haimovitz and Carol S. Dweck, "Parents' Views of Failure Predict Children's Fixed and Growth Intelligence Mind-Sets," *Psychological Science* 27, no. 6 (2016): 859–869.
13. These examples are drawn from Haimovitz and Dweck, "Parents' Views of Failure," 866.
14. Elizabeth A. Canning, Katherine Muenks, Dorainne J. Green, and Mary C. Murphy, "STEM Faculty Who Believe Ability Is Fixed Have Larger Racial Achievement Gaps and Inspire Less Student Motivation in Their Classes," *Science Advances* 5, no. 2 (February 15, 2019): eaau4734.
15. For a famous example of college students taking a similar approach to calculus, see Uri Treisman, "Studying Students Studying Calculus: A Look at the Lives of Minority Mathematics Students in College," *College Mathematics Journal* 23, no. 5 (November 1, 1992): 362–372.

16. "Our Story: The Story behind WeWantToKnow and the Development of DragonBox Games," https://dragonbox.com/about/story-story.
17. David S. Yeager and Carol S. Dweck, "What Can Be Learned from Growth Mindset Controversies?" *American Psychologist* 75, no. 9 (2020): 1269–1284, 1282.
18. Lisa Blackwell, "You Can Grow Your Intelligence: New Research Shows the Brain Can Be Developed Like a Muscle," Brainology Curriculum Guide for Teachers, www.brainology.us/websitemedia/youcangrowyourintelligence.pdf.
19. Joenna Driemeyer, Janina Boyker, Christian Graser, Christian Büchel, and Arne May, "Changes in Gray Matter Induced by Learning—Revisited," *PLoS ONE* 3, no. 7 (2008): e2669.
20. Susan Bobbitt Nolen, "Reasons for Studying: Motivational Orientation and Study Strategies," *Cognition and Instruction* 5, no. 4 (1988): 269–287.
21. Lisa S. Blackwell, Kali H. Trzesniewski, and Carol Sorich Dweck, "Implicit Theories of Intelligence Predict Achievement across an Adolescent Transition: A Longitudinal Study and an Intervention," *Child Development* 78, no. 1 (January–February 2007): 246–263.

THREE: CREATING A HOME THAT SUPPORTS LEARNING

1. If you feel unsure about how to help your kids get evidence-based help with school in general or with particular subjects, the internet can help. Here's one example of the growing number of resources available: "How to Find Free Tutoring and Homework Help Near You," National School Choice Week, updated March 26, 2024, https://schoolchoiceweek.com/free-tutoring/.
2. For a good example, on the topic of growth mindset and pitched at a seventh-grade reading level, see "You Can Grow Your Intelligence: New Research Shows the Brain Can Be Developed Like a Muscle," Brainology Curriculum Guide for Teachers, https://www.mindsetworks.com/websitemedia/youcangrowyourintelligence.pdf.
3. Specifically on the learning of phonics, here are some resources for use at home: "How to Practice Phonics with Kids at Home," Scholastic, August 7, 2023, https://www.scholastic.com/parents/books-and-reading/reading-resources/developing-reading-skills/teach-phonics-home.html; "Early Learning at Home Reading Tips," Teach Your Child to Read, https://teachyourchildtoread.com/early-learning-at-home/.

4. Steve Rees, interviews with authors, 2023.
5. More will be said about Paul Baker later in this book. For a compendium of materials he used in classes, see Paul Baker, *Integration of Abilities: Exercises for Creative Growth* (San Antonio, TX: Trinity University Press, 1972).
6. You can read more about Herschbach's boyhood adventures in Ken Bain, *What the Best College Students Do* (Cambridge, MA: Belknap Press of Harvard University Press, 2012), 215–220.
7. For more of the Jeffrey Hawkins story, see Bain, *What the Best College Students Do*, 32–34, 121–125.
8. James M. Lang, *Distracted: Why Students Can't Focus and What You Can Do about It* (New York: Basic Books, 2020).
9. Ken Bain with Marsha Marshall Bain, *Super Courses: The Future of Teaching and Learning* (Princeton, NJ: Princeton University Press, 2022), 16.
10. Candice Millard, *Destiny of the Republic: A Tale of Madness, Medicine, and the Murder of a President* (New York: Doubleday, 2011).
11. Bain, *What the Best College Students Do*, 133.
12. For a documentary about Lipman's work that helped bring the Philosophy for Children program to Great Britain, see Matthew Lipman, *Philosophy for Children*, BBC, 1990, https://www.youtube.com/watch?v=fp5lB3YVnlE.
13. See Renia Gasparatou and Maria Kampeza, "Introducing P4C in Kindergarten in Greece," *Analytic Teaching and Philosophical Praxis* 33, no. 1 (2012): 72–82.
14. The stories that the teacher read can all be found in your local public library: Kathryn Cave, *Something Else* (London: Puffin Books, 1994); David McKee, *Elmer* (London: Andersen Press, 2007); and Steve Smallman, *The Lamb Who Came for Dinner* (Wilton, CT: Tiger Tales, 2007).
15. Gasparatou and Kampeza, "Introducing P4C," 75.
16. Gasparatou and Kampeza, "Introducing P4C," 76.
17. "Resources for Parents, Grandparents, and Family Members," PLATO, https://www.plato-philosophy.org/for-parents-and-grandparents/.
18. The account of Sandel's course in this section draws on Ken Bain, *What the Best College Teachers Do* (Cambridge, MA: Harvard University Press, 2004), 109–111.
19. Quoted in Bain, *What the Best College Teachers Do*, 109.
20. Bain, *What the Best College Teachers Do*, 109.
21. See Ken Bain, "What Makes Great Teachers Great?" *Chronicle of Higher Education*, April 9, 2004.

22. Michael Sandel, "Justice: What's the Right Thing to Do?" Harvard University's Justice with Michael Sandel, http://justiceharvard.org/justicecourse/. Your college-bound children can take the course online for free, if they do not wish to receive certification, or they can pay to receive a certificate and have unlimited access to the material. See "HarvardX: Justice" EdX, accessed April 9, 2024, https://www.edx.org/learn/justice/harvard-university-justice?in.
23. Quoted in Bain, *What the Best College Teachers Do,* 110.
24. Sandel, "Justice: What's the Right Thing to Do? Episode 01 'The Moral Side of Murder,'" YouTube, https://www.youtube.com/watch?v=kBdfcR-8hEY&t=11s.

FOUR: **FOSTERING A CREATIVE MINDSET**

1. The account that follows is drawn from Ken Bain, *What the Best College Students Do* (Cambridge, MA: Belknap Press of Harvard University Press, 2012), 191–198.
2. This is the fourth book in which Ken has discussed Baker's ideas and work, in part because each time he revisits Baker's teachings, he discovers something new and important that he had not fully noticed and understood in the earlier telling.
3. For an introduction to Baker's thought, see Paul Baker, *Integration of Abilities: Exercises for Creative Growth* (San Antonio, TX: Trinity University Press, 1972).
4. Sir Ken Robinson, "Do Schools Kill Creativity?" TED Talk, February 2006, https://www.ted.com/talks/sir_ken_robinson_do_schools_kill_creativity.
5. The quotation from Laughton appears on the inside flap of Robert Flynn and Eugene McKinney, eds., *Paul Baker and the Integration of Abilities* (Fort Worth, TX: TCU Press, 2003), but it was first shared with us by Robyn Flatt, Baker's daughter, who heard Laughton say it in an oral interview with the press during the English actor's work with Baker at the Baylor Theater in the 1950s.
6. The quote is from notes Ken took from Baker's course in 1962, first published in Bain, *What the Best College Students Do,* 3.
7. Baker, *Integration of Abilities,* 61, quoted in Bain, *What the Best College Students Do,* 14.
8. Albert Einstein, "What Life Means to Einstein," interview by George Sylvester Viereck, *Saturday Evening Post,* October 26, 1929.
9. Sherry Kafka, quoted in Bain, *What the Best College Students Do,* 16.
10. Author's notes from Baker's course, quoted in Bain, *What the Best College Students Do,* 16.

11. Author's notes from Baker's course.
12. Bain, *What the Best College Students Do*, 16.
13. Baker often spoke of the need to overcome our "resistance to work."
14. We originally suggested some of these activities in Ken Bain with Marsha Marshall Bain, *Super Courses: The Future of Teaching and Learning* (Princeton, NJ: Princeton University Press, 2021), 134–135.
15. The teacher is Kate Walker, of the Booker T. Washington High School for the Performing and Visual Arts. In addition to teaching dance, Walker teaches a version of Baker's Integration of Abilities course. See Bain, *Super Courses*, 133.
16. Elizabeth Emery, "Have Students Interview Someone They Disagree With," *Heterodox Academy*, February 11, 2020, https://heterodoxacademy.org/blog/viewpoint-diversity-students-interview-someone/.
17. See Wendy A. Suzuki, "Editorial: Exercise to Enhance Mental Health," *Frontiers in Human Neuroscience* 16 (November 24, 2022); Yuen Shan Christine Lee, Teresa Ashman, Andrea Shang, and Wendy Suzuki, "Effects of Exercise and Self-Affirmation Intervention after Traumatic Brain Injury," *NeuroRehabilitation* 35, no. 1 (January 1, 2014): 57–65; Julia C. Basso and Wendy A. Suzuki, "The Effects of Acute Exercise on Mood, Cognition, Neurophysiology, and Neurochemical Pathways: A Review," *Brain Plasticity* 2, no. 2 (January 1, 2017): 127–152.
18. Talia is a pseudonym. Some minor details of her story have been changed to protect her privacy and to make our central point clearer.
19. Karl Duncker, "On Problem-Solving," *Psychological Monographs* 58, no. 5 (1945).
20. Katherine W. Phillips, Gregory B. Northcraft, and Margaret A. Neale, "Surface-Level Diversity and Decision-Making in Groups: When Does Deep-Level Similarity Help?" *Group Processes and Intergroup Relations* 9, no. 4 (2006): 467–482. See also Shane Frederick, "Cognitive Reflection and Decision Making," *Journal of Economic Perspectives* 19, no 4 (2005): 25–42; and Katherine W. Phillips, "How Diversity Makes Us Smarter," *Scientific American* 311, no. 4 (2014): 43–47.

FIVE: HELPING YOUR KIDS LEARN DEEPLY

1. Names in this story have been changed to protect individual privacy.
2. Ference Marton and Roger Säljö, "On Qualitative Differences in Learning: I—Outcome and Process," *British Journal of Educational Psychology* 46, no. 1 (February 1976): 4–11.
3. Noel Entwistle, "Motivational Factors in Students' Approaches to Learning," in *Learning Strategies and Learning Styles*, ed. Ronald R. Schmeck (Boston:

Springer, 1988), 21–51; D. I, Newble and N. J. Entwistle, "Learning Styles and Approaches: Implications for Medical Education," *Medical Education* 20, no. 3 (1986): 162–175; Noel Entwistle and Bela Kozeki. "Dimensions of Motivation and Approaches to Learning in British and Hungarian Secondary Schools," *International Journal of Educational Research* 12, no. 3 (1988): 243–255.

4. The TeamLEAD curriculum, developed by Duke-NUS Graduate Medical School Singapore, offers a fantastic example of what deep-learning approaches can accomplish in medical education. See "TeamLEAD at Duke-NUS," video, 9:03, November 28, 2011, https://www.youtube.com/watch?v=BlVPLYGdBLg. For earlier work on these issues, see Newble and Entwistle, "Learning Styles and Approaches."

5. For more on surface vs. deep learning, see Ken Bain, *What the Best College Students Do* (Cambridge, MA: Belknap Press of Harvard University Press, 2011), 37–46.

6. Newble and Entwistle, "Learning Styles and Approaches"; John B. Biggs, "Assessing Student Approaches to Learning," *Australian Psychologist* 23, no. 2 (1988): 197–206.

7. See Karen Arnold, *Lives of Promise: What Becomes of High School Valedictorians* (San Francisco: Jossey-Bass, 1995); D. W. MacKinnon, "The Nature and Nurture of Creative Talent," *American Psychologist* 17, no. 7 (1962): 484–495; Kay Cheng Soh, "Grade Point Average: What's Wrong and What's the Alternative?" *Journal of Higher Education Policy and Management* 33, no. 1 (December 31, 2010): 27–36; Leonard L. Baird, "Do Grades and Tests Predict Adult Accomplishment?" *Research in Higher Education* 23, no. 1 (March 1, 1985): 3–85; Adam Grant, "What Straight-A Students Get Wrong," *New York Times,* December 8, 2018; Louis Deslauriers et al., "Measuring Actual Learning versus Feeling of Learning in Response to Being Actively Engaged in the Classroom," *Proceedings of the National Academy of Sciences* 116, no. 39 (September 24, 2019): 19251–19257.

8. Jonathan Malesic, "The Key to Success In College Is So Simple, It's Almost Never Mentioned," *New York Times,* January 3, 2023.

9. The questions below have been adapted from Arnold B. Arons, *Teaching Introductory Physics* (New York: Wiley, 1997), 376–382.

10. You can get a good book on logic for children and read it together, doing exercises and puzzles around the breakfast table. You can find a multitude of such resources online and in good bookstores. Let your children pick out one that will tickle their fancy. Books will vary in their content, colors, and puz-

zles depending on age. That's one reason you and your kids pick out the best choice for your child at a given age. For children in late high school or early college, try Irving Copi, Carl Cohen, and Victor Rodych, *Introduction to Logic,* 15th ed. (New York: Routledge, 2019). It's the gold standard of logic texts for young adults, but don't buy it. It will cost you an arm and a leg. See if your local library has it instead. If not, go with whatever strikes your fancy from a local bookstore that doesn't cost an illogical amount of money. Get something with games and puzzles that will introduce both formal and informal logic. Steve Pearlman's Critical Thinking Institute also offers a range of programs for kids of all ages to enhance their critical thinking. "Empowering the Next Generation of Critical Thinkers," Critical Thinking Institute, https://www.thectinstitute.com/brighter-minds-better-futures-main.

11. See John B. Biggs and Kevin Collis, "Towards a Model of School-Based Curriculum Development and Assessment Using the SOLO Taxonomy," *Australian Journal of Education* 33, no. 2 (1989): 151–163.

12. The cow examples all come from an accessible introduction to Biggs's thought produced by Aarhus University: Claus Brabrand, "Teaching Teaching & Understanding Understanding," video, 19:00, 2006, https://www.youtube.com/watch?v=iMZA8oXpP6Y.

13. See John Biggs, "The Role of Metacognition in Enhancing Learning," *Australian Journal of Education* 32, no. 2 (August 1, 1988): 127–138, especially 134–136 for how to improve deep learning.

14. One experiment found that students who reread a passage four times performed worse on a subsequent test than those who read the passage just once and then took notes on what they could recall about the passage without looking at the text again. Henry L. Roediger III and Jeffrey D. Karpicke, "Test-Enhanced Learning: Taking Memory Tests Improves Long-Term Retention," *Psychological Science* 17, no. 3 (March 2006): 249–255.

15. See Peter C. Brown, Henry L. Roediger III, and Mark A. McDaniel, *Make It Stick: The Science of Successful Learning* (Cambridge, MA: Belknap Press of Harvard University Press, 2014), 31–32.

16. For an alternative (and deep) approach to learning physics (or anything else), see what Harvard professor Eric Mazur has done to create a whole new approach to schooling. Ken Bain with Marsha Marshall Bain *Super Courses: The Future of Teaching and Learning* (Princeton, NJ: Princeton University Press. 2021), 86–104.

17. The term "spaced repetition" comes from Brown, Roediger, and McDaniel, *Make It Stick*, x.
18. Brown, Roediger, and McDaniel, *Make It Stick*, 201–202.
19. For an overview of the science behind retrieval practice, see Brown, Roediger, and McDaniel, *Make It Stick*, chap. 2.
20. We've adapted the baseball example from Brown, Roediger, and McDaniel, *Make It Stick*, 79–83.
21. Ellen J. Langer and Alison I. Piper, "The Prevention of Mindlessness," *Journal of Personality and Social Psychology* 53, no. 2 (1987): 280–287.
22. Langer and Piper, "Prevention of Mindlessness," 282.
23. For a glimpse of a recent class's efforts, see Matt Goisman, "Reusable Rhythms: SEAS Students Present Musical Instruments Made from Found or Recycled Materials at Symposium Concert," press release, Harvard School of Engineering, December 13, 2021, https://seas.harvard.edu/news/2021/12/reusable-rhythms. Mazur's use of Abreu is also described in Bain, *Super Courses*, 96–97.
24. For more project-based learning ideas, see Buck Institute for Education, "PBLWorks," http://pblworks.org.
25. Bain, *Super Courses*, 81–84.
26. Daniel T. Willingham, *Why Don't Students Like School: A Cognitive Scientist Answers Questions about How the Mind Works and What It Means for the Classroom* (San Francisco: Jossey-Bass, 2009), 25.
27. Michael Gove, speech to Independent Academies Association, November 14, 2012, full text at "Secretary of State for Education Michael Gove Gives Speech to IAA," Gov.UK, https://www.gov.uk/government/speeches/secretary-of-state-for-education-michael-gove-gives-speech-to-iaa.
28. Peter Walker, "Tough Exams and Learning by Rote Are the Keys to Success, Says Michael Gove," *Guardian*, November 13, 2012; Sean Lyons, "Rethinking the Way We Learn: UVA Psychologist Debunks Myths about How the Brain Works," *Virginia Magazine*, Spring 2013, https://uvamagazine.org/articles/rethinking_the_way_we_learn. For a more thorough response from Willingham, see the post on his personal website, "Did Michael Gove Get the Science Right?," November 19, 2012, http://www.danielwillingham.com/daniel-willingham-science-and-education-blog/did-michael-gove-get-the-science-right.
29. For the keys to creating natural critical learning environments, see Ken Bain, *What the Best College Teachers Do* (Cambridge, MA: Harvard University Press, 2004), 99–109.

SIX: PREPARING YOUR CHILDREN FOR THE SLINGS AND ARROWS OF SCHOOL

1. Thomas Curran and Andrew P. Hill, "Perfectionism Is Increasing over Time: A Meta-Analysis of Birth Cohort Differences from 1989 to 2016," *Psychological Bulletin* 145, no. 4 (2019): 410–429.
2. Paul L. Hewitt et al., "Perfectionism and Its Role in Depressive Disorders," *Canadian Journal of Behavioural Science* 54, no. 2 (April 2022), 121–131; Fredrik Saboonchi and Lars-Gunnar Lundh, "Perfectionism, Self-Consciousness, and Anxiety," *Personality and Individual Differences* 22, no 6 (June 1997): 921–928; Tracey D. Wade, Anne O'Shea, and Roz Shafran, "Perfectionism and Eating Disorders," in *Perfectionism, Health, and Well-Being,* ed. Fuschia M. Sirois and Danielle S. Molnar (Cham, Switzerland: Springer, 2016), 205–222; Dora Gyori and Judit Balazs, "Nonsuicidal Self-Injury and Perfectionism: A Systematic Review," *Frontiers in Psychiatry* 12 (2021), 691147.
3. Jennifer Breheny Wallace, "Is Your Child a Perfectionist? Here's How to Help," *Washington Post,* March 8, 2022.
4. Graham Kates, "Lori Loughlin and Felicity Huffman Among Dozens Charged in College Bribery Scheme," CBS News, March 12, 2019, https://www.cbsnews.com/news/college-admissions-scandal-bribery-cheating-today-felicity-huffman-arrested-fbi-2019-03-12/.
5. Miriam Adderholt-Elliott, "Perfectionism and Underachievement," *Gifted Child Today Magazine* 12, no. 1 (1989): 19–21. Paul L. Hewitt, Walter Mittelstaedt, and Richard Wollert, "Validation of a Measure of Perfectionism," *Journal of Personality Assessment* 53, no. 1 (1989): 133–144; Adina Schwartz, "Equality, Liberty, and Perfectionism," *Ethics* 92, no. 1 (1981): 134–137; D. Louise Mebane and Charles R. Ridley, "The Role-sending of Perfectionism: Overcoming Counterfeit Spirituality," *Journal of Psychology and Theology* 16, no. 4 (1988): 332–339; Thomas Curran and Andrew P. Hill, "Young People's Perceptions of Their Parents' Expectations and Criticism Are Increasing over Time: Implications for Perfectionism," *Psychological Bulletin* 148, no. 1–2 (January 2022): 107–128.
6. Curran and Hill, "Young People's Perceptions."
7. "Kids under Pressure: A Look at Student Well-Being and Engagement during the Pandemic," Challenge Success, May 14, 2021, https://challengesuccess.org/resources/kids-under-pressure-a-look-at-student-well-being-and-engagement-during-the-pandemic/.

8. "Map of Gun Deaths Shows Cities Have Lower Rates Than Rural Counties in the U.S.," NBC News, April 27, 2023, https://www.nbcnews.com/health/health-news/map-gun-death-rates-lower-cities-than-rural-counties-rcna81462; Curran and Hill, "Young People's Perceptions."
9. Thomas Curran, quoted in "Rising Parental Expectations Linked to Perfectionism in College Students," AAAS EurekAlert! March 31, 2022, https://www.eurekalert.org/news-releases/947889.
10. *The Great Santini*, directed by Lewis John Carlino (Burbank, CA: Warner Bros., 1979), film, 115 minutes. The film was adapted from Pat Conroy, *The Great Santini* (Boston: Houghton Mifflin, 1976).
11. See, for example, Sho Chan et al., "Perfectionism and Worry in Children: The Moderating Role of Mothers' Parenting Styles," *Current Psychology* 42 (2023): 18291–18299.
12. Researchers who surveyed 25 school shootings between 2013 and 2019 found that 60 percent of the shooters reported being bullied either in person or online. Elizabeth Burgess Dowdell et al., "School Shooters: Patterns of Adverse Childhood Experiences, Bullying, and Social Media," *Journal of Pediatric Health Care* 36, no. 4 (July–August 2022): 339.
13. William E. Copeland et al., "Adult Psychiatric Outcomes of Bullying and Being Bullied by Peers in Childhood and Adolescence," *JAMA Psychiatry* 70, no. 4 (2013): 419–426; Maria N. K. Karanikola et al., "The Association between Deliberate Self-Harm and School Bullying Victimization and the Mediating Effect of Depressive Symptoms and Self-Stigma: A Systematic Review," *BioMed Research International* 2018 (2018), art. 4745791.
14. A. A. Mamun et al., "Adolescents Bullying and Young Adults Body Mass Index and Obesity: A Longitudinal Study," *International Journal of Obesity* 37 (2013): 1140–1146.
15. See Sandra Jo Wilson and Mark W. Lipsey, "School-Based Interventions for Aggressive and Disruptive Behavior: Update of a Meta-Analysis," *American Journal of Preventative Medicine* 33, no. 2, Supplement (August 2007): S130–S143; Sturla Fossum et al., "Psychosocial Interventions for Disruptive and Aggressive Behaviour in Children and Adolescents: A Meta-Analysis," *European Child and Adolescent Psychiatry* 17 (2008): 438–451. Both articles are cited in David Scott Yeager, Kali H. Trzesniewski, and Carol S. Dweck, "An Implicit Theories of Personality Intervention Reduces Adolescent Aggression in Response to Victimization and Exclusion," *Child Development* 84, no. 3 (May / June 2013): 970–988.

16. Lucy Bowes et al., "Families Promote Emotional and Behavioural Resilience to Bullying: Evidence of an Environmental Effect," *Journal of Child Psychology and Psychiatry* 51, no. 7 (July 2010): 809–817.
17. Yeager, Trzesniewski, and Dweck, "Implicit Theories."
18. Brian Shea and Kirby Williams are both pseudonyms. They are composites of several kids we've interviewed.
19. Quoted in David Scott Yeager and Carol S. Dweck, "Mindsets That Promote Resilience: When Students Believe That Personal Characteristics Can Be Developed," *Educational Psychologist* 47, no. 4 (2012): 302–314, 309.
20. For evidence that strict, zero-tolerance policies against bullying have done more harm than good, see Christopher Boccanfuso and Megan Kuhfeld, "Multiple Responses, Promising Results: Evidence-Based, Nonpunitive Alternatives to Zero Tolerance," ChildTrends Research-to-Results Brief, March 2011, https://web.archive.org/web/20150616072933/https://www.childtrends.org/wp-content/uploads/2011/03/Child_Trends-2011_03_01_RB_AltToZeroTolerance.pdf; Marvin J. Berlowitz, Rinda Frye, and Kelli M. Jette, "Bullying and Zero-Tolerance Policies: The School to Prison Pipeline," *Multicultural Learning and Teaching* 12, no. 1 (2017): 7–25.
21. Peter Felten and Leo M. Lambert, *Relationship-Rich Education: How Human Connections Drive Success in College* (Baltimore: John Hopkins University Press, 2020).
22. Yeager, Trzesniewski, and Dweck, "Implicit Theories," 972.
23. Yeager, Trzesniewski, and Dweck, "Implicit Theories," 972–973.
24. Yeager, Trzesniewski, and Dweck, "Implicit Theories," 976.
25. Yeager, Trzesniewski, and Dweck, "Implicit Theories," 976.
26. Yeager, Trzesniewski, and Dweck, "Implicit Theories," 971.
27. See, for example, Carol S. Dweck, Chi-yue Chiu, and Ying-yi Hong, "Implicit Theories and Their Role in Judgments and Reactions: A World from Two Perspectives," *Psychological Inquiry* 6, no. 4 (1995): 267–285; Lisa S. Blackwell, Kali H. Trzesniewski, Carol S. Dweck, "Implicit Theories of Intelligence Predict Achievement across an Adolescent Transition: A Longitudinal Study and an Intervention," *Child Development* 79, no. 1 (2007): 246–263.
28. For studies showing that active learning is better than passive learning for enhancing problem solving ability, see Yunfeng He et al., "A Comparison between the Effectiveness of PBL and LBL on Improving Problem-Solving Abilities of Medical Students Using Questioning," *Innovations in Educational and Teaching*

International 55, no. 1 (2018): 44–54; Andis Klegeris, Manpeet Bahniwal, and Heather Hurren, "Improvement in Generic Problem-Solving Abilities of Students by Use of Tutor-Less Problem-Based Learning in a Large Classroom Setting," *CBE—Life Sciences Education* 12 (Spring 2013): 73–79. For evidence that active learning techniques improve more traditional measurements of student performance, see Scott Freeman et al., "Active Learning Increases Student Performance in Science, Engineering, and Mathematics," *Proceedings of the National Academy of Sciences* 111, no. 23 (June 10, 2014): 8410–8415.

29. Yeager, Trzesniewski, and Dweck, "Implicit Theories," 976.
30. Yeager, Trzesniewski, and Dweck, "Implicit Theories," 976.
31. Yeager, Trzesniewski, and Dweck, "Implicit Theories," 978. The researchers tested the students' sensitivity to peer exclusion using a method developed in Kipling D. Williams and Blair Jarvis, "Cyberball: A Program for Use in Research on Interpersonal Ostracism and Acceptance," *Behavior Research Methods* 38 (2006): 174–180.
32. This point is made in Yeager, Trzesniewski, and Dweck, "Implicit Theories," 976.
33. We're not suggesting that you must turn your family into brain experts, but there are some great resources out there that can give your kids great insights into the workings of their own noggins. For young children, see Donald M. Silver and Patricia J. Wynne, *My First Book about the Brain* (Mineola, NY: Dover, 2013); Baby Professor, *My Little Brain! Explaining the Human Brain for Kids* (Newark, DE: Speedy Publishing, 2016). For older children and teenagers, see Lara Boyd, "After Watching This, Your Brain Will Not Be the Same," November 14, 2015, TEDx Talks, video, 14:24, https://www.youtube.com/watch?v=LNHBMFCzznE; Jeanette Norden, *Understanding the Brain,* 36-lecture course, The Great Courses, video, https://www.thegreatcourses.com/courses/understanding-the-brain. One lecture from *Understanding the Brain* is available for free as Jeanette Norden, "The Neuroscience of Learning and Memory," March 27, 2014, video, 1:20:38, https://www.youtube.com/watch?v=wtu-yAm4xik.
34. American Psychological Association Zero Tolerance Task Force, "Are Zero Tolerance Policies Effective in the Schools? An Evidentiary Review and Recommendations," *American Psychologist* 63, no. 9 (2008): 852–862, quote on 854.
35. Ps. 118:24.
36. 5 Thess. 16–18.

37. George H. Gallup, "Thankfulness: America's Saving Grace," paper presented at the National Day of Prayer Breakfast, Thanks-Giving Square, Dallas TX, May 1998, cited in Robert A. Emmons and Michael E. McCullough, "Counting Blessings versus Burdens: An Experimental Investigation of Gratitude and Subjective Well-Being in Daily Life," *Journal of Personality and Social Psychology* 84, no. 2 (2000): 377–389.
38. Emmons and McCullough, "Counting Blessings," 378.
39. Emmons and McCullough, "Counting Blessings," 379.
40. Emmons and McCullough, "Counting Blessings," 386.
41. Lourdes Rey et al., "Being Bullied at School: Gratitude as Potential Protective Factor for Suicide Risk in Adolescents," *Frontiers in Psychology* 10 (March 2019), article 662.
42. On the harms of "downward social comparison," see Judith B. White et al., "Frequent Social Comparisons and Destructive Emotions and Behaviors: The Dark Side of Social Comparisons," *Journal of Adult Development* 13, no. 1 (March 2006): 36–44.
43. Quoted in Jalen Brown and Meron Moges-Gerbi, "A Neighbor's Call to Police on a Little Black Girl while She Sprayed Lanternflies Exposes a Deeper Problem, Mom Says," CNN, November 23, 2022, https://www.cnn.com/2022/11/23/us/lanternflies-black-girl-new-jersey-police-reaj/index.html.
44. Maya King, "Someone Called the Police on a Girl Catching Lanternflies. Then Yale Honored Her," *New York Times,* February 3, 2023.
45. Brown and Moges-Gerbi, "A Neighbor's Call."
46. Grace Toohey, "Body Camera Video: 6-Year-Old Girl Cries, Screams for Help as Orlando Police Arrest Her at School," *Orlando Sentinel,* February 24, 2020, https://www.orlandosentinel.com/news/crime/os-ne-orlando-police-body-camera-6-year-old-arrest-20200224-rlg2ukttdvhehpoj2ki7irqe74-story.html.
47. Rebecca Epstein, Jamilia J. Blake, and Thalia González, "Girlhood Interrupted: The Erasure of Black Girls' Childhood," Georgetown Law Center on Poverty and Inequality, 2017, https://genderjusticeandopportunity.georgetown.edu/wp-content/uploads/2020/06/girlhood-interrupted.pdf, 1, 9.
48. See Phillip Atiba Goff et al., "The Essence of Innocence: Consequences of Dehumanizing Black Children," *Journal of Personality and Social Psychology* 106, no. 4 (April 2014): 526–545. The summarizing quote here is from Epstein, Blake, and González, "Girlhood Interrupted," 1.

49. Erica L. Green, Mark Walker, and Eliza Shapiro, "'A Battle for the Souls of Black Girls,'" *New York Times,* October 1, 2020. The American Civil Liberties Union has published an interactive map that shows, state by state, the rate at which Black girls are arrested in schools compared to white girls. In some states, the disproportion is as high as eleven to one. "Black-White Girl School Arrest Risk," American Civil Liberties Union, accessed July 30, 2024, https://www.aclu.org/issues/racial-justice/race-and-inequality-education/black-white-girl-school-arrest-risk.
50. See Kayla Susalla, "The Costs of School Policing," Cato Institute, blog post, December 20, 2023, https://www.cato.org/blog/costs-school-policing.
51. Amy Stuart Wells, Lauren Fox, and Diana Cordova-Cobo, "How Racially Diverse Schools and Classrooms Can Benefit All Students," Century Foundation, February 9, 2016, https://tcf.org/content/report/how-racially-diverse-schools-and-classrooms-can-benefit-all-students/.
52. Wells, Fox, and Cordova-Cobo, "Racially Diverse Schools."
53. Claude M. Steele and Joshua Aronson, "Stereotype Threat and the Intellectual Test Performance of African Americans," *Journal of Personality and Social Psychology* 69, no. 5 (1995): 797–811.
54. For research on age-based stereotype threat, see Sarah J. Barber, "The Applied Implications of Age-Based Stereotype Threat for Older Adults," *Journal of Applied Research in Memory and Cognition* 9, no. 3 (September 1, 2020): 274–285.
55. See, for example, Steven J. Spencer, Claude M. Steele, and Diane M. Quinn, "Stereotype Threat and Women's Math Performance," *Journal of Experimental Social Psychology* 35, no. 1 (January 1999): 4–28; Arielle M. Silverman and Geoffrey L. Cohen, "Stereotypes as Stumbling-Blocks: How Coping with Stereotype Threat Affects Life Outcomes for People with Physical Disabilities," *Personality and Social Psychology Bulletin* 40, no. 10 (2014): 1330–1340.
56. For more on the physiological effects of stereotype threat, see Wendy Berry Mendes and Jeremy Jamieson, "Embodied Stereotype Threat: Exploring Brain and Body Mechanisms Underlying Performance Impairments," in *Stereotype Threat: Theory, Process, and Application,* ed. Michael Inzlicht and Toni Schmader (New York: Oxford University Press, 2012): 51–68.
57. For evidence on the effects of stereotype threat in boys' education, see Bonny L. Hartley and Robbie M. Sutton, "A Stereotype Threat Account of Boys' Academic Underachievement," *Child Development* 84, no. 5 (September/October 2013): 1716–1733.

58. See Jean-Claude Croizet and Theresa Claire, "Extending the Concept of Stereotype Threat to Social Class: The Intellectual Underperformance of Students from Low Socioeconomic Backgrounds," *Personality and Social Psychology Bulletin* 24, no. 6 (1998): 588–594.
59. Thomas S. Dee, "Stereotype Threat and the Student-Athlete," *Economic Inquiry* 52, no. 1 (January 2014): 173–182.
60. Jason K. Clark, "Southern Discomfort: The Effects of Stereotype Threat on the Intellectual Performance of US Southerners," *Self and Identity* 10, no. 2 (2011): 248–262.
61. The account that follows is drawn from Akira Miyake et al., "Reducing the Gender Achievement Gap in College Science: A Classroom Study of Values Affirmation," *Science* 330, no. 6008 (November 26, 2010): 1234–1237.
62. Riana Elyse Anderson interviewed by Maryam Abdullah, "How Adults Can Support the Mental Health of Black Children," *Greater Good Magazine,* June 9, 2020.
63. "Starting Materials," SAPERE's P4C Resource Hub, https://p4c.com/topic/p4c-library/.
64. Good possibilities include Walter Dean Myers and Christopher Myers, *Looking Like Me* (Minneapolis: Carolrhoda, 2009); Jenn Bailey and Mika Song, *A Friend for Henry* (San Francisco: Chronicle, 2019); Kathryn Cave and Chris Riddell, *Something Else* (New York: Puffin, 1994); Hilda Eunice Burgos and Gaby D'Alessandro, *The Cot in the Living Room* (New York: Kokila, 2021); Fabian E. Ferguson, *Daddy's Arms* (Newark, NJ: F. Ferguson, 2018); Kofi Genfi, *Dark Girl* (self-pub., 2018); Blair Imani, *Modern HERstory: Stories of Women and Nonbinary People Rewriting History* (Berkeley, CA: Ten Speed Press, 2018); Cheryl Kilodavis and Suzanne DeSimone, *My Princess Boy* (New York: Aladdin, 2010). Some of these titles were suggested in "How to Help Your Black Child Develop Resilience in the Face of Racism and Discrimination," Texas Children's Hospital, https://www.texaschildrens.org/blog/how-help-your-black-child-develop-resilience-face-racism-and-discrimination. To discover more books for children by and about people of color, check out the We Read Too app, www.wereadtoo.com.
65. See James H. Dee, "Black Odysseus, White Caesar: When Did 'White People' Become 'White'?" *Classical Journal* 99, no. 2 (December 2003 / January 2004): 157–167; Ibram X. Kendi, *Stamped from the Beginning: The Definitive History of Racist Ideas in America* (New York: Bold Type Books, 2016); Jacqueline Battalora,

Birth of a White Nation: The Invention of White People and Its Relevance Today, 2nd ed. (New York: Routledge, 2021).

66. Ed Simon, "How 'White' People Were Invented by a Playwright in 1613," *Aeon*, September 12, 2017, https://aeon.co/ideas/how-white-people-were-invented-by-a-playwright-in-1613.

67. See Megan Gannon, "Race Is a Social Construct, Scientists Argue," *Scientific American*, February 5, 2016, https://www.scientificamerican.com/article/race-is-a-social-construct-scientists-argue/.

68. Dee, "Black Odysseus, White Caesar."

69. Shuchen Xiang, "Why the Confucians Had No Concept of Race (Part I): The Antiessentialist Cultural Understanding of Self," *Philosophy Compass* 14, no. 10 (2019): e12628.

70. See David R. Roediger, "Historical Foundations of Race," National Museum of African American History and Culture, https://nmaahc.si.edu/learn/talking-about-race/topics/historical-foundations-race.

71. Michelle Alexander, *The New Jim Crow: Mass Incarceration in the Age of Colorblindness*, 10th anniversary ed. (New York: New Press, 2020); Richard Rothstein, *The Color of Law: A Forgotten History of How Our Government Segregated America* (New York: Liveright, 2017); Joe R. Feagin, *Systemic Racism: A Theory of Oppression* (New York: Routledge, 2006).

72. Erin Pahlke, Rebecca S. Bigler, and Marie-Anne Suizzo, "Relations Between Colorblind Socialization and Children's Racial Bias: Evidence from European American Mothers and Their Preschool Children," *Child Development* 83, no. 4 (July / August 2012): 1164–1179.

73. Kate Kennedy-Moulton et al., "Maternal and Infant Health Inequality: New Evidence from Linked Administrative Data," NBER Working Paper no. 30693, November 2022, https://www.nber.org/papers/w30693.

74. Haley Weiss, "Study: Wealthiest Black Moms More Likely to Die in Childbirth Than Poorest White Moms," *Fatherly*, January 7, 2023, https://www.fatherly.com/health/wealthiest-black-moms-more-likely-die-childbirth-than-poorest-white-moms-study.

SEVEN: HELPING YOUR KIDS GET A HIGHER EDUCATION THEY CAN USE

1. Morris Baker is a composite figure based on hundreds of interviews conducted with high school and college students.

2. David J. Deming and Kadeem Noray, "Earning Dynamics, Changing Job Skills, and STEM Careers," *Quarterly Journal of Economics* 135, no. 4 (2020): 1965–2005.
3. David Deming, "In the Salary Race, Engineers Sprint, but English Majors Endure," *New York Times,* September 20, 2019.
4. Deming, "Salary Race."
5. Deming, "Salary Race."
6. National Association of Colleges and Employers, "Job Outlook 2024," November 2023, https://www.naceweb.org/docs/default-source/default-document-library/2023/publication/research-report/2024-nace-job-outlook.pdf.
7. Ken Bain with Marsha Marshall Bain, *Super Courses: The Future of Teaching and Learning* (Princeton, NJ: Princeton University Press, 2021), 49–56.
8. The notion of a "promising syllabus" was introduced in Ken Bain, *What the Best College Teachers Do* (Cambridge, MA: Harvard University Press, 2004), 74–75. But Ken didn't make up the idea—he simply observed what the fantastic instructors he was interviewing at the time were doing.
9. Adriana Butler is a pseudonym used to protect privacy.
10. Stephanie Saul, "At N.Y.U., Students Were Failing Organic Chemistry. Who Was to Blame?" *New York Times,* October 3, 2022.
11. Ken founded and directed teaching centers at Vanderbilt, Northwestern, NYU, and Montclair State, and while he enjoyed broad support and saw what the centers could do, a lingering regret is that he didn't create a way for parents to bolster continued administrative support for the centers and their ongoing struggle to bring research insights into learning and teaching.
12. Leslie Berntsen, "How Not to Handle Student Failure," *Chronicle of Higher Education,* October 13, 2022, https://www.chronicle.com/article/how-not-to-handle-student-failure.
13. Learning that even great scientists fail can help high school students change the way react to failure. See Xiaodong Lin-Siegler et al., "Even Einstein Struggled: Effects of Learning about Great Scientists' Struggles on High School Students' Motivation to Learn Science," *Journal of Educational Psychology* 108, no. 3 (April 2016): 314–328.
14. Between 2010 and 2021, the total number of students enrolled in higher education dropped from 18.1 million to 15.4 million. Although enrollment numbers recovered slightly in 2023, experts expect them to continue declining in the coming years. See Alejandra O'Connell-Domenech, "College Enrollment

Could Take a Big Hit in 2025. Here's Why," *The Hill,* January 10, 2024, https://thehill.com/changing-america/enrichment/education/4398533-college-enrollment-could-take-a-big-hit-in-2025-heres-why/.

15. Paul Tough, "Americans Are Losing Faith in the Value of College. Whose Fault Is That?" *New York Times Magazine,* September 5, 2023.

16. OECD data, reported in National Center for Education Statistics, "International Educational Attainment," *Condition of Education,* US Department of Education, Institute of Education Sciences, updated May 2024, https://nces.ed.gov/programs/coe/indicator/cac/intl-ed-attainment.

17. Tough, "Americans Are Losing Faith."

18. National Center for Education Statistics, "International Educational Attainment."

19. Philip Troustel, "It's Not Just the Money: The Benefits of College Education to Individuals and to Society," Lumina Issue Papers, October 14, 2015, https://www.luminafoundation.org/resource/its-not-just-the-money/.

20. Gallup and Lumina Foundation, "Education for What?" 2023, https://www.gallup.com/file/analytics/510092/Gallup-Lumina%20Education%20for%20What%20Report.pdf; Jan-Willem van Prooijen, "Why Education Predicts Decreased Belief in Conspiracy Theories," *Applied Cognitive Psychology* 31, no. 1 (2017): 50–58.

21. Neeraj Kaushal, "Intergenerational Payoffs of Education," *Future of Children* 24, no. 1 (Spring 2014): 61–78.

22. April Rubin, "Life Expectancy Gap in America Widens Depending on College Education," Axios, October 16, 2023, https://www.axios.com/2023/10/16/life-expectancy-educated-adults-mortality-rate.

23. In 2022, 62 percent of high school (or equivalent) graduates went on to postsecondary study, a decline of 7 percent from 2018. Melanie Hanson, "College Enrollment & Student Demographic Statistics," Education Data Initiative, August 31, 2024, https://educationdata.org/college-enrollment-statistics.

24. Derek Bok, *Our Underachieving Colleges: A Candid Look at How Much Students Learn and Why They Should Be Learning More* (Princeton, NJ: Princeton University Press, 2006).

25. See Colleen Flaherty, "A 'Growth' Field," *Inside Higher Ed,* May 29, 2014, https://www.insidehighered.com/news/2014/05/30/some-teaching-and-learning-centers-have-closed-after-recession-field-growing-over.

26. "North Carolina Man Sentenced to Four-Year Prison Term for Armed Assault at Northwest Washington Pizza Restaurant," press release, US Attorney's

Office, District of Columbia, June 22, 2017, https://www.justice.gov/usao-dc/pr/north-carolina-man-sentenced-four-year-prison-term-armed-assault-northwest-washington; Jessica Taylor, "'Lives Are at Risk,' Hillary Clinton Warns over Fake News, 'Pizzagate,'" NPR, December 8, 2016, https://www.npr.org/2016/12/08/504881478/lives-are-at-risk-clinton-warns-over-fake-news-pizzagate.

Acknowledgments

Not every book requires a large community of people to produce, but this one sure did. With great thanks we acknowledge the colleagues, family, and friends old and new whose research, experience, expertise, encouragement, and support made *The Learning Household* possible.

May the dozens of writers, researchers, and scholars cited here see yet another example of how their work has influence, and be freshly encouraged to continue adding to the world's knowledge of how children learn. May the many educators who have impressed us with their creative cultivation of deep learning recognize their voices and ideas in these pages.

Most of all—in the spirit of this whole project—may the parents we interviewed and observed in action see their roles celebrated here, just as they see every day their positive effects on the learners they are rearing.

This book has been in the works for more than twenty years and across two different households. Sharmila Sen, now editorial director at Harvard University Press, helped in early days with the basic concept. We have James Lang, who himself has contributed so much to the literature on learning, to thank for the title. (A close runner-up came from our new neighbor, Fred Rodriguez, who suggested *Stand Back!*) A multitude of readers reacted to early drafts, sharing notes and making suggestions. Rachel Field, the Press editor who inherited the project, brought us valuable peer reviews as well as her own smart input, and kept things on track. Once the manuscript was finally turned over, Julia Kirby enhanced it with a level of editing—and warmth and encouragement—most authors only dream of.

On the home front, much gratitude goes to the medical professionals and bevy of home health aides who, especially over the past year, have kept us well and happy enough to stay productive.

And above all, we thank the family members who have been such wellsprings of learning for us. One way to look at this book is as a product of our own educational journeys, starting with what we noticed as children about other kids and how they learned. Its major theme is that education doesn't come only from professional educators. We know we are indebted to teachers in many fields, and beyond them to untold taxi drivers, librarians, artists, students, and others making observations that caused us to stop and think. We also know that, in a household, everyone stands to learn from each other—and no one has provided more insight and inspiration to us than our beloved children and grandchildren.

Index

Abreu, José Antonio, 171–172, 258n23
academic achievement: ladder metaphor for, 127; learning *versus*, 10–11, 16, 24; racial gap in, 73–75. *See also* grades and grading
active learning, 195–197, 261n28
adaptive expertise, 12–13, 14–15, 145, 162
agency, sense of, 5, 7–8, 18
altruism, 171–172, 193–194
Amemiya, Jamie, 66
American Psychological Association, Zero Tolerance Task Force, 199–200
Anderson, Riana Elyse, 210
anxiety, 5, 56–57, 97, 179, 182, 184–185, 201, 205
arguments: agreements and disagreements, 18, 112–113; analytical approach to, 88, 176; deep learning approach to, 147, 152, 156, 160
Aristotle, 113
Arons, Arnold, 155–156
Aronson, Joshua, 206
art and art-related activities, 16, 38, 40, 43, 90, 189; art education, 126, 216, 217, 219, 238, 241; autobiographical collages, 135–136; creativity-enhancing role of, 12, 120, 122, 129, 131–132, 135–137, 139
artificial intelligence (AI), 22, 112
assumptions, 19–20, 21, 40, 43–44, 153, 156
attention deficit hyperactivity disorder, 98, 141
autonomy, 3, 27–29, 32, 186. *See also* agency, sense of

Baker, Paul, 12, 95, 121–122, 138, 255n13; Integration of Abilities course, 123, 125–133, 141, 246n7, 253n5, 254nn3–5
Bandura, Albert, 53–55, 57
Barker, Bob, 2
Barnard College, 55
Bei, Zhou, 229
belonging, sense of, 27
Berntsen, Leslie, 234–235
Biggs, John, 157–161, 257n12
Binet, Alfred, 61–62
birth order, 44, 66–67
Black children and young people, 245n4; broad education for, 245n4; discriminatory discipline toward, 200, 203–204, 264n49; racial prejudice toward, 200, 202–214, 251n10

Blackwell, Lisa, 81–82
Black women, maternal mortality rates, 212–213
Bok, Derek, *Our Underachieving Colleges,* 31
Booker T. Washington High School for the Performing and Visual Arts, 126
Books Behind Bars (Kaufman), 225
Bowes, Lucy, 188–189
brain and brain functions, 262n33; behavior change, 194–195; in dyslexia, 48–49; information storage and retrieval, 138, 163–164, 170; learning, 9, 77, 81–83, 87–88, 124, 175, 198; mindfulness of, 168–170; reading skill development, 47, 48–49; threat response, 206. *See also* mental models
brainstorming, 39–40, 139
Brown, Michael, 5–8, 21
Bryn Mawr College, Andrew W. Mellon Teaching and Learning Institute, 50, 70
Buchner, Linda, 91–95, 200
bullying, 53, 187–202, 210, 224, 261n20; active learning approach to, 195–199; growth mindset approach to, 189–191, 193–199; impact on friends and friendship, 188, 190–191, 194, 198–199; resilience approach to, 188–189, 191–195; zero-tolerance policies for, 199–200

careers: careerism, 154–155; deep learning as preparation for, 10, 161; education as preparation for, 8, 14, 102–106, 154–155, 238, 245n4, 247n17

change: children's preparation for, 6–7, 8–10, 14–15, 16, 18; conservative approach to, 21–22
children's literature, 35, 162; with diversity and inclusivity themes, 210, 212, 213–214, 265n64; with philosophical themes, 110, 256n10
climate change, 14, 140–141, 230
Clinton, Hillary, 242
cognitive development, 20
Cohen, Geoffrey, 67
collaboration, 7, 111, 229, 238, 239
college faculty: guidelines for students' selection of, 223–228; perspectives on grades, 232–235; research activities of, 222–223, 224, 225, 233, 240; teaching methods of, 232–235, 240–241
college majors and courses: course syllabus, 226–227; economic value of, 216–219; guidelines for students' selection of, 223–228; parental advice about, 215–217
colleges and universities: admission test scores, 181–182; enrollment, 237–238, 239; gender balance in, 44; public, 236–237; quality and ranking of, 181–182. *See also* higher education; *names of individual colleges and universities*
college students: philosophical thinking in, 110, 115, 116–118; research involvement, 37; selection guidelines for teachers and courses, 223–230
Columbia University, 107–109
communication skills, 7, 95, 176, 229, 238. *See also* reading; writing

INDEX

community colleges, 236
community service, 225
compassion, 7, 28, 38, 60, 179, 181, 220, 238
competency, 2–3, 7, 27–28, 56, 60, 238
competition, 84, 127, 180–182, 184, 186
confidence. *See* self-confidence
conflict management skills, 188, 193. *See also* arguments
contentment, 7, 238
control, children's sense of: as autonomy, 3, 27–29, 32, 186; deep learning-based, 10; growth mindset-based, 60; in learning, 5, 17, 28–29, 197, 232; loss of, 28–29; parental encouragement of, 36–37; in play, 2–4; self-control, 3, 4, 29, 30
Covid-19 pandemic, 44, 142–143, 184–185
Crain, Sabato, 146–147, 149–150, 151, 153
creative mindset, 5, 6, 7, 8, 11–14, 91, 119–144, 184, 209, 219; activities and exercises for, 128–137; basics of, 121–133; for decision-making, 139–141; growth mindset and, 121, 137–138; higher education-based, 221, 226, 238; imagination and, 125, 126, 133, 134, 136, 137, 138, 139, 247n15; Integration of Abilities course, 123, 125–137, 138, 144, 168–169, 246n7, 253n5; invention education approach to, 12, 99; looking inward and outward components of, 12, 122–124, 133, 138, 210; relation to deep learning, 147–148, 153, 160; self-examination component of, 12, 95

critical thinking, 5, 21–22, 60–61, 144, 145, 181, 256n10; basic processes in, 155–156; deep learning approach to, 156–161, 221; deficits in, 107–108; definition of, 40, 158; higher education-based, 219, 221, 224–225, 229, 238; memorization *versus*, 36, 107–109, 115, 152, 158, 164; philosophical thinking approach to, 107–118
criticism, 63–66, 182, 185
Curé, Marie, 35
curiosity, 7, 18, 23–49, 148, 238; deep learning-based, 152; loss of, 24, 25, 26–29, 37, 107; parental encouragement of, 183–184; psychological needs and, 26–29; revival of, 29–30, 112, 113; role of motivation in, 24–30
Curran, Thomas, 185

Darwin, Charles, 35
Deci, Edward L., 26–28, 32, 34
decision-making, 2–3, 4, 99–100, 107, 184; activities to promote, 34–35; creative, 139–141; deep learning-based, 145–146, 151; evidence-based, 112, 142–143, 152, 155; moral decisions, 7
deep learning, 10–11, 13–14, 15, 97, 145–177; bullying and, 190; conditioning process in, 153–156; definition of, 156–161; group approach in, 168; growth mindset and, 147–148; higher education-based, 224; interleaving technique in, 167–168; memorization *versus*, 7, 21–22, 104, 111–112, 145,

deep learning (*continued*)
  148, 150, 152, 162, 174–175, 176–177, 226, 251n11, mental models based on, 80, 152, 153; mindful approach in, 168–170; obstacles to, 92–93; promotion of, 15, 153–161; racism and, 204; relation to problem solving, 145, 151–152, 156, 169–173; retrieval practices in, 105, 163–164, 165–167, 170, 258n19; study techniques based on, 147, 160, 161–173; surface learning *versus*, 146–156, 256n5
De La Salle Education Center, 91–92
dementia, 97–98
Deming, David, 217–219
depression, 5, 28, 119, 179, 187–188, 190, 197, 201
Descartes, René, 23
Destiny of the Republic (Millard), 102
Diener, Carol, 57–60
digital and electronic devices, positive alternatives to, 100–101
discipline: parental approach to, 186–187; racially prejudiced, 200, 203–204, 264n49
diversity, benefits of, 127, 143–144, 204–205, 209, 212
DIY Girls project, 173
downward social comparison, 202
Duncker, Karl, 143
Dweck, Carol, 55–61, 70, 76, 137–138, 192–195, 196
dynamic power of the mind, 12, 127, 246n7
dyslexia, 48–49

early childhood education, 30–32; philosophy instruction in, 108, 113–116
eating disorders, 179
education: agricultural, 103–106; as basis for a creative life, 122–123; broad / general, 125, 126, 219–222, 221–222, 241, 245n4, 247n17; as career preparation, 8, 14, 102–106, 154–155, 238, 245n4, 247n17; inequalities in, 17, 44, 73–75; parental goals for, 13; as preparation for the future, 8–10; technical, 12, 173, 217–221, 245n4, 246n8; value of, 10–11. *See also* academic achievement; early childhood education; higher education; schools and schooling
Einstein, Albert, 14–15, 24, 124, 125–126
El Sistema, 171–172
Emery, Elizabeth, 140
Emmons, Robert A., 201–202
empathy, 7, 189, 202, 209. *See also* altruism
ethics and morality, 11; in college curriculum, 229; philosophical thinking as basis for, 106–110, 111–112, 117–118
eugenics, 62, 63
evidence-based approach, 252n1; in curiosity development, 38; in decision-making, 35, 140, 142–143; in deep learning, 30, 147, 152, 155, 156, 164, 176, 252n1; in higher education, 226, 234, 240, 241; in learning research, 11; parental role in, 88, 139–140; philosophical thinking and, 111–113; in reading instruction, 47

exercise, 141, 201–202
experiential learning, 33–37, 40–41, 77–78; relationship with intelligence, 57, 59, 60

facts: as basis for learning, 174–177; creative mindset approach to, 124; disputes about, 112–113
failure, 16, 18, 50–85; fear of, 179–180; growth mindset perspective on, 16, 51–63, 75–76, 80–83, 247; intelligence and, 69–76, 80–83; as learning opportunity, 18, 50–51, 71, 72–73, 186, 235; perfectionism and, 179–180, 184–185
fake news, 242
family tree exercise, 209–210
far transfer, 13–14, 163–164
fixed mindset, 17–18, 80; applied to personality traits, 189–191, 193; bullying and, 189–191; learning *versus*, 76–77, 82, 155; in older children, 65–66, 137–138; parental belief in, 63, 68, 69, 82; parental influence on, 63–66, 72, 75, 100; research on, 53–63; of teachers and school administrators, 73–74, 82–83, 226. *See also* growth mindset
Flatt, Robyn, 126
friends and friendship, 3, 13, 27, 31–32, 38, 70, 86, 208, 210; decision-making with friends, 145–146; deep learning and, 146–147, 161–162; differences in study habits, 146–147; diversity of, 123–124, 144, 209, 212; impact of bullying on, 188, 190–191, 194, 198–199; individuality of, 123–124; involvement in learning environment, 53, 66, 68–69, 74, 91, 128, 136; lack of, 188, 190–191; philosophical questions about, 111, 113–114, 130
Frigidaire, 20
Future Farmers of America, 103–105

games and game playing: chess, 97–98; competition for grades as, 180–181, 186; as learning opportunities, 97–98, 101; online, 100–101; road games, 35; street games, 1–3; studying as, 170
Garfield, James, 102
gender bias, 43–44, 218–219, 235–236
General Motors, 20
Georgetown Law Center on Poverty and Inequality, 203–204
Geraldine R. Dodge Foundation, 43
GI Bill, 236
Gothenburg University, 148
Gove, Michael, 174–175
grades and grading, 25, 30, 32; college faculty's perspectives on, 232–235; competitive approach toward, 180–182, 184, 186; interests and, 105; parental attitudes toward, 70–73, 97, 104, 105–106, 180–182, 185–186, 232; relation to critical thinking, 158; relation to economic success, 154; relation to learning, 70–73, 75, 83–85, 147, 158, 160–161, 230–235, 251n11; students' focus on, 230, 232; study skills and, 83–85; surface learning and, 146–147, 148–149, 151, 154. *See also* testing and test scores

Grande, Reyna, 119–120
Grant, Adam, 22
Grant, David, 43
gratitude, 200–202
Gray, Peter, 2–5
Great Santini, The (film), 186
Greider, Carol, 48–49, 161, 222–223
growth mindset, 51–66, 121; among older children, 53, 81–83, 137–138; among younger children, 53, 87–88; as bullying intervention, 189–191, 193–195, 196–199; community-based approach to, 53, 66, 68–69, 71–75; definition of, 51, 58; higher education-based, 224; learning and, 83–85, 87–88; parental influence on, 52–53, 63–76; relation to deep learning, 147–148, 153; research on, 52–63, 76; as response to racism, 210–212

Haimovitz, Kyla, 69–70
Hanford, Emily, 46; *Sold a Story* (podcast), 47–48
Hao, Li, 229
Harvard University, 116–118, 169, 171, 217, 240
Hatano, Giyoo, 12–13
Hawkins, Jeffrey, 99, 138
Head Start, 31
helplessness, sense of, 5, 8, 27, 56–57, 58, 60
Herschbach, Dudley, 50–51, 96–97
higher education: access to, 235–238; cost of, 216, 236–237, 240, 241; democratization of, 236; economic benefits of, 215–219, 238–240; government funding for, 216, 236–237, 240; individual and societal benefits of, 238–240; parental role in, 215–217, 240–241; preparation for, 19; selection of courses and teachers in, 223–230; white privilege in, 235–236. *See also* college faculty; colleges and universities; liberal arts education
Holocaust, 62
homophobia, 206
Huynh, Jean-Baptiste, 74–75

ideas: deep learning approach to, 151, 152, 155–156, 163, 167–168; questioning of, 21–22
imagination, 6–7, 42, 45, 95, 151, 238; Einstein on, 14–15, 124; knowledge compared with, 14–15, 124–125; in puzzle and problem solving, 42, 43, 143, 169; relation to creativity, 95, 126, 133, 134, 136, 137, 138, 139, 247n15
immigrants, 119–120, 236
Inagaki, Kayoko, 12–13
individuality / uniqueness, 11–12, 15–16, 43–44, 123–124, 209
informal fallacies, 156
innovation, 12–13, 22, 122–123, 134, 137, 152, 221. *See also* creative mindset
inquiry. *See* questions and questioning
Integration of Abilities course, 123, 125–133, 138, 144, 246n7, 253n5; core activities of, 129–137, 168–169
intelligence: imaginative, 55–57; nature-nurture debate about, 61; relation

to failure, 69–76; relation to mental models, 80–83. *See also* fixed mindset; growth mindset
intelligence quotient (IQ) tests, 61–63
interests, as motivation for learning, 88–106; in deep learning, 164–165, 175–176; intrinsic, 2–3, 70; parental encouragement of, 29–36, 37, 38, 40–41, 86–87, 95–96, 183–184; teachers' encouragement of, 33. *See also* curiosity
internet, 37, 42, 98, 117, 153, 220, 242; learning resources on, 36, 48, 90, 101, 182, 252n1
invention education, 12

Jefferson, Thomas, 112–113
Jinkins, Carol, 146–147, 149–150, 153
Johnson, Steven, 19–20
Jones, Maitland, Jr., 233–235
journals, 34–35, 96, 135

knowledge, imagination compared with, 14–15, 124

Lang, James M., 100–101
Langer, Ellen, 169–170
language(s): descriptive of ideas, 155–156; development of, 77–78; foreign, study of, 143, 144; influence on deep learning, 169–170
Laughton, Charles, 121
lead poisoning, 20–21, 22, 247n19
learning, 76–83; for adaptation to change, 8–10; children's control over, 5, 28–29; as focus of learning household, 97–106; goals of, 10; inventive, 98–102; levels (taxonomy) of, 158–160; mental models and, 77–83, 143, 152, 153; mindful, 168–170; parental models of, 86–87; problem-based, 172–173, 175–177, 228–230; project-based, 91–95, 172–173, 225, 229; psychological needs in, 26–29; quality of, 158–160; relation to grades, 70–73, 75, 83–85, 147, 158, 160–161, 230–235, 251n11; research on, 9–10; reward and punishment approach, 25–26, 28–29. *See also* deep learning; strategic learning; surface learning
learning environments, 17, 52–53, 66–67; deep learning-based, 150, 181–182; growth mindset-based, 197–198; in higher education, 224, 227, 241; natural critical, 175–177, 258n29; safety of, 199–200
learning household, 9, 37, 83, 86–118; creation of, 86–88; definition of, 5; learning activities in, 95–106
learning opportunities, 36–37, 45–46; grades as, 230–235; mistakes as, 18, 32, 51, 55, 59, 70–71, 180, 181, 184, 186, 224, 232–233; multidisciplinary, 228–230; questions and questioning as, 29, 30, 33, 35–37, 87, 92, 175
Lemelson-MIT Program, 12, 246n8
liberal arts education, 216–222, 241
life, enjoyment of, 16–17, 146
lifelong learning, 218, 222

Lincoln, Abraham, 235–236
Lipman, Matthew, 107–110, 112, 113, 116, 210, 253n12

Make It Stick (Brown et al.), 165–167
Make Just One Change (Rothstein and Santana), 39–40
Malesic, Jonathan, 155
Marshall, Trinity, 102–106, 172, 186
Marton, Ference, 148–149
mathematics: children's introduction to, 32, 33; growth mindset approach to, 73–75; problem-solving activities in, 42–43, 46; racial achievement gap in, 73–75
Mazur, Eric, 171–172, 257n16, 258n23
McCullough, Michael E., 201–202
medical education, 150–151
memorization, 122; application to standardized testing, 174–175; critical thinking *versus*, 36, 107–109, 115, 152, 158, 164; deep learning *versus*, 7, 21–22, 104, 111–112, 145, 148, 150, 152, 162, 174–175, 176–177, 226, 251n11; in surface / strategic learning, 148–150
memory, 158, 162; benefits of chess on, 97–98; in deep learning, 163–164, 166–167; exercises for, 141, 164, 166–167; in surface learning, 149; understanding-based, 163–164
mental health: bullying and, 187–188; parental expectations and, 185; play and, 3, 5. *See also* anxiety; depression
mental models, 77–83, 143; deep learning-based, 80, 152, 153; failure of, 80–83; relation to growth mindset, 80–85, 143; relation to intelligence, 80–83
metacognition, 40
Microsoft, 236–237
Midgley, Thomas, 19–21, 22, 112, 247n19
MindDrive program, 91–95, 161, 164–165, 171, 175–176, 186, 200, 229
mindfulness, 168–170
mistakes: children's attitudes toward, 29, 51, 59, 152, 180; as learning opportunities, 18, 32, 51, 55, 59, 70–71, 180, 181, 184, 186, 224, 232–233; parental responses to, 32, 37, 70–71, 100, 215
Montclair State University, 109
morality. *See* ethics and morality
motivation, for learning, 17; effort praise and, 66; grades as, 231; in higher education, 225, 235, 240–241; reward-and-punishment approach, 25–26, 28–29, 70–71; science of, 4, 25–30; as self-motivation, 8, 24, 28, 57, 133. *See also* interests, as motivation for learning
music and music-related activities, 39, 136, 138, 160, 168–169, 171–172

narcissism, 5
National Association of Colleges and Employers, 221
nature, children's interactions with, 96, 98, 131
neurodivergence, 16
New York University, 163, 233–235; Center for Teaching Excellence, 234

Nobel Prize laureates, 38, 49, 50–51, 71, 109, 222–223
Nolan, Susan Bobbitt, 84
Noray, Kadeem, 217–219
Northwestern University, 39, 163

Oberlin College, 235
Organization for Economic Cooperation and Development (OECD), 237
ozone layer, damage to, 19–20, 21

paradigms. *See* mental models
parenting styles: authoritarian, 186; helicopter, 3, 98; permissive, 186; submarine, 98
parents, time spent with their children, 183–184
passion-based learning. *See* interests, as motivation for learning
Pell, Claiborne, 236
perfectionism, 97–99, 149, 179–187, 224, 231
Perks, Charlotte, 5–8
personality traits: entity *versus* incremental theories of, 194–195, 196, 199; growth mindset theory of, 189–191, 193–199
philosophical questions and questioning, 36, 105–125, 238; deep learning approach to, 145, 152–153, 161, 169–171, 175–176; in higher education, 116–118, 228–230; in the home environment, 115–116
Philosophy Learning and Teaching Organization (PLATO), 35, 115

Philosophy with and for Children (PW4C), 108–110, 112, 113–116, 210, 253n12
Piper, Alison, 169–170
Plato, 109, 113
play: adequate time for, 184; adult-managed, 3–5; free play, 1–3, 5, 97, 98; functions of, 2–3; inventive, 91, 97, 98. *See also* games and game playing
poetry, 43, 86, 132
poverty, 17, 109, 119, 171–172, 182, 202, 206–207, 212, 213, 245n4
praise, task *versus* person types of, 63–66
prejudices, 68, 73, 79, 198; of college faculty, 226; mental model-based, 79. *See also* racism
problem-based learning, 228–230
problem solving, 2–3, 6, 8, 22, 89, 97–98, 196, 213, 221, 238; active learning-based, 196–197, 261n28; adaptive expertise in, 12–13, 14–15, 92; in corporate environment, 205, 221; creativity in, 14, 93–94, 142–144; deep learning approach to, 145, 151–152, 156, 169–173, 175–177; fixed mindset perspective on, 16, 56; growth mindset perspective on, 16, 59–60, 64, 81–82; higher education and, 219, 229, 238, 239; impact on brain, 81–82, 175; perceived self-efficacy in, 54–55; puzzle solving, 41–43, 58–60, 72; racial prejudice and, 205; of structural problems, 156
project-based learning, 173
psychological needs, in learning, 26–29

punishment: physical, 28, 187; for poor grades, 70, 72, 105; as response to bullying, 190–191, 192, 199; for violation of rules, 33

questions and questioning: closed-ended questions, 40; creativity-enhancing, 134, 140, 168–169; in decision-making, 140; in deep learning, 155–156, 164, 165–166; double questions, 40; fixed mindset approach to, 155; as indication of lack of intelligence, 64; as learning opportunities, 29, 30, 33, 35–37, 36–37, 87, 92, 175; open-ended questions, 38, 40, 161, 217; parental encouragement of, 35–40; question-based curriculum, 228–230; questioning of convictions, 112; questioning of ideas, 21–22; in school environment, 92–93; spaced repetition technique, 165–166; in young children, 23–24. See also critical thinking; philosophical questions and questioning

Quiz Kids (radio program), 62–63

Rabi, Isidor Isaac, 38
race, as historical fiction, 210–212
racism, 202–214, 224; growth mindset response to, 210–212; in higher education, 235, 236; institutional or systemic, 213
reading, 24, 36, 46–49, 86–88; aloud, 87, 102; for deep learning, 154, 162–163, 166; dyslexia and, 48–49; parents as role models for, 37, 86–88; phonics method, 47–48, 87, 88, 252n3; research-based principles for, 163;

Starfall Learn to Read app, 48, 250n22; strategic and surface learners' approach to, 161–163, 148o; whole-word method, 47–48. See also children's literature

reasoning, 155–156, 164, 176, 226, 238. See also critical thinking

Rees, Steve, 91–95, 161, 171, 200, 229
relatedness, 27–28
Relationship-Rich Education (Felten and Lambert), 191
research: college faculty's involvement in, 222–223, 224, 225; creativity of, 12; in psychology, 54; students' involvement in, 36–37, 49, 98, 222–223
research universities, 236–237
resilience, 191–195
responsibility, 99–100
retrieval practices, 105, 135, 166–167, 258n19
Right Question Institute, 39–40
Robinson, Ken, 121
Rockefeller family, 236
role-playing, 197
Rolle, Kaia, 203–204
Roosevelt, Franklin, 185, 236
Ross, Lee, 67
rules and regulations: children's engagement with, 2–3; for good conduct, 33, 114–115; in schools, 28–29, 199–200; zero-tolerance policies, 199–200
Ryan, Richard M., 26–28, 32, 34

Sahlberg, Pasi, 229
Säljö, Roger, 148–149

INDEX

Sandel, Michael, 116–118, 196
schools and schooling: adverse effect on learning, 28–29, 92–93; bullying prevention in, 188–191, 199–200; children's adverse experiences in, 30–31; deep learning-based curriculum, 176; expulsions and suspensions, 200, 204; ladder metaphor for, 127; performance-oriented approach of, 65, 70; rules and regulations, 28–29, 199–200; traveling to, 184–185. *See also* colleges and universities; higher education
school shootings, 187, 204, 260n12
self-confidence: development of, 18, 50, 64–67, 123, 145–146, 238; growth *versus* fixed mindsets approaches to, 63, 64–66, 189; lack of, 54, 56–57, 63, 64–65, 189, 231; as perceived self-efficacy, 54–55, 57
self-control, 3, 4, 29, 30
self-efficacy, perceived, 54–55, 57
self-esteem, 65, 66, 179, 185
self-harm, 179, 187–188
self-reflection, 213–214
self-worth, 179–180; contingent, 123
sexism, 206
Sharp, Ann Margaret, 109, 110
Simon, Ed, 210–211
Skinner, B. F., 25–26
slavery, 211, 221
smart learning, 145. *See also* deep learning
social media, positive alternatives to, 100–101
social psychology, 191–195

social threats, to academic success, 178–179. *See also* bullying; perfectionism; racism
Socrates, 117
sororities, 105, 106
Southwest Jiaotong University, 229
sports, parental involvement in, 4–5
Stanford University, 53–54, 61, 62, 67, 69
Steele, Claude, 67–68, 206, 251n10
STEM education, 173, 217–219
stereotyping / stereotypes: gender-biased, 203–204, 206, 208–209; judgments based on, 68; mental models-based, 79; responses to, 208–212; stereotype threat, 205–208, 251n10, 264n56
storytelling, 96–97, 98
strategic learning, 149–151, 161–163; conditioning process in, 153–154; perfectionism associated with, 180–181
student debt, 216, 237
student success programs, 240
study habits, 18; deep learning-based, 147, 160, 161–173; growth mindset-based, 83–85; interleaving, 167–168; mindful learning, 168–170; retrieval practices, 105, 135, 166–167, 258n19; spaced repetition, 165–166; strategic learning-based, 161–163
suicide, 188–189, 202
Super Courses (Bain), 53, 173, 225, 230, 241
surface learning, 146–156, 256n5. *See also* strategic learning
syllabus, 226–227; promising or invitational, 227
sympathy, 189, 202

Tarleton State University, 104
teachers: approaches to reading instruction, 46–47; growth and fixed mindsets of, 73, 75; learning-supportive, 33, 40, 45. *See also* college faculty
teaching centers, 182, 234–235, 240–241, 267n11
television watching, 101, 134, 154
Terman, Lewis Madison, 61–62
testing and test scores: for college admission, 181–182; competitive approach toward, 180–182; standardized, 174–175, 181
think / pair / share discussions, 113–114
Tough, Paul, 237–238
Truman Show, The, 34, 79–80
Trzesniewski, Kali H., 192, 193–195, 196–197

uncertainty, 16, 112, 145–146, 155
University of Bath, 185
University of California: at Davis, 201; at San Diego, 201; at Santa Barbara, College of Creative Studies, 49; at Santa Cruz, 119
University of Colorado, 208–209
University of Illinois, 57–58
University of Michigan, 210
University of Pittsburgh, 66
University of Rochester, 260
University of Southern California, 234–235
University of Texas at Austin, 236
University of Virginia, 173–174, 225

values, 6, 8–10, 15–16; conflicts in, 14, 101, 140; parental promotion of, 17–18, 28; questions about, 38, 101, 128
Vanderbilt University, 39, 163
Varsity Blues college admission scandal, 181–182
violence: among high school students, 193; gun-related, 187, 204, 242, 260n12; parental fear of, 184–185; police violence, 203, 204; racial violence, 203, 204, 207–208; as response to bullying, 187, 190–191, 192, 198

Wallace, Jennifer, 179–180
Wang, Ming-Te, 66
Washington University, 165
Welch, Edgar Maddison, 242
What the Best College Students Do (Bain), 220
Why Don't Students Like School? (Willingham), 174–175
Willingham, Daniel, 173–175
Wilson, Bobbi, 202–203
writing, 176; as active learning, 196; automatic, 128–129; creativity-enhancing approaches to, 128–129, 135; grading of, 231–232; journals, 34–35, 96, 135; parental encouragement of, 66, 67, 87, 95–96; stereotyping-related, 208–209; un-essays, 135–136

Yale University, 55, 121, 203
Yeager, David, 76, 193–195, 196–197
Yihong, Fan, 229